National Association o
Silver Spring

feminist visions for social work

Nan Van Den Bergh &
Lynn B. Cooper,
editors

Library of Congress Cataloging-in-Publication Data

Feminist visions for social work.

    1. Social services—United States. 2. Feminism—United States. 3. Social work with women—United States. I. Van Den Bergh, Nan. II. Cooper, Lynn B.
HV91.F45   1986   361.3'024042   86-5137
ISBN 0-87101-132-8

contents

Nan Van Den Bergh
Lynn B. Cooper

introduction

In the past 25 years, social, cultural, and political institutions in the United States have experienced a tremendous upheaval. The practices and policies of these institutions have been directly challenged by large-scale, broad-based movements of people demanding changes in the existing distribution of rights, resources, and opportunities. Feminism and the feminist movement have been significant components of this process, which has actively questioned the allocation of power and privilege in American society.

The feminist vision for a different society includes the demand for gender equality as well as a commitment to altering the processes and the manner in which private and public lives are organized and conducted. This vision does not accept the existing competitive, hierarchical, and authoritarian organization of decision making and action. A feminist vision is dedicated to creating new styles and new dynamics of interaction and relationships.

Feminism is a transformational politics, a political perspective concerned with changing extant economic, social, and political structures.[1] Basically, feminism is concerned with ending

1

domination and resisting oppression. Consequently, as a world view, it can lend perspective to any issue and is not limited to a separate ghetto called "women's issues."[2] Feminism, therefore, is infinitely broader than an "Add women and stir" perspective on social change, that is, maintaining the status quo but simply adding more women to where there used to be only or predominantly men. As a politics of transformation, feminism is relevant to more than a constituency of women. It is a vision born of women, but it addresses the future of the planet with implications accruing for males as well as females, for all ethnic groups, for the impoverished, the disadvantaged, the handicapped, the aged, and so on.[3] Feminism is a politics for the future of the world, not just for an isolated handful of the converted.

Many areas of public and private life have been affected by feminism. This can be seen in the development of child care programs and policies, self-help and community-based health care clinics, rape crisis centers, battered women's shelters, and more. Feminism's encouragement of women to have choices in their life pursuits has also effected the influx of females into the labor market within the last two decades. In 1982, 53 percent of all women aged 16 and older were paid workers, and they constituted more than 43 percent of the civilian labor force.[4] It has been noted that nine out of every ten women will be in the paid labor force at some time in their lives.[5] Feminism has suggested that women can pursue careers as well as raise children. Perhaps this accounts for the fact that 59 percent of all mothers with children under 18 years of age were paid workers in 1982, and 50 percent with preschool children were also in the labor force.[6] Women can also choose not to be mothers. In general, women have accounted for 52 percent of the civilian labor force increase since 1970.[7]

Within education, feminist pedagogy has made significant inroads in challenging the traditions that have served to reinforce the existing relationships of patriarchal power and authority. This has, in part, been accomplished by the evolution of women's studies as an appropriate and important discipline within the academy. In addition, legitimacy has been provided for the study of topics such as pornography, rape, domestic violence, and incest. Also, significant attention has been directed toward the generation of nonsexist reading materials for children. Many elementary, secondary, and college texts have been critiqued in efforts to purge sex-stereotypical content as well as to make them more inclusive

2   in subject matter pertaining to women. Within almost all aca-

Feminist Visions

demic disciplines there has been a spate of scholarship devoted to feminist issues. There are still, however, obstacles to being published that seem attributable to insidious structural sexism.

Despite the myriad outcomes of feminism generating an impact within society, it seems to have touched the field of social work only peripherally. Research has indicated that traditional and stereotypic views of women have often been prevalent among social workers.[8] Gender stereotypes continue to exist within social work texts and journal articles.[9] Moreover, studies have noted significant discrimination against women social workers in status and salary within agencies and academia. Research has also suggested that role strain and conflict frequently exist for women who choose to combine family responsibilities with a social work career or who are in an educational program preparing for an MSW.[10] It has also been suggested that a bias exists within the delivery of social services that tends to reinforce sex-stereotypical behaviors for female clients by encouraging dependency, rather than independence.[11] In summation, although the majority of social work practitioners and recipients of service are women, feminist visions seem to have had a difficult time pervading the profession.

Ironically, at its base, social work is supposed to share many of the fundamental concerns of feminism, particularly the relationship between individual and community, between individually and socially defined needs, as well as the concern with human dignity and the right to self-determination. Social work, like feminism, is theoretically committed to improving the quality of life for all people.

The codes for both social work educators (Council on Social Work Education [CSWE]) and practitioners (National Association of Social Workers [NASW]) mirror, at many points, the feminist commitment to explain, confront, and resolve the conditions of life for oppressed people and for society in general.[12] Those professional codes underscore a feminist principle related to the need for addressing collective welfare as equivalent in importance to individual well-being. In fact, within NASW's Code of Ethics it is stated that concern for the welfare of individuals includes action for improving social conditions. Similarly, feminism has been described as "a theory of individuality that recognizes the importance of the individual within the social collectivity."[13] A social worker advocating for individual as well as societal change is intrinsically behaving in terms of feminist principles.

3

Feminist principles specifically relevant to social work education and practice include: eliminating false dichotomies and artificial separations, reconceptualizing power, valuing process as equally important as product, validating renaming, and believing that the personal is political. These premises, or feminist visions, can inform education and practice related to sundry populations and social problems. The task now is to define the five premises, noting how their incorporation into the profession can generate a profound impact within social work.

Eliminating False Dichotomies and Artificial Separations

Feminist analysis mandates viewing reality in a holistic, integrated, and ecological fashion. The ecological concept pertains to the interrelatedness inherent between persons and their environments.[14] This feminist concern counters the prevalent trend within Western thought of classifying knowledge and observations around principles that *separate*.[15] For example, within conventional thinking, intuition and empiricism are viewed as incompatible. Mind, spirit, and body are considered individually and not in an interrelated fashion. In addition, masculinity and femininity are not only falsely accepted as biologically ordered categories, but are also viewed as mutually exclusive entities that should be manifest for one gender but not the other. Distinctions between the sexes, rather than commonalities, are emphasized, and the isolation of individuals is reinforced.

False dichotomies, in terms of domination versus subordination politics, abound and can be thought of as "either-or" and "zero-sum" models in that someone must lose for another to gain. So pervasive is the effect of creating false dichotomies that it undergirds the infighting that occurs among oppressed groups. Trying to get a "slice of the pie," minorities tend to view each other competitively in an "us versus them" mode rather than perceive commonalities and work collaboratively against a common oppressor.

These artificial separations are particularly true for women of color, who are constantly forced to place themselves at either one end or the other of an oppression continuum. Minority women are forced to identify their discrimination as *primarily* racist or *primarily* sexist rather than as an interaction of both. Working-class people of color are dichotomized into categorizing themselves as hampered by classism or racism. Feminists of color are often chastised by ethnic men for their concern with women's rights. Such splitting tactics are an outcome of a systemic propensity to dichotomize.

The feminist concern with interrelatedness derives primarily from recognizing the inability of existing social, political, and economic arrangements to provide adequately satisfying and meaningful lives for the overwhelming number of people in this society. Feminism, committed to creating and building a new culture, utilizes a holistic, ecological, and spiritual perspective as the force behind the evolving societal paradigms.[16] Feminist political analysis has also consistently stressed the need to eliminate separating and alienating power structures. Consequently, feminist politics have focused on collective, integrative decision-making processes.[17] Equally important is the recognition that making separations out of unities and dividing a whole into conflicting components is the quintessence of patriarchal processes which isolate, separate, and divide, and is the model for hierarchical organization and order.[18]

Reconceptualizing Power

Power is a central concern within feminist analysis. A significant amount of discourse has related to considering ways in which patriarchy can be challenged.[19] Patriarchal processes are characterized by creating power dichotomies—in essence, generating conditions of "haves and have-nots." The concept of patriarchy has most usually been employed to describe situations of male domination and female submission. It can be generalized, however, as a paradigm describing all inequitable situations whereby many must lose so that a few can gain. Within a patriarchal mode, power is seen as a finite commodity to be controlled, particularly in determining the distribution of rights, resources, and opportunities. In most traditional models, power is viewed as property, analogous to money, involving control and domination of subordinates to make them subservient. Accordingly, those who control power manage the environment and determine goals, information is withheld, and rules are created to censure behavior.[20]

Through control of power, patriarchal modes breed subordination by promoting dependency and not providing persons with the ability to have full control over their lives. Powerlessness can

5

be considered an inability to manage emotions, skills, knowledge, and material resources in a way leading to effective performance of valued social roles.[21] It is through performing in certain capacities, such as worker, head of household, parent, partner, and spouse, that individuals derive a sense of purpose and self. Powerlessness can prevent persons from performing optimally and can lead to isolation, anomie, and social problems.

As an alternative to the patriarchal finite notion of power, feminists have sought to reconceptualize power as infinite, a widely distributed energy of influence, strength, effectiveness, and responsibility. Power is viewed as facilitative; empowerment to action occurs rather than domination.[22] Empowerment, or claiming personal power, is a political act because it allows people control over their own lives and the ability to make decisions for themselves.

To redefine power does not mean to deny the reality of differentials that exist between persons in knowledge, influence, skills, resources, or responsibility. It is a myth to believe that persons are equally powerful or that everyone must have an equivalent amount of power. Types of power, such as knowledge power or skill power, must be recognized and acknowledged as merely being different and not more legitimate than other types of power. From time to time, certain individuals might be more expert than others and their opinion could weigh more heavily than that of others. Structures can be created, however, that give persons more equal access to issues, resources, and information.[23] Disclosing certain data can provide the conditions by which individuals can make choices—and that is part of the process of empowering.

Valuing Process Equally with Product

The feminist agenda of valuing process equally with product is related to both the interconnectedness and false dichotomy notions. Basically, it maintains that how one pursues a goal is as important as the accomplishment of the goal. Because of patriarchal separating processes, means and end, as well as process and product, have been dichotomized. Only what one achieves tends to be considered, rather than, with equal interest, how one arrives at goals. One consequence of this type of process is the amassing of wealth and power as an end in itself, despite the generally unethical and harmful behaviors involved in the pursuit of that end. Competition, conquest, and individualism are all reinforced when

Feminist Visions

the ends are rewarded and the means to those ends are ignored.

A feminist vision of process and outcome is based on an assumption that the merit of a goal is directly related to the way in which it is achieved. Goals achieved through bad processes must always be mistrusted. How one pursues an objective becomes a goal in and of itself. Processes utilized to make decisions are as important as the final determinations.

Process can be conceptualized as an enabling and facilitative force akin to an empowering experience. Redefinition of power and attention to means are highly interrelated. For example, feminist organizational style has attempted to ensure that all participants are aware of the agenda, encouraged to speak, and comfortable in requesting clarity on issues. Moreover, being aware of process means taking time for the personal concerns of colleagues, co-workers, and supervisees, within work settings. It also means generating vehicles for feedback and critique so that persons can express both validations and dissatisfactions.

Validity of Renaming

Having the right to name one's own experience is a feminist agenda that that has significance for all oppressed people. Inspired by the example of civil rights activists, feminists deemed early in the movement's resurgence that there was power in naming. Initially identified by Betty Friedan in 1963 as "the problem which has no name," sexism has since been defined, along with other terms denoting a new reality for women, including the term "consciousness raising" and the use of Ms.

It was through black activism that the right to name was first articulated as the cry for "Black Power" was made by Stokely Carmichael. Following this example, other ethnic minorities chose to name themselves no longer as "hyphenated" Americans but adopted terms such as Chicano, La Raza, Atzlan, and Pacific Islander, in order to describe their unique cultural identities. In addition, to emphasize the significance of being racial minorities so as to differentiate themselves from other groups also using the label "minority" (women, lesbians and gay men, the physically handicapped), some ethnic people have chosen to name themselves as "people of color" or "women of color."[24] How one names oneself is highly related to one's identity and sense of self.

Renaming includes four processes: (1) applying new labels

7

Introduction

(words) to persons, places, or things; (2) changing meanings by altering the format of language; (3) reclaiming archaic definitions; or (4) conceptually broadening the meaning of existing language. It is helpful to provide a brief indication of what each process entails.

An example of renaming would be referring to persons as black rather than Negro, Afro-American, or colored. Similarly, use of the word Ms. as an article of address for women, regardless of their marital status, exemplifies that process.

The second potential renaming action, changing meanings by altering the formats of words, can be accomplished by the utilization of hyphens or slashes. Daly, for example, refers to renaming as an "a-mazing process."[25] Hidden deceptions within language can be revealed by dividing words and employing alternative meanings for prefixes. Also, slashes and hyphens can be used to create more inclusive words, such as s/he.

Renaming via reclaiming archaic definitions entails "going back to basics" in order to purge racism and sexism in language. By searching out archaic meanings it may be possible to discern original definitions diametrically opposite to current conventional language, which may have been affected by prejudiced attitudes. For example, the word hag is typically associated with an ugly old woman. However, it emanates from the Greek word *hagios* (meaning holy), which aludes to the eminent positions women once held as spiritual leaders in society. For both feminists and ethnic activists, renaming includes reclaiming knowledge and pride in cultural, historical, and current experiences.

Finally and perhaps most important, to rename also means to expand the conceptual boundaries of words by going beyond conventional definitions. For example, the conceptual picture conjured up most frequently by the word family is a nuclear unit with a mother, father, and children. However, society is increasingly bearing witness to the burgeoning of alternative family forms, and social forecasting predicts the continuation of that phenomenon. Currently, only 16 percent of American families conform to the traditional nuclear family stereotype of an employed father, a homemaker wife-mother, and offspring.[26] Feminists have articulated the need to have a plural vision of families. In fact, it has been suggested that "families" is a more inclusive concept than "family" because it denotes the right and need of people to create a variety of loving and caring structures for their daily lives.[27] Consequently, it may be that the future will see seemingly uncon-

Feminist Visions

troversial words, such as family, renamed in a conceptually broadened way so as to provide a change impetus for evolving social institutions.

The Personal Is Political

"The personal is political" was first articulated in conjunction with consciousness-raising activities during the early years of the current feminist movement. When women talked about their personal experiences in a group context, they were able to "speak bitterness" and perceive the commonalities among their lives. Consequently, it became possible to evolve beyond personal faulting and to develop an empirically based understanding of institutionalized sexism. Women learned that the problems they encountered were not individualized; they were part of a pattern generalizable to sexism. This type of awareness signaled the evolution of political consciousness—a sense of individual connectedness to a system of oppression.

As a tenet of feminist analysis, this premise suggests that the values and beliefs a person harbors, the goals that one sets, and the type of life style one chooses to pursue can be considered a political statement. It demonstrates an interconnectedness between individual activities and societal structures. The social movement can influence personal behavior, just as individual activities can exert influence on society. In addition, this proposition suggests that institutional change can be effected by personal, social, and political action.

An assumption underlying the personal is political is that working to bring about changes within societal institutions can also alter the course of one's life. Challenging systems may precipitate establishing new priorities among one's personal values. Such a change could be an impetus for modifying an individual's dysfunctional patterned behaviors. Simultaneously, alterations within institutional structures can allow persons new opportunities that may facilitate individual change. This process is exemplified by Figure 1.

A focus on social change to bring about individual and institutional modifications is in sharp contrast to both Freudian psychology and the American ethic of "rugged individualism," which have a victim-blaming component and do not address structural inequality. The feminist agenda validates that indi-

9

Introduction

Figure 1
Interaction Between Institutional and Individual Change

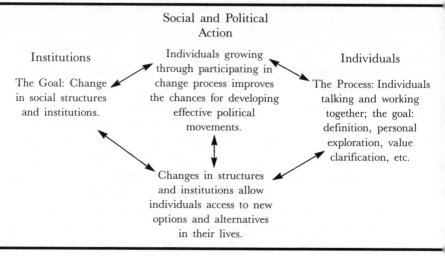

Social and Political
Action

Institutions

The Goal: Change
in social structures
and institutions.

Individuals growing
through participating in
change process improves
the chances for developing
effective political
movements.

Individuals

The Process: Individuals
talking and working
together; the goal:
definition, personal
exploration, value
clarification, etc.

Changes in structures
and institutions allow
individuals access to new
options and alternatives
in their lives.

Source: Adapted and reprinted with the permission of the publisher from N. B. Gluckstern, "Beyond Therapy: Personal and Institutional Change," in E. I. Rawlings and D. K. Carter, eds., *Psychotherapy for Women* (Springfield, Ill.: Charles C Thomas, Publisher, 1977), p. 429.

vidual experiences can be related to systemic structures and out-comes. Individual distress can be seen as having an etiology within system-based inequalities, just as institutional change can be facilitated through individual actions.

> It means that women's distinctive experience as women occurs within that sphere that has been socially lived as the personal-private, emotional, interiorized, particular, individuated, intimate—so that what it is to *know* the politics of woman's situation is to know women's personal lives.[28]

Summary of Feminist Visions

The five premises of feminist analysis—eliminating false dichotomies and artificial separations, reconceptualizing power, valuing process equally with product, renaming, and the personal is political—have the potential to alter dramatically all aspects of social work education and practice. Their incorporation into the core of social work will not be easy. These premises are intimately linked to challenging power, prestige, and the dynamics of existing practices, policies, and programs. All of these visions are relatively

10

Feminist Visions

new; they are in the process of being developed and understood.

Feminist analysis is not static, but rather a continually evolving and expanding process. Each vision is filled with ambiguities, uncertainties, and complexities. For example, how does one utilize good processes when a crisis demands an immediate response? How does a feminist administrator convince workers accustomed to hierarchical decision making that their opinions and feelings are valid? Challenges and changes are never easy or simple, and they are often met with resistance. Feminist social work practitioners, educators, and consumers of social services must be prepared to confront and overcome resistance from others, as well as from their own insecurities and uncertainties, and to begin to make feminist visions an integral part of their lives. The implications of these visions for specific areas of social service provision, education, and research will now be suggested.

False Dichotomies and Artificial Separations. *Specialist vs. generalist practice.* Historically, social work has been composed of two primary types of services—direct and indirect. Direct practice typically refers to services provided for individuals, families, and small groups, whereas indirect practice has referred to community organization, planning, policy making, administration, and research. At different times within the history of social work, one type or the other seems to have been emphasized. At the turn of the century, an emphasis on creating settlement houses and scientifically documenting living conditions in urban areas was an important synthesis of direct and indirect service provision.

In the early 1900s, with the development and growth of monopoly capitalism, the strengthened ideological commitment to the separation of private and public lives, as well as the intensification of class and racial divisions, dramatically altered the practice of social work. Similar to medicine, and influenced by Freudianism, social work began to focus solely on the individual's personal responsibility for life's difficulties. For example, poverty was no longer primarily a problem of slum housing, poor wages, or discrimination; it began to be treated as an individual psychological difficulty.[29]

The overwhelming impact of the Great Depression beginning in 1929 sparked a renewed social work interest in societal responsibility for poverty and suffering. Many social workers, led by Bertha Reynolds, Mary Van Kleeck, and others, were actively involved in organizing unemployment councils and demonstra- **11** tions and in making demands for government aid to the poor, the homeless, the unemployed, and the exploited. There was a rekindling of the commitment to understanding suffering within the context of social responsibility. Social work involvement in the development of social security and unemployment insurance during this time documents this renewed commitment.

In the 1950s, the Cold War and McCarthyism helped once again to push the social work profession away from social and political activism. There was a reemphasis on individual difficulties and responsibilities. Social workers were concerned with helping people to adjust and accept the conditions of their lives, rather than to challenge the existing order.

The 1960s civil rights dissent gave birth to the Great Society social policy, which refocused attention on the need to intervene within communities as well as with individuals. The dismantling of social programs during the 1970s, along with a trend toward engaging in private clinical practice, has swung the professional pendulum away from concern with system intervention in the 1980s.

Today, social work has bred an ethic of specialization whereby individuals are trained to practice one type of service to the exclusion of other types. This pattern can be attributed in part to an oversubscription to Taylorism and professionalism. Taylorism required that work be divided into specialized, discrete components. Professionalism demanded that only an elite group of people, specially trained and qualified, were capable of performing certain types of work. Both Taylorism and professionalism were means to increase profit through greater worker efficiency and productivity, without regard to growing worker or client alienation and ennui.

Social work practice has tended to be dichotomized so that an individual worker is a specialist, rather than a generalist. To be a generalist practitioner is to be as adept in intervening with macro systems as with individuals, families, and small groups. Because social work emphasizes the concept of "person-in-situation," it could be argued that generalist practice is the only approach true to social work's ecological foundation. In order to deal with the myriad social problems within contemporary society and the commensurate distress experienced by individuals, generalist practice appears the most tenable approach. Consequently, there needs to be reemphasis on social work embodying a dual service delivery commitment to individuals, families,

12

Feminist Visions

and small groups intricately linked with community, organizational, administrative, and research efforts.

Conceptually, social work supports a practice that stresses concern for the welfare of individuals concomitant with action for improving social conditions. The dualism is more theoretical than actual, however, as persons tend to be dichotomized as caseworkers or administrators, clinicians or community organizers, researchers or practitioners. A social work practitioner operating on one end of the continuum or another cannot be of greatest aid to clients or systems. Implanting a feminist vision within social work education and practice is highly warranted in order to integrate components that have been artificially separated.

By eliminating false dichotomies, social work would move toward more of a generalist model. That is not to imply that practitioners would be without areas of expertise. Individuals would still have domains of particular competence. However, the overall training and practice model would be more integrated and generalist; social work practice would be more holistic, ecological, and preventive. Practitioners would be as committed to working for social change as to ameliorating individual client problems.

Indirect services. The development of social planning, programs, and policies, as well as administrative responsibilities, would be reoriented from short-sighted and limited visions to the feminist theme of interconnectedness. Currently, most planning and policy generation tends to be orchestrated through a "here and now" perspective. Short-term gains are addressed and long-term implications tend not to be assessed. This reflects a finite rather than more infinite perception of reality. Industrial pollution, the environmental crisis, and nuclear proliferation are all testimonies to the pervasiveness of short-term gain planning. An inevitable outcome of this approach is perpetual crisis resolution as resources have to be invested today in order to solve problems created yesterday. Perceiving phenomena in a more interrelated fashion could generate greater integration between actions taken in the present and their future consequences. That is, policies would be implemented with a clearer sense of responsibility for their outcome in the future. A sense of social contract would undergird the planning process.

For example, consider the issue of connectedness as it applies to traditional housing planning and policy. Political, economic, and social values shape the kinds of buildings that are constructed, and buildings affect the type of social interaction that 13 takes place within them. Views of the poor, the mentally ill, elderly people, and delinquent children influence the location and design of housing for those population groups. Housing design affects the self-image and self-esteem of those residing in the domiciles and shapes relationships among inhabitants, staff, and the surrounding community.[30] If a belief in interconnectedness were more prevalent, housing environments might be planned with greater concern for the quality of life they shape.

Research. Challenging false dichotomies, in conducting studies, means eliminating the separation between research and practice. Research needs to be seen as part of practice itself, a process of evaluating effort and outcome. Greater utilization of single-subject designs could bridge the existing gap between practice and research; such designs allow an evaluation of both process and outcome, do not require substantial statistical knowledge, and can be used by clients as a method for self-monitoring.

In addition, employing this agenda challenges positivism. The positivist tradition maintains that research should be objective, neutral, and value-free, with empirical knowledge separated from the pursuit of moral aims, and that all knowledge must be definable, measurable, and testable.[31] Basically, the positivist stance is antiactivist, and therefore antifeminist. Studies undertaken by feminist researchers tend to be precipitated by a strong value stance that the experiences of women and other oppressed groups may be best examined by persons of like affiliation. An extraordinary amount of social science knowledge has been formulated from studies done by and on white males and generalized to be the experience of all persons. Feminist researchers see a need to engage in research with an activist perspective in order to engender social change.

Furthermore, feminists validate the efficacy of intuitive knowing, which is derided as invalid data within the positivist tradition. To value learning gained from intuitive insights would be to eliminate a false dichotomy between left-brain analytical knowing and right-brain creative understanding. It has been postulated that scientific insights are characteristically intuitive; only later are they described and verified by linear analytical argument. Moreover, it has been suggested that the most significant creative activities of our culture have only been made possible through the collaborative work of the left and right hemispheres.[32]

Education. Within the educational experience, eliminating false separations means advocating for generically based core curricu-

14

Feminist Visions

lum content on both the undergraduate and graduate levels. This implies providing "equal time" for course work stressing macro knowledge and practice principles as well as clinical knowledge and skills. A burgeoning of social work private practitioners within the last decade has caused curriculum to become skewed in the clinical direction. Although undergraduate preparation tends to be more generalist, it is equally important to supply indirect services information on the MSW level—and not just for nonclinical students. To practice social work, an MSW should be familiar with concepts, theories, and skills pertaining to organizational, community, and social change. Despite private career ambitions, social workers need to retain their public "roots." They must be cognizant of the clearly articulated mission of social change. Seeing clients privately does not preclude concern for pervasive societal inequities, nor the ability to engage in activism.

Eliminating false dichotomies also suggests the need to ensure that conceptual frameworks are "in contact with reality." That is, theories that are taught need to be based on people's actual experiences, not on speculative conjecture formulated by "informed observers." Too many conceptual frameworks utilized in social work point to individual rather than social pathology. Theories that blame people for their victimization or distress, or that view them out of the context of the historical period and social order in which they live, need to be replaced. Concepts need to be promulgated that indicate that people have the ability to ameliorate individual difficulties *and* that, collectively, we can solve social problems.

Reconceptualizing Power. *Direct services.* Applying this premise to direct services suggests that therapeutic strategies would be modeled to facilitate client empowerment. The emphasis would be on aiding clients to develop skills that could be used to influence their environment. For example, assertiveness training, improving communication abilities, and stress and time management, as well as conflict resolution and negotiation and bargaining skills, would be appropriate parts of the therapeutic process. These approaches are significantly different from the examination of client intrapsychic dynamics that is the hallmark of insight-based psychoanalytic approaches. Drawing from feminist therapy, which is based upon empowerment principles, clients are encouraged to take risks in assuming personal power. Often this entails **15** encouraging the client to express anger and to role-play ways in which that anger can be channeled toward constructive change.[33]

Feminist therapists also take the position that power between therapist and client should be either equal or continually approaching equality. This is not to negate those situations in which clients may attribute to their therapists a certain amount of power based upon the practitioners' knowledge and skills. The assumption is, however, that therapists must not exploit that difference between themselves and their clients by using professional jargon or obscure clinical terms. Clients are viewed as being experts on their own behavior, competent to understand both the impressions and the techniques of their therapists.[34]

Indirect services. Reconceptualizing power on a macro level includes encouragement of planning, policy, and decision-making processes that are more collective and horizontal in structure rather than autocratic and hierarchical. In facilitating such models, it is important to recognize expertise differentials between persons; however, responsibility, as well as opportunities to exert influence, can be shared. Leadership skills can be built by offering individuals new experiences in which they are the primary facilitators of an activity.

It might also be possible to consider the incorporation of "flextime" and job-sharing options as a type of indirect services empowerment. Instead of accepting employment based solely on fixed criteria established by employers, unions representing employees could negotiate for work to take place during times and under conditions more beneficial to the workers. Working collectively in unions, employees would have more latitude and power in creating the conditions of their employment; potential "burnout" could be mediated.

Also related to the empowerment notion for indirect services might be working to decrease the number of managers and supervisors by encouraging workers to utilize peer accountability. Implementing that process could be facilitated through a team model encouraging job sharing, task rotation, and multiskill development. The use of consensus management also provides workers with the opportunity to exert more influence on decisions regarding productivity. An outcome of such processes could be the creation of close working relationships; hence, enhanced job satisfaction.[35]

Similarly, reconceptualized power might be facilitated in **16** agencies by organizing personnel into work groups in which tasks

Feminist Visions

are shifted. Such an arrangement could allow for workers to have a greater sense of integration within and connection to agency services. For example, through the process of rotating workers and job responsibilities within a public welfare department, child protective workers could gain greater experience as well as insight into the entire range of services from finding placements to doing investigations, testifying in court, and providing treatment.

Finally, reconceptualizing power for indirect services would include eliciting consumer input during the planning and policy-making process. Clearly, consumers are more likely to utilize a service if they feel that their input has been sought by decision makers. This has obvious implications for client satisfaction and is empowering because it provides consumers with the ability to exert influence on their environment.

Research. Research must be designed and conducted in order to facilitate client empowerment. Typically, research is viewed as an intrusive act replete with oppressive processes usually not helpful to social work recipients. It is conceptualized as something not readily integrated into practice—something that does not provide rewards to those studied, only to the researcher.

However, research can be an empowering process for clients and can assist in their growth. Single-subject designs can be easily employed with clients and can aid their empowerment by providing ongoing feedback on their movement toward achieving their goals. The process of regularly recording self-assessments on some behavioral or affective dimension can help clients understand their problems. Furthermore, there are built-in incentives to work toward change in order to see alterations in the pattern of a behavior or feeling.

Reconceptualizing power within a research context also means that the purposes of a study, as well as the findings, should not be isolated from respondents. This is to ensure that informants are not excluded from important aspects of the research process, such as determining the study questions, deciding on methodology, analyzing findings, and providing interpretation analysis. Moreover, client feedback can be elicited on the perceived appropriateness of conceptual frameworks or theoretical paradigms used to inform the study.

To employ this vision is to include clients within the research process as active rather than passive participants. It assumes that clients have knowledge, based on their personal experiences, and should be approached to ascertain their "expert" opinion on study **17** issues. In essence, this vision suggests utilization of nonhierarchical research methods so that studies are not generated "from the top down." Rather, they will be guided by a commitment to serve those who are powerless.

Education. What are some potential outcomes of reconceptualizing power for social work education? Social work classes can be considered laboratories for persons experimenting in becoming empowered. Theories and issues related to power should be utilized as unifying themes in order to bridge connections between the sundry manifestations of institutionalized inequality for all oppressed groups. Rather than address the reconceptualization of power solely through a lecture or discussion context, students should experiment with becoming empowered. Role playing would allow individuals to experience being in powerless situations and then asserting influence, strength, and responsibility so as to become empowered. Students could be required to keep a journal about their experiences with powerlessness and empowerment by mandating that they attempt some risk-taking actions within their social environment. Also, students might be encouraged to role play a planning or administrative process where tasks and responsibilities are shifted among different work groups. Didactically, in fact, classroom groups could be established with learning goals that varied over the course of the semester. Students could shift responsibility in facilitating the accomplishment of certain group tasks. One benefit of using social work courses as a laboratory for experimenting with reconceptualized power is that there will be heterogeneity in the classroom population, allowing for a simulation of actual organizational and societal experience.

Students can gain a sense of empowerment by receiving validation for the knowledge they have acquired through life experience. They have information and skills to offer, and faculty can learn from student experiences. Providing reinforcement for learner knowledge establishes a model that can be replicated by the student in work with clients and within agencies.

Another vehicle for teaching empowerment through classroom experiences is utilizing contract grading. Some situations are obviously more conducive to this approach than others; but some opportunity to formulate a self-design evaluation plan should be considered by faculty as a part of the grading scheme. Relatedly, students should be encouraged to provide feedback on their experience with the course and to suggest additional directions or revisions.

18

Feminist Visions

Valuing Process Equally with Product. *Direct services.* Facilitating client independence and empowerment utilizes the principle of valuing process as equal to product. Discouraging dependency on the therapist and encouraging challenging as well as risk-taking behaviors engender a therapeutic process by which independence is learned and validated. The therapist is not envisioned as an omnipotent person who "cures" a client, but, rather, as a facilitator of individuals' innate abilities to heal themselves.

Therapy is acknowledged as a learning experience. Clients are aided in acquiring skills that can be generalized to other problems encountered in life situations, beyond the problem(s) that caused them to seek professional intervention. Direct practice approaches that fail to aid individuals in dealing with problems beyond the presenting issue(s) suggest questionable therapeutic value. *Indirect services.* Incorporating this feminist agenda within indirect services could ensure that the way in which programs are implemented would not contradict service provision goals. Often the ostensible merit of a service becomes contradicted through the processes generated for its implementation. For example, AFDC income maintenance programs have been theoretically created for the purpose of providing security to indigent families with dependent children. Frequently, however, programs have stipulated that in order to receive benefits, a father must not live with his family. The result has been not to provide security but rather to generate insecurity. If a program is founded on principles that generate separations, then the result can only be divisive. Programs utilizing segregating processes will likely create insecurities and alienation. Integrating processes can engender a sense of security and connectedness.

Considering process and product as equivalent in importance also has implications for administrative practice. Traditional bureaucratic management has assumed that administrators must employ a value-free, neutral style in order to expedite getting the job done. In contradiction to that model, being concerned with process includes valuing different experiences and perspectives. For example, an administrator with feminist values will validate multidimensional thinking.[36] She or he recognizes the richness of varied explanatory systems being brought to bear on any decision. This means that how one "feels" about an issue, or one's intuition about a dynamic, is given a value equivalent to concrete facts or realities.

19

Introduction

In a related vein, relationships between co-workers are also recognized as important rather than discounted as inefficient or a waste of time. Valuing relationships, a feminist administrator tries to achieve a fit between individual and organizational needs. For example, support would be given to staff who are dealing with personal problems. Concern with process would also be exemplified by implementing flextime, job sharing, or jobs that could be partially completed at home.[37] These alternatives indicate that providing an environment sensitive to human needs is a component of concern with process.

Another example of the focus on process within a feminist administrative style would be the administrator's showing concern at the beginning of a meeting with participants sharing what is going on with them personally. This is in contrast to the traditional rap of the gavel to start a meeting on time in order to address an agenda. Process time would be structured for critique, sharing opinions, praise, and affirmation.[38] Conflict would be dealt with as it arose rather than being tabled or dismissed. The importance of compromise, of avoiding polarities, is also recognized. Concern with process makes a feminist administrative style more focused on effectiveness than efficiency, which can be seen as the difference between long- and short-range planning.[39] Will a coercive process that engenders short-term goals be able to sustain over time? Multidimensional thinking suggests that the answer is "No."

Education. Teaching students empowering processes will facilitate the development of a commitment to valuing process and product. Social work pedagogy should serve as an example of participatory learning process. Educators need to be keenly aware of creating an environment that maximizes opportunities for people to make connections with each other and become empowered. For example, the beginning and end of each class can allow for personal sharing, with individuals feeling comfortable in stating "what's good and new" for them. Also, the teacher should encourage the students to express anger and pose challenges, which is a difficult and often painful task for the educator. However, by feeling that they can share their process, students may be better able to accept the instructor's process in terms of potential disappointment with student performance. Also, encouraging the articulation of conflict and providing a vehicle for its resolution can serve as a modeling experience to be applied beyond the classroom.

20

Feminist Visions

Renaming.   *Direct services.* Renaming, when applied to direct services, has implications for the support of individual client choice and life experiences. This feminist vision is particularly important for work with minorities. Encouraging clients to examine the strengths of their cultural experience validates renaming. Claiming and renaming one's heritage is an empowering process and is integral within both ethnic-sensitive and feminist practice.

Emphasizing client experience in diagnosis and treatment is a part of this renaming process. Practitioners should never assume that their ethnic clients all have the same cultural frame of reference or interpret events in the same way. Similarly, it should not be assumed that all women or all men view sex-role experiences comparably. Nor should it be assumed that all gay male and lesbian clients have had the same experience and interpret their sexuality in a similar fashion. Practitioners must constantly ask clients to define presenting problems concretely, based on the clients' own experience.

In addition, practitioners should help their clients to understand that they, the clients, have choices in how they name their experiences. In other words, to rename being a wife and mother might mean choosing to work outside the home on a part- or full-time basis, rather than being solely a homemaker. The practitioner's role is to support the idea of clients' having choices.

Another direct practice implication is facilitating group treatment for people of color. By experiencing a collective sharing and problem-solving process, oppressed persons can evolve renamed definitions of personal and collective identity. Group treatment can serve a consciousness-raising function by bringing to an individual's attention the recognition that her or his experience has been shared, to a greater or lesser degree, by others. It was through group consciousness-raising practices in the early years of feminist activism that women began to reclaim and rename what it was to be female. This same phenomenon was experienced by ethnic persons involved in civil rights activism.

Indirect services. Renaming has important implications for indirect practice, including altering the perception of social workers from being "do-gooders" to being agents for social change. Most people appear to consider social workers as friendly visitors distributing alms to the poor, hoping to save souls. Social work needs to be renamed as including organizers and advocates for the elimination of institutionalized inequality and economic oppression. **21**

Validating renaming also suggests supporting gender-centered and ethnic-centered social services, such as battered women's shelters, rape crisis centers, women's health services, and ethnic-oriented services and programs. The issue of special services for special populations is constantly debated within social work, raising such questions as the following: Should there be ethnic agencies that only serve ethnic clientele? Should ethnic foster or adoptive children only be placed within comparable ethnic homes? Should services for battered and raped women be provided by programs that are separate from existing agencies? To support renaming would seem to include validation of the need to allow special services to serve special populations.

Finally, social work must be open to accepting redefinitions of seemingly uncontroversial terms, like family. The receipt of social services is often predicated on conforming to narrowly defined criteria. Social institutions are constantly being challenged and redefined according to cultural exigencies. Consequently, a concept such as family needs redefining as more than a nuclear unit. Family should also mean single parents and children, nonbiologically affiliated persons, extended units with grandparents or other blood relatives, as well as single adults living together. There are obvious implications for adoption and foster parenting related to redefining family. Single adults, both male and female, should be allowed to adopt or act as foster parents. In addition, same-sex partners or couples who are not legally married should be considered eligible adoptive or foster parents.

Research. Renaming in research demands that what has been typically considered as unimportant or not scientific be reexamined as valid. This includes a premise expounded on previously, concerning the need to validate intuition and nonempirical phenomena as sources of knowledge.

Renaming also connects to the personal is political theme by underscoring the significance of individual experience. Personal issues need to be seen as politically important and scientifically valid for the generation of new knowledge and understanding. As applied to research, renaming means that clients have the right to name what is important to study and the methods that should be undertaken within research.

Education. Social work education must examine the experiences of oppressed groups in order to develop the potential to rename what it is to be ethnic, female, aged, gay, and so on. This includes a past, present, and future perspective. The realities of oppressed people must be explicitly studied and renamed in order to reflect the diversity of their experiences.

Although all accredited programs are mandated to cover ethnic and gender content, there seems to be no uniform pattern as to how this mandate is actualized. Unfortunately, too often that content is "ghettoized" in the curriculum and is not inclusively covered in most classes. Care must be taken not to focus solely on demographic characteristics, because this can lead to the promulgation of stereotypes.

In practice classes, students should be aided in learning techniques that allow them to define and validate client experiences. Basically, a strong need exists to ensure that students' work with clients will not be based on stereotypes. Future social workers must understand that there are continuums of experience and that good practice entails determining how clients name and define their own realities.

The Personal Is Political. *Direct services.* Practitioners must aid their clients in understanding that personal problems can be related to political realities. Individuals can be helped to identify both external and internal restraints. External restraints, based on political, economic, and social systems, are manifest as stereotypes, prejudices, discriminatory actions, and blocked opportunities. Internal restraints can be considered the individual's own resistances to changing her or his dysfunctional behavior patterns.[40] When a client encounters resistance in the way of a desired goal and is able to differentiate whether the restraint is internal or external, then that individual is indicating an evolving political consciousness. In essence, the client is renaming her or his experience in a more holistic and therapeutically beneficial way. The tendency to be self-blaming, guilty, and isolated is being mediated. Consequently, political education should be considered a legitimate and necessary component of the therapeutic process. It helps clients to be cognizant of how personal conflicts are connected to contradictions within society. It reinforces that the personal is political.

A second implication of incorporating this premise into direct social work is that the practitioner would be serving as an activist role model. She or he needs to break out of the constraints of the traditional counselor role. This means challenging the sexism, racism, and other prejudices within service delivery systems, as well as in the larger society. Typically, mental health workers have not taken the risks involved in initiating **23**

Introduction

meaningful social action. Social workers need to serve as advocates for the individuals and groups they want to serve. If they do not play that role, then they act as agents of social control by maintaining the status quo.[41]

Indirect services. The personal is political entails sharing professional skills and knowledge. In part, the power of any profession lies in its monopoly over knowledge and skills. To train or to share practice methodologies with community members is to facilitate the empowerment of others. Many human services that have evolved during the last decade as outgrowths of the feminist movement, such as rape crisis centers, battered women's shelters, and women's health services, have systematically trained community persons. This same dynamic has been true for ethnic activism. Many ethnic professionals have taken responsibility to share their knowledge and skills by training others in order to aid in the empowerment of their communities. Practitioners who participate in such training are personally making a political statement that part of their social work responsibility is to share their expertise with others.

Related to sharing knowledge and skills is personal effort undertaken in order to build competent communities. Such communities would be able to challenge existing power structures. This means aiding localities with needs assessment, resource mobilization, and program planning and implementation, as well as evaluative techniques. The practitioner does not need to act out his or her professional role when aiding in these activities but can share "how-to's" as a concerned citizen. Again, this kind of personal commitment clearly has political implications by allowing for community empowerment.

Education. In the classroom students need to be encouraged to share their own experiences when discussing issues of ethnicity, sex, and class. They should be helped to see how their personal experiences are indicators of systemic patterns in society. "Reaction" papers can be assigned whereby students relate how their gender, ethnicity, and class have influenced both personal and work experiences. They can be asked to reflect on the kinds of cultural messages they received concerning roles they should and should not perform.

In addition, it would be beneficial for students to read biographies and memoirs of social workers, such as Jane Addams and Bertha Reynolds, who modeled social change concern with their personal lives. Also, students could be asked to interview community activists in order to ascertain how those individuals' personal lives reflect their social change vision.

24

Feminist Visions

Students should be required to embark upon some kind of social change activity during their academic career. This could include distributing leaflets, participating in a march or demonstration, writing letters to the editor, acting as a spokesperson for a cause, and so on. It is essential that students be clear about the inherent linkage between social work and social change. That awareness is best facilitated by requiring that they engage in activist behaviors.

Conclusion

Feminist visions for social work education and practice are much broader and more inclusive than they would be if they solely addressed "women's issues." Analysis utilizing these visions sharpens the focus on individual as well as societal change. Feminist visions aid in understanding the relationship between personal hardship and institutionalized oppression, validating the unity between public and private life. In addition to eliminating false dichotomies, such a focus also values personal experience; individuals and collectivities are encouraged to rename their realities. Empowerment of persons and communities is envisioned, which means redefining power as an energy of influence and responsibility rather than a commodity to be controlled. As much attention is focused on the process by which a goal is pursued as its accomplishment; means must justify ends.

Examining social work through feminist visions provides a focus for professional practice and education that is integrative, holistic, and ecological. As such, these perspectives can be a synergistic force allowing for accomplishment of social work's unique mission—facilitating social change in order to improve the quality of life.

notes

1. Feminism has raised fundamental questions as to the underlying structure and assumptions of capital economy, professionalism, and bureaucracy. See Ann Withorn, *Serving the People: Social Services and Social Change* (New York: Columbia University Press, 1984).

2. Charlotte Bunch, *Going Public with Our Vision* (Denver, Colo.: Antelope Publications, 1983), p. 19.

25

3. Ibid.

4. Women's Bureau, *Time of Change: 1983 Handbook of Women Workers* (Washington, D.C.: U.S. Department of Labor, 1983), p. 3.

5. Women's Bureau, *Twenty Facts on Women Workers* (Washington, D.C.: U.S. Department of Labor, 1980), p. 1.

6. Women's Bureau, *Time of Change.*

7. Ibid.

8. See Diane Kravetz, "An Overview of Content on Women for the Social Work Curriculum," *Journal of Education for Social Work,* 18 (Spring 1982), pp. 42–49; Caree Rozen Brown and Marilyn Levitt Hellinger, "Therapists' Attitudes toward Women," *Social Work,* 20 (July 1975), pp. 266–270; Dennis M. Dailey, "Are Social Workers Sexist? A Replication," *Social Work,* 25 (January 1980), pp. 46–50; Judith Davenport and Nancy Reims, "Theoretical Orientation and Attitudes toward Women," *Social Work,* 23 (July 1978), pp. 306–309; Trudy Bradley Festinger and Rebecca L. Bounds, "Sex-Role Stereotyping: A Research Note," *Social Work,* 22 (July 1977), pp. 314–315; Joel Fischer et al., "Are Social Workers Sexists?" *Social Work,* 21 (November 1976), pp. 428–433; Linda Hall Harris and Margaret Exner Lucas, "Sex Role Stereotyping," *Social Work,* 21 (September 1976), pp. 390–395; John L. Hipple and Lee Hipple, "Concepts of Ideal Woman and Ideal Man," *Social Work,* 25 (March 1980), pp. 147–149; and Ann Weick and Susan T. Vandiver, eds., *Women, Power, and Change* (Silver Spring, Md.: National Association of Social Workers, 1981).

9. See Pat Diangson, Diane Kravetz, and Judy Lipton, "Sex-Role Stereotyping and Social Work Education," *Journal of Education for Social Work,* 11 (Fall 1975), pp. 44–49; Mary S. Hanlan, "Women in Social Work Administration: Current Role Strains," *Administration in Social Work,* 1 (Fall 1977), pp. 259–265; Mary C. Schwartz, "Sexism in the Social Work Curriculum," *Journal of Education for Social Work,* 9 (Fall 1973), pp. 65–70; and Jean K. Quam and Carol D. Austin, "Coverage of Women's Issues in Eight Social Work Journals, 1970–81," *Social Work,* 29 (July–August 1984), pp. 360–364.

10. See Kravetz, "An Overview of Content on Women"; Cynthia J. Belon and Ketayun H. Gould, "Not Even Equals: Sex-Related Salary Inequities," *Social Work,* 22 (November 1977), pp. 466–471; Gould and Bok-Lim C. Kim, "Salary Inequities between Men and Women in Schools of Social Work: Myth or Reality?" *Journal of Education for Social Work,* 12 (Winter 1976), pp. 50–55; James Gripton, "Sexism in Social Work: Male Takeover of a Female Profession," *The Social Worker,* 42 (Summer 1974), pp. 78–89; Dorothy Chave Herberg, "A Study of Work Participation by Graduate Female Social Workers: Some Implications for Professional Social Work Training," *Journal of Education for Social Work,* 9 (Fall 1973), pp. 16–23; Dorothy Zietz and John L. Erlich, "Sexism in Social Agencies: Practitioners' Perspectives," *Social Work,* 21 (November 1976), pp. 434–439;

Feminist Visions

and Esther Sales, Barbara K. Shore, and Floyd Bolitho, "When Mothers Return to School: A Study of Women Completing an MSW Program," *Journal of Education for Social Work,* 16 (Winter 1980), pp. 57–65.

11. See Phyllis J. Day, "Sex Role Stereotypes and Public Assistance," *Social Service Review,* 53 (March 1979), p. 114; and Miriam Dinerman, "Catch 23: Women, Work, and Welfare," *Social Work,* 22 (November 1977), pp. 472–477.

12. See *Curriculum Policy for the Master's Degree and Baccalaureate Degree Programs in Social Work Education* and *Handbook of Accreditation Standards and Procedures* (New York: Council on Social Work Education, 1982 and 1984, respectively); and *Code of Ethics* (Silver Spring, Md.: National Association of Social Workers, 1980).

13. Z. Eisenstein, *Capitalist Patriarchy and the Case for Socialist Feminism* (New York: Monthly Review Press, 1976), p. 1.

14. Carel B. Germain, *Social Work Practice: People and Environments* (New York: Columbia University Press, 1979), p. 1.

15. A. Mander, "Feminism as Therapy," in E. I. Rawlings and D. K. Carter, *Psychotherapy for Women* (Springfield, Ill.: Charles C Thomas, Publisher, 1977), p. 298.

16. See Z. Budapest, *The Feminist Book of Lights and Shadows* and *The Holy Book of Women's Mysteries* (Venice, Calif.: The Feminist Wicce, 1975 and 1976, respectively); and M. Stone, *When God Was a Woman* (New York: Harcourt Brace Jovanovich, 1976).

17. K. Millett, *Sexual Politics* (New York: Ballantine Books, 1970); S. Firestone, *The Dialectic of Sex* (New York: Bantam Books, 1971); J. Mitchell, *Women's Estate* (New York: Vintage Books, 1973); B. Deckard, *The Women's Movement* (New York: Harper & Row, 1975); A. Kuhn and A. Wolpe, *Feminism and Materialism* (Boston: Routledge & Kegan Paul, 1978); and Eisenstein, *Capitalist Patriarchy.*

18. Eisenstein, *Capitalist Patriarchy,* p. 16.

19. See Millett, *Sexual Politics;* Firestone, *Dialectic of Sex;* Mitchell, *Women's Estate;* and *Feminist Revolution* (New Paltz, N.Y.: Redstockings, 1973).

20. N. Hooyman, "Toward a Feminist Administrative Style." Paper presented at the National Association of Social Workers' First National Conference on Social Work Practice in a Sexist Society, Washington, D.C., September 1980, p. 6.

21. B. Solomon, *Black Empowerment* (New York: Columbia University Press, 1976), p. 16.

22. Hooyman, "Toward a Feminist Administrative Style," p. 7.

23. Ibid., p. 8.

24. June G. Hopps, "Oppression Based on Color," Editorial, *Social Work,* 27 (January 1982), pp. 3–5.

25. M. Daly, *Gyn/Ecology: The Metaethics of Radical Feminism* (Boston: Beacon Press, 1978), p. 2.

Introduction

26. B. Thorne, *Rethinking the Family: Some Feminist Questions* (New York: Longman, 1982), p. 5.

27. Bunch, *Going Public,* p. 10.

28. G. MacKinnon, "Feminism, Marxism, Method and the State: An Agenda for Theory," *Signs,* 7 (Spring 1982), p. 535.

29. For an in-depth discussion of the economic and social transformation occurring at this time, see Herman and Julia R. Schwendinger, *The Sociologists of the Chair* (New York: Basic Books, 1974); Roy Lubove, *The Professional Altruist* (Cambridge, Mass.: Harvard University Press, 1975); and Barbara Ehrenreich and Deirdre English, *For Her Own Good* (New York: Anchor Press, 1978).

30. Germain, *Social Work Practice,* p. 437.

31. L. Rosenman and R. Ruckdeschel, "Catch 1234B: Integrating Material on Women into the Social Work Research Curriculum," *Journal of Education for Social Work,* 17 (Spring 1981), p. 6.

32. R. Valet, "Creative Imagination: To Man's Advancement," *Fresno Bee,* February 13, 1983, p. G1.

33. E. Kaschak, "Feminist Psychotherapy: The First Decade," in S. Cox, ed., *Female Psychology: The Emerging Self* (New York: St. Martin's Press, 1981), pp. 393–399.

34. Ibid., p. 396.

35. Hooyman, "Toward a Feminist Administrative Style," p. 13.

36. C. Ellsworth et al., "Toward a Feminist Model of Planning for and with Women." Paper presented at the National Association of Social Workers' First National Conference on Social Work Practice in a Sexist Society, Washington, D.C., September 1980, p. 9.

37. Hooyman, "Toward a Feminist Administrative Style," p. 5.

38. M. Lapton and A. Thompson, "Living with Conflict on the Journal," *Women: A Journal of Liberation,* 2 (1980), pp. 48–50.

39. Hooyman, "Toward a Feminist Administrative Style," p. 6.

40. N. B. Gluckstern, "Beyond Therapy: Personal and Institutional Change," in Rawlings and Carter, eds., *Psychotherapy for Women,* p. 437.

41. E. I. Rawlings and D. K. Carter, "Psychotherapy for Social Change," in Rawlings and Carter, eds., *Psychotherapy for Women,* p. 47.

28

Feminist Visions

Diane Goldstein Wicker

combating
racism in
practice and in
the classroom

in its section on the social
worker's ethical responsibility to society, the Code of
Ethics of the National Association of Social Workers states that

> the social worker should act to prevent and eliminate
> discrimination against any person or group on the basis
> of race, color, sex, sexual orientation, age, religion,
> national origin, marital status, political belief, mental
> or physical handicap, or any other preference or
> personal characteristic, condition, or status.[1]

Yet discrimination persists, both by individual social workers and
by the institutions in which they practice, even though many
social workers have allied themselves with antiracist work such
as the civil rights movement.

This chapter is directed to white educators, practitioners,
and administrators and focuses on the issue of white racism
within the field of social work and its broader influence in society.
Because feminism systematically analyzes power relationships and **29**

hierarchical structures and offers ideas for fundamental change, feminist theory can and must be applied to evolve solutions to the central issue of racism: dealing with the prejudice and power of whites over people of color.

Looking at racism in social work from a feminist perspective forces us to deal with racism not as "something out there in society," "something too big to handle," or "something I don't participate in because I'm not racist," but as something endemic to whites, related to our personal lives. This perspective then moves to understanding racism at the political and institutional level. Racism is understood in the context of the personal and the political. A feminist analysis allows us to drop the competition among oppressions and to look at how all kinds of discrimination serve the power structure; a feminist analysis can be used to see through these artificial divisions.

Two concepts are crucial in understanding how white racism works: The first holds that all whites are racist; the second, that racism hurts whites as well as people of color.[2]

All Whites Are Racist

The first concept, that *all whites are racist*, has as its corollary that only whites can be racist in a white-controlled society. Although people of color (as well as whites) can be prejudiced, that is, can nurture "unfavorable opinions or feelings formed beforehand without knowledge, thought, or reason," racism is more than prejudice.[3] It is *power plus prejudice;* in this society, power is clearly vested with whites and white institutions.[4] It is essential to understand that racism refers to systematic discrimination within our institutions and uses institutional power to distribute benefits and resources to white people and to withhold them from people of color. (Within this system, whites benefit in varying degrees, with poor white women benefiting the least and wealthy white males benefiting the most.)

The concept that all whites are racist is difficult for white people to accept. Seeing ourselves as racist is uncomfortable, particularly for those who may have been active in the civil rights movement or other organized antiracist groups. After much work struggling with the concept and definition of white racism, most people begin to understand the specific truth—that all whites are racist and benefit from white privilege in a racist system

Feminist Visions

simply by virtue of being white. In order for us to be effective antiracists, we must understand the distinctions between prejudice and racism. If all prejudice could be expunged from white consciousness, the systematic discrimination built into the fiber of U.S. institutions—in racist textbooks, racist housing policies, and the sterilization abuse of Third World women, for example— would still remain because changing prejudiced attitudes does not change racist laws and policy. Only organized political action and lobbying will change institutional racism.

Once white people begin to accept their racism, a certain freedom arises from being able to let go of defenses. Pretending to be nonracist in a white racist society takes as much energy and time as keeping racist attitudes intact.[5] To look at racism and prejudice, we must first recognize them in ourselves and those like ourselves; in order to root out racist attitudes, we must understand clearly and feel how racism damages all of us and then move toward purposeful antiracist action.

Racism Damages White People

The second concept—that *racism damages white people, too*—is essential if white people are to escape from the "do-gooder" mentality, which prevents us from coming to terms with our own pain and losses in a fundamental way.

How, exactly, does racism damage white people? Bowser and Hunt state that the costs of prejudice and discrimination include: (1) personality distortions arising from tensions inherent within chronic dilemmas of "moral ambivalence"; (2) economic waste stemming from the dollar cost of supporting discriminatory programs, inefficiencies in the use of labor resources, lower tax yield, and depressed productivity; (3) the political debilitation of a divided society; and (4) disorderly international relations.[6]

When one group is pitted against another, especially among the poor, both groups are effectively prevented from identifying the real enemy and from recognizing true allies, and are hindered in becoming effective organizers for all working people. Teaching one group that they are better than another because of skin color produces a false sense of psychological security.

Racist lies are taught to children early; thus we receive false information about people and about the world. This false information hinders our ability to think clearly about ourselves, other **31** people, and our capacity to live our lives in harmony with the environment. False information distorts reality and keeps us from loving one another freely; it robs us of the richness of knowing people different from ourselves and challenging ourselves with the differences. Racism forces white people to blend in with one another and deprives them of their own cultural heritage. On an institutional level, it misleads people into thinking that there are individual solutions to social and political problems.

Antiracist Education

Feminist pedagogy (feminist theory applied to classroom situations) can offer social work education some unique concepts about nonhierarchical teaching methodologies that enable social work students to deal more effectively and nondefensively with their racism. Many of the teaching methodologies in this chapter come from careful attention to feminist principles, such as: connecting theory to personal practice ("The personal is political"), bringing theory close to everyday-life activities, working on both cognitive and emotional levels, and attention to power issues leading to a nonhierarchical classroom setting. Whenever possible, I acknowledge the power structure in the classroom and work toward creating a cooperative, nondefensive atmosphere. If I believe in nonhierarchical structures in society but function hierarchically in the classroom, I have not learned how to integrate my beliefs into practice. Although it is impossible to equalize the teacher-student relationship in a traditional setting, acknowledging power and problem solving with students on how to make that relationship less oppressive often results in a classroom environment that allows students to participate more fully and challenges both teachers and students to work more creatively together.[7]

To develop strongly antiracist social workers, social work education programs must make combating racism a priority. In keeping with this priority, social work programs must create task forces composed of faculty, students, and community representatives to discuss how to develop antiracist strategies. Careful attention should be paid to community issues involving racism and the quality of life for people of color in the community.

The curriculum should include a required course devoted to racism; this course can often be taught in conjunction with the topic of sexism. Although there are important differences between these two types of oppression, they also overlap. It is necessary to recognize the differences but equally important to recognize the connections: Both kinds of oppression work to further the prosperity of a few and the suppression of the majority. Focusing on the differences prevents people from developing effective strategies for social change.

The Council on Interracial Books for Children defines racism as "any action or institutional structure which subordinates a person or group because of their color."[8] Sexism is defined as any action or institutional structure that subordinates individuals or groups because of their sex. Racism and sexism particularly overlap when we study the lives of women of color, who have to struggle daily with both "isms." Telling examples of this struggle emerge in statistics such as the following: (1) In 1978, black women died in childbirth at a rate almost four times that of white women, and (2) between 1975 and 1980, black adult women had the largest percentage increase in unemployment, making black female heads of households the group most severely affected by unemployment during that time. In 1980, 34.4 percent of Latina women lived below the poverty level, as compared to 19 percent of white women.[9]

Because both racism and sexism require full exploration, an entire course should be devoted to each topic. In teaching these courses, however, the instructor should discuss the connections between them. Course content should include an in-depth understanding of institutional racism, personal work on racism, and methods for developing strategies in the struggle against racism. In the following sections, material is offered related to content and process, both of which must be addressed in education.

Institutional Racism.   When teaching about institutional racism, it is helpful to work first with basic definitions of racism and prejudice. The Council on Interracial Books for Children has a list of definitions, statistical information, and a variety of films for this purpose.[10] A full explanation of the two basic concepts is essential.

After these concepts are fully understood, readings on people of color, guest lectures from people of color, and films and literature by and about people of color can be used as classroom material. There is a growing collection of literature written by **33** women of color that is particularly important to draw on now.[11]

The instructor should require projects (instead of exams) that have to do with the struggle against racism. Each student could make a contract with other students and the instructor on three tasks she or he would like to accomplish during the semester. A list of suggestions provided by the instructor could include: a paper on a personal experience of racism ("What did you do about it then? How would you change your response now?"); an interview with a person of different color, focusing on issues of race, class, and sex; antiracist community work; joining an organization and writing a paper on what was done; or an analysis of racism and sexism in a social work agency.[12] A class organizing project on racism could entail bringing together campus groups that are unfamiliar with one another.

In addition to a required course on racism, programs should make available an ongoing study group or consciousness-raising group on racism that meets outside of class. Both faculty and students could participate nonhierarchically; students could receive credit. This group should be structured to provide shared facilitation and equal participation. Content could emphasize the reading of current books or articles on racism or books written by people of color. This group should not be an academic group but one that shares on a personal level. For example, Alice Walker's book *The Color Purple* can be read and discussed on an emotional level, then examined for its piercing look at institutional racism as it is experienced by Walker's characters.[13] Feminist principles should be applied in organizing this group: agreements on structure and ground rules must be made to provide an adequately safe environment.

Another suggestion for making racism a priority is to have students entering the MSW program be required to read and respond to a statement—which might be included in the application packet—that clearly indicates that the program is antiracist and expects students to look at their own racism on a personal level as well as to study and understand institutional racism. A short definition of "personal work" should be included. At this time students should be asked to respond to the question, "How do you struggle against racism?"

Another classroom issue for social work programs involves students' confronting those who may enjoy more power in such relationships as student-teacher or worker-employer relationships.

34 My own approach in the classroom is to state that although I have been struggling against racism for years, I still benefit from a racist society and have not eliminated my racism. I point out that I am racist because I benefit from white privilege and that I am antiracist because I actively struggle against racism. I encourage students to point out my racism or prejudice if they recognize it. Teachers must be open to struggling with their racism in public and private settings. Making statements such as the one above facilitates more openness among students. Setting a permissive, nondefensive tone is an effective technique in helping students deal honestly with their racism.

Workable techniques for confronting people in power positions about racism could be role-played in the classroom setting. Students and instructors could volunteer incidents that they did not know how to handle, and new approaches could be discussed. Some examples are: a worker confronting an employer about the employer's racism; confronting parents; and a student confronting a teacher. It is important to think of goals and strategies concerning the desired outcome.

Personal Work. Personal work on racism and prejudice has often been neglected. Even though we hold contrary intellectual beliefs, racism is still deeply rooted in our emotions. Unlearning racism requires a commitment to attack the roots of our prejudices from a feeling level.[14] It is particularly important for teachers to have done their own personal work before conducting the following exercises in the classroom.[15]

In personal work, we identify early childhood experiences of prejudice. In identifying where we learned these attitudes, ideas, feelings, and their "roots," we attempt to purge ourselves. Even though intellectually we know that these attitudes are wrong and are not how we want to think, we cannot get rid of them easily. First we must face them, and, in doing so, recognize the full weight of our racist heritage, which is inescapable. Racist ideas have a hold on us deep within; only special examination of them will allow us to begin to rid ourselves of them.

These racist attitudes are exemplified by the racist words we all learned as children. Most whites are embarrassed, guilt-ridden, and immobilized by these words and the attitudes they embody. We want to ignore and deny them, but they are so ingrained that ignoring or denying them will not make them go away. Only dealing with them head on can demystify their hold. **35**

Personal work should be interspersed throughout the course with learning about institutional racism and the lives of people of color. It is important to give students an understanding and full explanation of why we need to do personal work.

Personal work can be facilitated in class by using a series of exercises designed for this purpose. One exercise that can help bring racism to the surface is to have students work in dyads, saying out loud all the racist and prejudiced words, phrases, and attitudes they know. Say them, write them, own them! Whether we know it or not, these words roll around inside of us; when white people are around people of color, we struggle to suppress these words. Though often unintentionally, our racist attitudes distort relationships with people of color. We have become too busy choosing our words carefully, and thus we are stilted in our communication.[16]

Another helpful exercise for tracing the roots of our personal racism is to answer a series of questions about early childhood experiences. "When did you first meet a person of a different skin color than your own? What were your feelings and thoughts? What did you know about people from that culture? What were you taught at that time about people from different ethnic groups? How did you feel about yourself at that time?"[17] This exercise can be done in dyads or small groups, followed by a more general class discussion. Students may divide themselves into groups; sometimes people of color prefer to work together so that they do not have to hear white people's racist experiences.

A crucial part of personal work involves knowing your own cultural heritage and validating the parts of it that feel positive. This can be done in groups or in pairs. Participants each have five minutes to describe themselves and the positive things they receive from their heritage. Often white people parasitize people of color. We may idolize people of color as having fascinating and colorful roots and customs—in fact wanting or envying that heritage and denying our own. This romanticizing of people of color only perpetuates their objectification. Whites can only become antiracist by knowing who they are and owning their own cultural history. Many whites lack a sense of their cultural heritage because a racist system teaches us that being different is bad; those who are different, or "others," are often persecuted. Taught to blend in with the rest, white people often have difficulty finding anything positive in their origins. For some, this realization can be startling and painful; during these exercises,

Feminist Visions

for example, people can often become emotional and feel sad.

In the classroom setting, the exercise of validating cultural roots can be incredibly empowering for both whites and people of color. Instructors should allow time for discussion of the links and connections between personal and institutional racism, using personal experiences to illustrate how they support institutional racism. Instructors should also be certain to give students time to deal with the deep emotions that the exercises can arouse.

Rooting Racism from Direct Practice

Just as schools of social work must make struggling against racism a priority, so must individual practitioners. To be effectively antiracist, clinicians need to work on three areas: personal racism, prejudice in clinical practice with clients, and political activism.

Social workers, as well as other helping professionals, have a special mandate to scrutinize their racism in working with clients of color. People coming to them for help are already in a vulnerable, powerless position and do not need further racist injury inflicted by unaware practitioners.

Many clinicians believe it is enough to look at their own racism on a superficial level and do not really deal with the depths of their prejudices. Some social workers verbally deplore racism but are timid when it comes to confronting the racist policies of their agency (hiring practices, unavailability of service to people of color, not having bilingual workers, whites developing programs for Third World people). It is important that practitioners join together at the workplace to evaluate how Third World people are being treated there and in the local community.

Racism can be unintentional and naively perpetuated by frontline workers because it is so institutionalized that we often do not notice it.[18] As social workers, we must be prepared to do creative problem solving and have the courage to push ourselves, our co-workers, and our administrators to struggle effectively against racism. Passive acceptance of racist situations—even ones created by others—ensures the perpetuation of a racist system.

Personal Work.   Clinicians can work on their personal racism in a variety of ways:

1. Form nonhierarchical peer-supervision groups at work to discuss basic definitions of racism and prejudice; then use a variety **37**

of therapeutic techniques, such as role-playing, psychodrama, and gestalt, to help one another look at prejudice and racism in clinical work with people of color. Set up mock racist situations that are possible in your agency—for example: "analyzing why people of color are not using a primarily white agency." Role-play these situations, encourage discharge of feelings, and then move into problem solving. Do not be afraid to face racist and prejudiced attitudes; do not be afraid to say racist words. This group can probe early childhood experiences of racism in order to ferret out racist attitudes. Consider setting up gestalt or psychodrama experiences to allow participants to go back and confront racist experiences with parents, teachers, or friends, this time with the power to change those experiences. In doing this work, it is important to pay attention to feelings: Racism is painful; it hurts all of us.

To create a safe environment in which to do this work with colleagues, every participant must have a thorough understanding of what the ground rules are and "why we are doing this." Participants must strive for an attitude of helpfulness instead of one of competition—for example, stating that "You are more racist than I am" is pointless.

2. Reading literature and nonfiction written by people of color is vital to educate ourselves about people who are different and who live in different cultures.[19]

3. Attend multicultural events. Learn about ethnocentrism and how it alienates the group in power by presuming that only one culture—the dominant culture—exists. Support multicultural events in your community. Feel what it is like to be in the minority. What does this experience teach us about racism?

4. Attend "unlearning racism" workshops.

Working with Clients. Some suggestions follow that enable clinicians to scrutinize their racism concerning clients of a different color.

1. Ask the client how she or he feels about working with you. What are the drawbacks? Are there any positive factors?

2. Are you aware of and do you have information about the client's cultural heritage? What does it mean to the client? How important is it? How did it help shape her or his personality and belief systems? Read about the client's culture. If the client is paying an agency for the sessions, can you arrange free sessions with the client to help educate yourself? If you are in private

38

practice, do not charge the client for sessions that are primarily teaching you about her or his culture.

3. Ask yourself about your assumptions, hidden or blatant, about this client. The material these questions elicit can be examined more closely in the peer-supervision group suggested earlier. If such a group is not available, consult with another antiracist clinician. Verbalize your assumptions out loud, look at them, face them; if they make you feel guilty, where can you go next with them? White guilt not only immobilizes us, it inhibits effective struggle against our racism. By keeping us patronizing and sympathetic, white guilt prevents us from empathizing and empowering.

4. Be clear on how racism affects clients' lives on a daily basis. If you are a member of another minority group—gay, female, Jewish—try to identify the oppression of racism with the kind of oppression you have dealt with on a daily basis. What are *your* survival skills? Recognize and validate those survival skills; do not treat your client as a victim. Clinical labeling has been used to paper over the effects of racism and prejudice. Labeling "powerlessness," for example, which is an effect of racism, as a "lack of assertiveness or competence" on the client's part ignores the client's reality and her or his experience of racism, thus perpetuating a racist system. Clinicians do not need to ignore intrapsychic material to understand the social and political context of the client's life. In the example cited here, assertiveness training might make the client feel better but does nothing to change the system of racism on an institutional or political level. Unless clinicians and clients acknowledge the reality of racism, clinicians will only frustrate the clients further by denying their experiences.

5. Interrupt racism in the therapeutic setting. This is going to be a controversial suggestion, because the therapeutic setting is supposed to be sacred and provide total permission for the client. I believe that good clinical skills can be used to interrupt the internalized oppression of people of color or white racism within the clinical setting. Interrupting internalized oppression—defined here as the oppressed taking on stereotyped views that the oppressor holds about them—with clients of color is essential. Both these issues—internalized oppression and white racism—must also be dealt with in group settings.

6. Encourage clients to get involved in antiracist organizations as a constructive way to deal with feelings of hopelessness and powerlessness.

7. Under certain circumstances, antiracist clinicians must be able to exercise the option not to work with a client. Often this option simply is not available; clinicians are taught that they should be able to work with anyone. But when clinicians feel that their personal racism will interfere with working effectively with a client, they should not inflict that racism on the client. Once they have removed themselves from the case, such clinicians must make a commitment to wage an overt struggle with their racism.

Political Activism. To deal with systematic racism, clinicians need to be politically active within their community. To be antiracist also means to work actively to stop racism. Political awareness gives the clinician a better understanding of the racist policies and practices that affect us all.

Antiracist organizations, such as anti-Klan groups, fair housing groups, or welfare rights groups, are opportunities for political activity that social workers should become involved in. Local ad hoc groups that form around certain issues in the community offer another possibility for political activism. Participation in local campaigns for antiracist politicians is another way of getting involved. National organizations with local chapters—such as the National Committee Against Racist and Political Oppression and CISPES (U.S. Committee in Solidarity with the People of El Salvador)—also provide opportunities for activism. It is important to be aware of the stand on racism of groups you may already be involved in. How do all the issues of racism, classism, and sexism connect in your community?

Dealing with Racism in Administration

If we examine primary and secondary social work settings in agencies and institutions from a feminist perspective, we can see that many racist policies need to be changed. Racism can be found in agency hiring practices and job advancement policies. Racist policies affect delivery of services, and racist workers carry out these policies. What can individuals do to change this situation?

To evaluate racism, it is crucial to evaluate first how power is handled, who has it, how it is distributed, and who is involved in the decision-making process. If the agency setting is a traditionally hierarchical one, then racism will be institutionalized. **40** Even if the agency is struggling with a consensual organizational style within a predominantly white organization, racism will still exist, but it will not be bureaucratic in nature and should be more easily remedied. Alternate structures are more likely to be found in nontraditional women's organizations, such as battered women's shelters.

The administration of feminist programs needs to be studied for information on the implementation of nonhierarchical structures such as consensual democracy, an organizational form that represents a stable compromise between the values and rewards of the collective and the necessities of existing in the real world. The connection between authoritarianism and racism has already been studied[20]; studies measuring the extent of racism in a hierarchical structure versus a more collective structure would be beneficial in developing new strategies for combating institutional and administrative racism.

Clinicians must realize that many of our social service programs are systematically racist and that such racist programs affect both poor white people and people of color. This is most often true in geographical areas where there are many people of color; racist welfare programs can result in the distribution of fewer funds in comparison to overall need. White people in these areas are similarly affected.[21]

People of color who are frontline workers in social work programs are sometimes just one step above the clientele served in economic security. A racist system will give some people of color a little more power than service recipients, thus furthering racist injury by having policies carried out by the client's own brothers and sisters. Such a system will reinforce internalized oppression in workers of color, causing some to believe, for example, that people of color are lazy, whereas in fact they are without adequate resources. Only further up the hierarchical ladder do white faces begin to emerge. This particular strategy of institutional racism confuses and divides us, making us angry at each other rather than at the administrators of policy, and diffuses our power. Racism hides true information, preventing effective organizing. Obscure policies need to be ferreted out, and fundamental structural changes need to be made. Given the current political climate, however, it is unlikely that radical changes will take place. We must, therefore, continue to whittle away at this racist system and slowly break it down.

Demeaning programs can be renamed, thus diffusing racist language; special service programs should be developed by the **41** people the programs will serve; recruitment of people of color must be a priority and should entail developing innovative ways to deal with recruitment; administrators must do personal and institutional work on racism; worker evaluations should include questions probing how practitioners are struggling against racism; and agency administrators need to be open to outside evaluation. Job interviews and licensing boards should include questions on racism. We need to continue to lobby in Washington, D.C., for creative human service programs and to keep up the fight against the enormous cutbacks in this area.

Summary   Unlearning racism can be greatly enhanced by using a feminist perspective because of the emphasis in feminist pedagogy on integrating political theory with personal practice and creating classroom environments that share responsibility and power. These same concepts can be applied to struggling against racism outside the classroom, in the agency, and in the community.

Moving from nonracism to antiracism is a challenge. Social work programs, agencies, and practitioners need to take up this challenge in order to strategize effectively and systematically against racist policies. Unlearning racism and struggling against it must be a number one priority.

notes

1. *Code of Ethics* (Silver Spring, Md.: National Association of Social Workers, 1980), p. 9.

2. Benjamin Bowser and Raymond Hunt, eds., *Impact of Racism on White Americans* (Beverly Hills, Calif.: Sage Publications, 1981).

3. Council on Interracial Books for Children, *Definitions of Racism* (New York: Racism/Sexism Resource Center for Educators, 1983), p. 1.

4. Ibid.

5. Bowser and Hunt, eds., *Impact of Racism on White Americans,* passim.

Feminist Visions

6. Ibid., p. 17.

7. Many of the strategies and ideas about racism discussed here were originally developed while I was team-teaching with Linda Shaw. For an in-depth description of materials and exercises, see Linda Shaw and Diane Wicker, "Teaching about Racism in the Classroom and the Community," *Heresies*, 15 (1982), pp. 9–14.

8. Council on Interracial Books for Children, *Definitions of Racism*, p. 1.

9. *Fact Sheet on Institutional Racism* (New York: Council on Interracial Books for Children, 1984), p. 18.

10. Ibid.; and Council on Interracial Books for Children, *Definitions of Racism*.

11. See, for example, Cherrie Moraga, *Loving in the War Years* (Boston: South End Press, 1983); Gloria T. Hull, Patricia Bell Scott, and Barbara Smith, eds., *All the Women Are White, All the Blacks Are Men, But Some of Us Are Brave: Black Women's Studies* (Old Westbury, N.Y.: Feminist Press, 1982) (this book also includes an enormous bibliography on black women); Alice Walker, *The Third Life of Grange Copeland* (New York: Harcourt Brace Jovanovich, 1977); and Audre Lorde, *Zami* (Trumansburg, N.Y.: Crossing Press, 1983).

12. Council on Interracial Books for Children, *Fact Sheet on Institutional Racism*.

13. Alice Walker, *The Color Purple* (New York: Washington Square Press, 1982).

14. Sara Winter, "Rooting Out Racism," *Issues in Radical Psychiatry*, 17 (Winter 1975), p. 18.

15. Shaw and Wicker, "Teaching about Racism in the Classroom and the Community."

16. Winter, "Rooting Out Racism."

17. A more detailed list of questions can be found in Tia Cross et al., "Face-to-Face, Day-to-Day—Racism CR," *Heresies*, 15 (1982), p. 66; also in Hull, Scott, and Smith, eds., *All the Women Are White, All the Blacks Are Men, But Some of Us Are Brave*, pp. 52–56.

18. For an in-depth discussion of racism and poverty policies pertaining to the administration of Aid to Families with Dependent Children, see Kenneth Neubeck and Jack L. Roach, "Racism and Poverty Policies," in Bowser and Hunt, eds., *Impact of Racism on White Americans*, pp. 160–172.

19. Some particularly relevant works are: Joyce Ladner, *Tomorrow's* **43**

Tomorrow (Garden City, N.Y.: Doubleday & Co., 1972); Zora Neale Hurston, *Their Eyes Were Watching God* (Urbana: University of Illinois Press, 1978); Frantz Fanon, *The Wretched of the Earth* (New York: Grove Press, 1965); Paula Gunn Allen, *The Woman Who Owned the Shadows* (Austin, Tex.: Thorp Spring Press, 1984); Maxine Hong Kingston, *China Men* (New York: Alfred A. Knopf, 1980); Herbert Biberman, *Salt of the Earth: The Story of a Film,* Carlos E. Cortes, ed., Chicano Heritage Series (Salem, N.H.: Ayer Co. Publishers, 1976), also printed in *California Quarterly* (1953); and Rosaura Sandez and Rosa Martinez Cruz, *Essays on La Mujer* (Los Angeles: University of California at Los Angeles, Chicano Studies, 1977).

20. Bowser and Hunt, eds., *Impact of Racism on White Americans.*

21. Ibid.

Barbara Smith

some home truths on the contemporary black feminist movement

in "Some Home Truths on the Contemporary Black Feminist Movement," Barbara Smith writes eloquently on the unity of feminism and antiracism. By carefully examining various myths about black women and feminism, she systematically demonstrates the strength and power of this unity in struggling for a society in which oppression, domination, and degradation have been replaced by liberation and freedom. There is "no use for ranking oppressions," she writes; it is "the simultaneity of oppressions," the interlocking nature of racism and sexism, that propels all of us in the struggle for creating a new society. A feminist vision for social work is committed to this unity. Smith helps point the way.

All women of color experience multiple oppressions based on race, gender, and income. Smith's analysis of these conditions for black women documents the importance and necessity for social work educators and practitioners to recognize and act on these multiple conditions. Comprehensiveness in service delivery is ensured by focusing on the different and specific needs of women of color. Agencies and policymakers must support funding services for ethnic populations. Creative and sensitive programs must be developed by and with women of color to define these unique needs. For example, when women of color experience family violence, can they be expected to ask for police protection **45** *without reluctance? It is not likely, because the police have a brutal record of killing and violence in ethnic communities. And, when women of color go to a shelter for battered women, where there are few, if any, women of color on staff, will their experiences there be different from those of white women? Low-income women of color are the most at risk for mental illness, particularly depression. The social reality for these women includes an unpredictable income, the lack of child care, poor housing, inadequate employment opportunities, dependence on social agencies, and the experience of discrimination and violent crime.*

We must ask, What services and programs can social workers develop to respond to these unique problems? Supporting ethnic-sensitive services is not enough. Ethnic- and gender-based services must be created. The issues faced by women of color are a central part of a feminist vision of social work. Therefore, we must recommit ourselves to altering the existing pattern of social work education and practice. —Eds.

In the fall of 1981, before most of *Home Girls*[1] was compiled, I was searching for a title. I'd come up with one that I knew was not quite right. At the time I was also working on the story which later became "Home" and thought that I'd like to get some of the feeling of that piece into the book. One day while doing something else entirely, and playing with words in my head, "home girls" came to me. Home Girls. The girls from the neighborhood and from the block, the girls we grew up with. I knew I was onto something, particularly when I considered that so many black people who are threatened by feminism have argued that by being a black feminist (particularly if you are a lesbian) you have left the race, are no longer a part of the black community, in short, no longer have a home.

I suspect that most of the contributors to *Home Girls* learned their varied politics and their shared commitment to black women from the same sources I did. Yet critics of feminism pretend that just because some of us speak out about sexual politics *at home*, within the black community, we must have sprung miraculously from somewhere else. But we are not strangers and never have been. I am convinced that black feminism is, on every level, organic to black experience.

Black women as a group have never been fools. We could not afford to be. Yet, in the last two decades, many of us have been deterred from identifying with a liberation struggle which might say significant things to women like ourselves, women who believe that we were put here for a purpose in our own right, women who are usually not afraid to struggle.

46

Feminist Visions

Although our involvement has increased considerably in recent years, there are countless reasons why black and other Third World women have not identified with contemporary feminism in large numbers.[2] The racism of white women in the women's movement has certainly been a major factor. The powers-that-be are also aware that a movement of progressive Third World women in this country would alter life as we know it.

As a result, there has been a concerted effort to keep women of color from organizing autonomously and from organizing with other women around women's political issues. Third World men, desiring to maintain power over "their women" at all costs, have been among the most willing reinforcers of the fears and myths about the women's movement, attempting to scare us away from figuring things out for ourselves.

It is fascinating to look at various kinds of media from the late 1960s and early 1970s, when feminism was making its great initial impact, in order to see what black men, Native American men, Asian American men, Latino men, and white men were saying about the irrelevance of "women's lib" to women of color. White men and Third World men, ranging from conservatives to radicals, pointed to the seeming lack of participation of women of color in the movement in order to discredit it and to undermine the efforts of the movement as a whole. All kinds of men were running scared because they knew that if the women in their midst were changing, they were going to have to change too. In 1976, I wrote:

> Feminism is potentially the most threatening of
> movements to Black and other Third World people
> because it makes it absolutely essential that we
> examine the way we live, how we treat each other,
> and what we believe. It calls into question the most
> basic assumption about our existence and this is the
> idea that biological, i.e., sexual identity, determines all,
> that it is the rationale for power relationships as well
> as for all other levels of human identity and action.
> An irony is that among Third World people biological
> determinism is rejected and fought against when it is
> applied to race, but generally unquestioned when it
> applies to sex.[3]

In reaction to the "threat" of such change, black men, with the collaboration of some black women, developed a set of myths to divert black women from our own freedom.   **47**

Contemporary Black Feminist Movement

Myths   *Myth No. 1: The Black Woman Is
                   Already Liberated.*   This myth
                   confuses liberation with the fact
                   that black women have had to take
on responsibilities that our oppression gives us no choice but to
handle. This is an insidious, but widespread, myth that many
black women have believed themselves. Heading families, working outside the home, not building lives or expectations dependent on males, seldom being sheltered or pampered as women,
black women have known that their lives in some ways incorporated goals that white middle-class women were striving for,
but race and class privileges, of course, reshaped the meaning
of those goals profoundly.

As W. E. B. DuBois said so long ago about black women:
" . . .our women in black had freedom contemptuously thrust
upon them."[4] Of all the people here, women of color generally
have the fewest choices about the circumstances of their lives.
An ability to cope under the worst conditions is not liberation,
although our spiritual capacities have often made it look like a
life. Black men did not say anything about how poverty, unequal pay, no child care, violence of every kind, including battering, rape, and sterilization abuse, translated into "liberation."

Underlying this myth is the assumption that black women
are towers of strength who neither feel nor need what other
human beings do, either emotionally or materially. White male
social scientists, particularly Daniel P. Moynihan with his
"matriarchy theory," further reinforce distortions concerning black
women's actual status. A song inspired by their mothers and sung
by Sweet Honey in the Rock, "Oughta Be A Woman," with lyrics
by June Jordan and music by Bernice Johnson Reagon, responds
succinctly to the insensitivity of the myth that black women are
already liberated and illustrates the home-based concerns of black
feminism. Its final stanza states:

> A way outa no way is flesh outa flesh
> Courage that cries out at night
> A way outa no way is flesh outa flesh
> Bravery kept outa sight
> A way outa no way is too much to ask
> Too much of a task for any one woman.[5]

Myth No. 2: Racism Is the Primary (or Only) Oppression Black
48 *Women Have to Confront.*   This myth goes hand in hand

Feminist Visions

with the one that the black woman is already liberated. The notion that struggling against or eliminating racism will completely alleviate black women's problems does not take into account the way that sexual oppression cuts across all racial, nationality, age, religious, ethnic, and class groupings. Afro-Americans are no exception.

It also does not take into account how oppression operates. Every generation of black people, up until now, has had to face the reality that no matter how hard we work, we will probably not see the end of racism in our lifetimes. Yet many of us keep faith and try to do all we can to make change now. If we have to wait for racism to be obliterated *before* we can begin to address sexism, we will be waiting for a long time. Denying that sexual oppression exists or requiring that we wait to bring it up until racism, or in some cases capitalism, is toppled, is a bankrupt position. A black feminist perspective has no use for ranking oppressions, but instead demonstrates the simultaneity of oppressions as they affect Third World women's lives.

Myth No. 3: Feminism Is Nothing but Man Hating. It is important to make a distinction between attacking institutionalized, systematic oppression (the goal of any serious progressive movement) and attacking men as individuals. Unfortunately, some of the most widely distributed writing about black women's issues has not made this distinction sufficiently clear. Our issues have not been concisely defined in these writings, causing much adverse reaction and confusion about what black feminism really is.[6]

This myth is one of the silliest and at the same time one of the most dangerous. Antifeminists are incapable of making a distinction between being critically opposed to sexual oppression and simply hating men. Women's desire for fairness and safety in our lives does not necessitate hating men. Trying to educate and inform men about how their feet are planted on our necks does not translate into hatred either. Centuries of antiracist struggle by various people of color are not reduced, except by racists, to our merely hating white people. If anything, it seems that the opposite is true. People of color know that white people have abused us unmercifully and it is only sane for us to try to change that treatment by every means possible.

Likewise, the bodies of murdered women are strewn across the landscape of this country. Rape is a national pastime, a form of torture visited upon all girls and women, from babies to the **49** aged. One out of three women in the United States will be raped during her lifetime. Battering and incest, those home-based crimes, are pandemic. Murder, of course, is men's ultimate violent "solution." If you think that I exaggerate, please get today's newspaper and verify the facts.

If anything is going down here it's woman hatred, not man hatred, a veritable war against women. But wanting to end this war still doesn't equal man hating. The feminist movement and the antiracist movement have in common trying to insure decent human life. Opposition to either movement aligns one with the most reactionary elements in American society.

Myth No. 4: Women's Issues Are Narrow, Apolitical Concerns. People of Color Need to Deal with the "Larger Struggle."

This myth once again characterizes women's oppression as not particularly serious and by no means a matter of life and death. I have often wished I could spread the word that a movement committed to fighting sexual, racial, economic, and heterosexist oppression, not to mention one which opposes imperialism, anti-Semitism, the oppressions visited upon the physically disabled, the old and the young, at the same time that it challenges militarism and imminent nuclear destruction, is the very opposite of narrow.

All segments of the women's movement have not dealt with all these issues, but neither have all segments of the black population. This myth is plausible when the women's movement is equated only with its most bourgeois and reformist elements. The most progressive sectors of the feminist movement, which include some radical white women, have taken the above issues, and many more, quite seriously. Third World women have been the most consistent in defining our politics broadly. Why is it that feminism is considered "white minded" and "narrow" while socialism or Marxism, from verifiably white origins, is legitimately embraced by Third World male politicos, without their having their identity credentials questioned for a minute?

Myth No. 5: Those Feminists Are Nothing but Lesbians. This

may be the most pernicious myth of all and it is essential to understand that the distortion lies in the phrase "nothing but" and not in the identification lesbian. "Nothing but" reduces lesbians to a category of beings deserving only the most violent attack, a category totally alien from "decent" black folks—not

50

Feminist Visions

your sisters, mothers, daughters, aunts, and cousins but bizarre outsiders like no one you know or *ever* knew.

Many of the most committed and outspoken feminists of color have been and are lesbians. Since many of us are also radicals, our politics, as indicated by the issues merely outlined above, encompass all people. We are also as black as we ever were. (I always find it fascinating, for example, that many of the black lesbian-feminists I know still wear their hair natural, indicating that for us it was more than a "style.")

Black feminism and black lesbianism are not interchangeable. Feminism is a political movement, and many lesbians are not feminists. Although it is also true that many black feminists are not lesbians, this myth has acted as an accusation and a deterrent to keep nonlesbian black feminists from manifesting themselves, for fear it will be hurled against them.

Fortunately this is changing. Personally, I have seen increasing evidence that many black women of whatever sexual preference are more concerned with exploring and ending our oppression than they are committed to being either homophobic or sexually separatist. Direct historical precedent exists for such commitments. In 1957, black playwright and activist Lorraine Hansberry wrote the following in a letter to *The Ladder*, an early lesbian periodical:

> I think it is about time that equipped women began to take on some of the ethical questions which a male-dominated culture has produced and dissect and analyze them quite to pieces in a serious fashion. It is time that "half the human race" had something to say about the nature of its existence. Otherwise—without revised basic thinking—the woman intellectual is likely to find herself trying to draw conclusions—moral conclusions—based on acceptance of a social moral superstructure which has never admitted to the equality of women and is therefore immoral itself. As per marriage, as per sexual practices, as per the rearing of children, etc. In this kind of work there may be women to emerge who will be able to formulate a new and possible concept that homosexual persecution and condemnation has at its roots not only social ignorance, but a philosophically active anti-feminist dogma.[7]

I would like a lot more people to be aware that Lorraine Hansberry, one of our most respected artists and thinkers, was asking **51**

Contemporary Black Feminist Movement

in a lesbian context some of the same questions that we are asking today and for which we have been so maligned.

Black heterosexual panic about the existence of both black lesbians and black gay men is a problem that they have to deal with themselves. A first step would be for them to understand better their own heterosexuality, which need not be defined by attacking everybody who is not heterosexual.

Home Truths

Above are some of the myths that have plagued black feminism. The truth is that there is a vital movement of women of color in this country. Despite continual resistance to women of color defining our specific issues and organizing around them, it is safe to say in 1985 that we have a movement of our own.

I have been involved in building that movement since 1973. It has been a struggle every step of the way and I feel that we are still in just the beginning stages of developing a workable politics and practice. Yet the feminism of women of color, particularly of Afro-American women, has wrought many changes during these years, has had both obvious and unrecognized impact upon the development of other political groupings and upon the lives and hopes of countless women.

The very nature of radical thought and action is that it has exponentially far-reaching results. But because all forms of media ignore black women, in particular black feminists, and because we have no widely distributed communication mechanisms of our own, few know the details of what we have accomplished. The story of our work and contributions remains untold.

One of the purposes of *Home Girls* was to get the word out about black feminism to the people who need it most: black people in the United States, the Caribbean, Latin America, Africa— everywhere. It is not possible for a single essay to encompass all of what black feminism is, but there is basic information I want every reader to have about the meaning of black feminism as I have lived and understood it.

In 1977, a black feminist organization in Boston of which I was a member from its founding in 1974, the Combahee River Collective, drafted a political statement for our own use and for inclusion in Zillah Eisenstein's anthology, *Capitalist Patriarchy and the Case for Socialist Feminism.* In our opening paragraph we wrote:

Feminist Visions

> . . .we are actively committed to struggling against
> racial, sexual, heterosexual, and class oppression and see
> as our particular task the development of integrated
> analysis and practice based upon the fact that the major
> systems of oppression are interlocking. The synthesis of
> these oppressions creates the conditions of our lives. As
> Black women we see Black feminism as the logical
> political movement to combat the manifold and simul-
> taneous oppressions that all women of color face.[8]

The concept of the simultaneity of oppression is still the crux of a black feminist understanding of political reality and one of the most significant ideological contributions of black feminist thought.

We examined our own lives and found that everything out there was kicking our behinds—race, class, sex, and homophobia. We saw no reason to rank oppressions, or, as many forces in the black community would have us do, to pretend that sexism, among all the "isms," was not happening to us.

Black feminists' efforts to comprehend the complexity of our situation, as it was actually occurring, almost immediately began to deflate some of the cherished myths about black womanhood, for example, that we are "castrating matriarchs" or that we are more economically privileged than black men. Although we made use of the insights of other political ideologies, such as socialism, we added an element that has often been missing from the theory of others: what oppression is comprised of on a day-to-day basis or, as black feminist musician Linda Tillery sings, ". . .what it's really like/To live this life of triple jeopardy."[9]

Multi-Issue Approach

This multi-issue approach to politics has probably been most often used by other women of color who face similar dynamics, at least as far as institutionalized oppression is concerned. It has also altered the women's movement as a whole. As a result of Third World feminist organizing, the women's movement now takes much more seriously the necessity for a multi-issue strategy for challenging women's oppression. The more progressive elements of the Left have also begun to recognize that the promotion of sexism and homophobia within their ranks, besides being ethically unconscionable, ultimately undermines their ability to organize. **53**

Even a few Third World organizations have begun to include the challenging of women's and gay oppression on their public agendas.

Approaching politics with a comprehension of the simultaneity of oppressions has helped to create a political atmosphere particularly conducive to coalition building. Among all feminists, Third World women have undoubtedly felt most viscerally the need for linking struggles and have also been most capable of forging such coalitions. A commitment to principled coalitions, based not upon expediency but upon our actual need for each other is a second major contribution of black feminist struggle. Many contributors to *Home Girls* wrote out of a sense of our ultimate interdependence. Bernice Johnson Reagon's essay, "Coalition Politics: Turning the Century," should be particularly noted. She wrote:

> You don't go into coalition because you just *like* it. The only reason you would consider trying to team up with somebody who could possibly kill you, is because that's the only way you can figure you can stay alive. . . . Most of the time you feel threatened to the core and if you don't you're not really doing no coalescing.[10]

The necessity for coalitions has pushed many groups to examine rigorously the attitudes and ignorance within themselves that prevent coalitions from succeeding. Most notably, there has been the commitment of some white feminists to make racism a priority issue within the women's movement, to take responsibility for their racism as individuals, and to do antiracist organizing in coalition with other groups.

Because I have written and spoken about racism during my entire involvement as a feminist and presented workshops on racism for white women's organizations for several years during the 1970s, I have not only seen that there are white women who are fully committed to eradicating racism, but that new understandings of racial politics have evolved from feminism which other progressive people would do well to comprehend.[11]

Having begun my political life in the civil rights movement and having seen the black liberation movement virtually destroyed by the white power structure, I have been encouraged in recent years that women can be a significant force for bringing about racial change in a way that unites oppressions instead of isolating them. At the same time, the percentage of white **54** feminists who are concerned about racism is still a minority of the movement, and even within this minority those who are personally sensitive and completely serious about formulating an *activist* challenge to racism are fewer still.

Because I have usually worked with politically radical feminists, I know that there are indeed white women worth building coalitions with, at the same time that there are apolitical, even reactionary, women who take the name of feminism in vain.

Black and Female

One of the greatest gifts of black feminism to ourselves has been to make it a little easier simply to *be* black and female. A black feminist analysis has enabled us to understand that we are not hated and abused because there is something wrong with us, but because our status and treatment is absolutely prescribed by the racist, misogynist system under which we live.

There is not a black woman in this country who has not, at some time, internalized and been deeply scarred by the hateful propaganda about us. There is not a black woman in America who has not felt, at least once, like "the mule of the world," to use Zora Neale Hurston's still apt phrase.[12] Until black feminism, few people besides black women actually cared about or took seriously the demoralization of being female *and* colored *and* poor *and* hated.

When I was growing up, despite my family's efforts to explain, or at least describe, attitudes prevalent in the outside world, I often thought that there was something fundamentally wrong with me because it was obvious that I and everybody like me was held in such contempt. The cold eyes of certain white teachers in school, the black men who yelled from cars as my sister and I stood waiting for the bus, convinced me that I must have done something horrible.

How was I to know that racism and sexism had formed a blueprint for my mistreatment long before I had ever arrived here? As with most black women, others' hatred of me became self-hatred, which has diminished over the years but has by no means disappeared. Black feminism has, for me and for so many others, finally given us the tools to comprehend that it is not something we have done that has heaped this psychic violence and material abuse upon us, but the fact that, because of who we are, we are multiply oppressed.

Contemporary Black Feminist Movement

Unlike any other movement, black feminism provides the theory that clarifies the nature of black women's experience, makes possible positive support from other black women, and encourages political action that will change the very system that has put us down.

The accomplishments of black feminism have been not only in developing theory but in day-to-day organizing. Black feminists have worked on countless issues, some previously identified with the feminist movement and others that we, ourselves, have defined as priorities. Whatever issues we have committed ourselves to, we have approached them with a comprehensiveness and pragmatism that exemplify the concept "grassroots." If nothing else, black feminism deals in home truths, both in analysis and in action. Far from being irrelevant or peripheral to black people, the issues we have focused on touch the basic core of our community's survival.

Some of the issues we have worked on are reproductive rights, equal access to abortion, sterilization abuse, health care, child care, the rights of the disabled, violence against women, rape, battering, sexual harassment, welfare rights, lesbian and gay rights, educational reform, housing, legal reform, women in prison, aging, police brutality, labor organizing, anti-imperialist struggles, antiracist organizing, nuclear disarmament, and preserving the environment.

It is frustrating that it is not even possible to know all the work black and other Third World women have done, because, as I already stated, we have had no consistent means of communication, no national Third World feminist newspaper, for example, that would link us across geographic boundaries.[13] It is obvious, however, that with every passing year, more and more explicitly feminist organizing is being done by women of color. There are many signs: Women of color have been heavily involved in exposing and combating sterilization abuse on local, state, and national levels. Puertorriqueñas, Chicanas, Native American women, and Afro-American women have been particularly active, since women in these groups are most subject to forced sterilization.

For a number of years, health issues, including reproductive freedom, have been a major organizing focus. Within the last year, a Third World women's clinic has been established in Berkeley and a black women's Self-Help Collective has been established in Washington. The National Black Women's Health Project in Atlanta held its first conference on black women's health issues in 1983, bringing together two thousand women, many of them low-income women from the rural South.

Feminist Visions

Black and other Third World women have been centrally involved in all aspects of organizing to combat violence against women. Many women of color first became involved in the women's movement through this work, particularly working or volunteering in battered women's shelters. Because battering is so universal, shelters have characteristically offered services to diverse groups of women. There are now shelters that serve primarily Third World communities, such as Casa Myrna Vásquez in Boston.

In 1980, the First National Conference on Third World Women and Violence was held in Washington, D.C. Many precedent-setting sexual harassment cases have been initiated by black women, both because black women are disproportionately harassed in school and on their jobs, and because it seems that they are more willing to protest their harassment. A group in Washington, D.C., the African Women's Committee for Community Education, has been organizing against the harassment of black women by black men on the street. In Boston, the Combahee River Collective was a mobilizing force in bringing together Third World and feminist communities when 12 black women were murdered in a three and a half- month period during 1979.

Third World women are organizing around women's issues globally. Activists in the Caribbean, Latin America, Africa, India, New Zealand, England, and many other places are addressing issues that spring simultaneously from sexist, heterosexist, racist, imperialist, and economic oppression. Some of these individuals and groups specifically identify as feminist. For example, in the Virgin Islands, there are a growing number of battered women's organizations on various islands. Some Afro-American women and Virgin Islanders have worked together on issues of violence against women. In Jamaica, Sistren, a community-based women's theater collective founded in 1977, organizes around basic survival issues, including sexual violence and economic exploitation. In Brazil, black women are active in the women's movement and have been especially involved in neighborhood organizing among poor women. Maori, Pacific Island, and other black women in New Zealand have been doing extensive organizing on a local and national level. The first National Hui (conference) for black women was held in September 1980 in Otara, Auckland, and the first Black Dyke Hui occurred in June 1981.

Economic exploitation, poor working conditions, inadequate health care, and anti-imperialist and antinuclear campaigns are just a few of the issues black women in New Zealand are address- **57** ing. At the same time, they are challenging sexist attitudes and practices within their specific cultural groups.

Black women's organizing, which is often specifically feminist, has been going on in England since the mid-1970s. National black women's conferences, which include all women of color currently living in Great Britain, that is, women born in England and women who have emigrated from India, Pakistan, the Caribbean, and Africa, are held annually. A Black Women's Center, which works on a wide range of community concerns, was established several years ago in the black community of Brixton, and since that time dozens of other black women's centers have opened all over London.

Black and Indian women in South Africa, who have always been central in the struggle against apartheid, are beginning to address specifically women's issues such as rape, which is widespread in the cities. In the future, Third World feminists in the United States and Third World women in other countries will no doubt make increasing contact with each other and continue to build a movement that is global in geographic range and political scope.

A number of black and Third World lesbian organizations are addressing a variety of issues as "out" lesbians, such as Salsa Soul Sisters in New York City and Sapphire Sapphos in Washington, D.C. They are doing education and challenging homophobia in their various communities as well as working on issues that affect lesbians, women, and people of color generally. The National Coalition of Black Lesbians and Gays (NCBLG), which has seven chapters in various cities and currently has several thousand members, has sponsored National Third World Lesbian and Gay conferences in Washington (1979) and Chicago (1981), attended by hundreds of participants.

NCBLG was also successful in the struggle to include a lesbian speaker, Audre Lorde, in the rally at the 20th Anniversary March on Washington in 1983 and was instrumental in increasing the accountability of Jesse Jackson's presidential campaign toward lesbian and gay issues.

A Flourishing Culture

Black feminist cultural work is flourishing, particularly in literature and in music. *Azalea,* a literary magazine for Third World lesbians began publishing in 1977. The Varied Voices of Black Women concert tour, featuring musicians Gwen Avery, Linda Tillery, and Mary

Feminist Visions

Watkins and poet Pat Parker, appeared in eight cities in fall 1978. Third World women's bands, singers, poets, novelists, visual artists, actors, and playwrights are everywhere creating and re-defining their art from a feminist perspective.

We have done much. We have much to do. Some of the most pressing work before us is to build our own autonomous institutions. It is absolutely crucial that we make our visions real in a permanent form so that we can be even more effective and reach many more people. I would like to see ongoing multi-issue political organizations, rape crisis centers, battered women's shelters, women's centers, periodicals, publishers, buying cooperatives, clinics, and artists' collectives started and run by women of color. The Third World Women's Archives and Kitchen Table: Women of Color Press in New York City, both founded in 1981, are examples of institutions controlled by women of color. We need more. I believe that everything is possible. It must be understood that black feminist organizing has *never* been a threat to the viability of the black community, but instead has enhanced the quality of life and ensured the survival of every man, woman, and child in the community.

In the 1980s, every one of us faces a great deal of danger. The reign of Reagan is more blatantly opposed to people's economic, civil, human, and land rights in this country and inter-nationally than any U.S. government for the last 50 years. We are living in a world at war, but at the same time we are also in a period of increasing politicization and conscious struggle.

If we are going to make it into the 21st century, it will take every last one of us pulling together. The unswerving commit-ment and activism of feminists of color, of home girls, are es-sential to making this planet truly fit for human habitation. And, as Bernice Johnson Reagon explains: "We are not on the de-fensive. . . . 'Cause like it is, it is our world, and we are here to stay."[14]

notes

1. This essay is excerpted from the Introduction to Barbara Smith, ed., *Home Girls: A Black Feminist Anthology* (New York: Kitchen Table: Women of Color Press, 1983). Reprinted with permission of the author and Kitchen Table: Women of Color Press, New York, New York. Also reprinted in *The Black Scholar,* 14 (March–April 1983), pp. 4–13.

2. The terms "Third World women" and "women of color" are used here to designate Native American, Asian American, Latina, and Afro-American women in the United States and the indigenous peoples of Third World countries wherever they may live. Both these terms apply to black American women. At times in the introduction black women are specifically designated as black or Afro-American and at other times the terms women of color and Third World women are used to refer to women of color as a whole.

3. Barbara Smith, "Notes for Yet Another Paper on Black Feminism, Or Will the Real Enemy Please Stand Up?" *Conditions: Five, The Black Women's Issue* (Autumn 1979), p. 124.

4. W. E. B. DuBois, *Darkwater, Voices from Within the Veil* (New York: AMS Press, 1969), p. 185.

5. June Jordan and Bernice Johnson Reagon, "Oughta Be A Woman," *Good News* (Chicago: Flying Fish Records, Songtalk Publishing Co., 1981). Quoted by permission.

6. See Linda C. Powell's review of Michele Wallace's *Black Macho and the Myth of the Super Woman* ("Black Macho and Black Feminism") in *Home Girls* and my review of Bell Hooks' (Gloria Watkins) *Ain't I a Woman: Black Women and Feminism* in *The New Women's Times Feminist Review,* 9 (November 1982), pp. 10, 11, 18, 19, and 20 and in *The Black Scholar,* 14 (January–February 1983), pp. 38–45.

7. Quoted from Jonathan Katz, ed., *Gay American History: Lesbians and Gay Men in the U.S.A.* (New York: T. Y. Crowell, 1976), p. 425. Also see Adrienne Rich's "The Problem with Lorraine Hansberry," in "Lorraine Hansberry: Art of Thunder, Vision of Light," *Freedomways,* 19 (1979), pp. 247–255, for more material about her woman-identification.

8. "The Combahee River Collective Statement," in *Home Girls,* p. 272.

9. Linda Tillery, "Freedom Time," *Linda Tillery* (Oakland, Calif.: Olivia Records, Tuizer Music, 1977).

10. Bernice Johnson Reagon, "Coalition Politics: Turning the Century," in *Home Girls,* p. 356.

11. Some useful articles on racism by white feminists are Elly Bulkin's "Racism and Writing: Some Implications for White Lesbian Critics," *Sinister Wisdom,* 13 (Spring 1980), pp. 3–22; Minnie Bruce Pratt's "Rebellion," *Feminary,* 11 (1980), pp. 6–20; and Adrienne Rich's "Disloyal to Civilization: Feminism, Racism, Gynephobia," *On Lies, Secrets and Silence: Selected Prose 1966–1978* (New York: W. W. Norton, 1979), pp. 275–310.

12. Zora Neale Hurston, *Their Eyes Were Watching God* (Urbana: University of Illinois, 1937, 1978), p. 29.

13. *Between Ourselves: Women of Color Newspaper* (P.O. Box 1939, Washington, D.C. 20038) was first published in February 1985.

14. Reagon, "Coalition Politics," p. 368.

Feminist Visions

Richard M. Tolman
Donald D. Mowry
Linda E. Jones
John Brekke

developing a profeminist commitment among men in social work

the feminist vision is essentially rooted in the experience of being a woman. Yet it is a vision that has touched some men who have come to share a belief in the potential benefits of a feminist society. Feminist authors have noted that it is predictable that men will resist feminism.[1] Male privilege is threatened by feminist actions to end the patriarchal oppression of women. Men will not, perhaps cannot, renounce that privilege voluntarily. If this is so, how might men be productively involved in shaping a feminist society? This chapter will address how men, specifically men in social work, can contribute to a realization of feminist visions for the future.

Kravetz reminds us that social work "traces its beginnings to the activism and vision of women who were pioneers of social change as charity workers, clubwomen, reformers, and suffragists."[2] Despite its traditional identification as a woman's profession and a value base consistent with feminism,[3] social work has warranted criticism for being sexist in its educational and professional practices and in its occupational structure.[4]

Empirical studies examining whether men in social work **61** are overtly sexist in their attitudes and professional practices have produced mixed results.[5] The results of some of the studies of attitudes have been questioned from the standpoint of "social desirability bias, that is, subjects responding to items in a socially acceptable manner even if it does not reflect their own attitudes or judgments."[6] Studies of attitudes and sexist behavior are suspect if they only measure a single behavioral component.[7] The entire line of research into the relationship between attitudes and behaviors is a difficult enterprise because there are multiple determinants of behavior, including past experiences of the individual, normative pressures, and specific demands of the setting in which the behavior occurs.[8] Even a carefully disguised, controlled laboratory experiment using multiple behavioral measures may fail to find significant behavioral differences between antifeminist and profeminist men.[9]

Overt sexist attitudes and professional practices aside, we believe that few men have taken an active role in promoting feminist values within the profession. As is the case in society in general, the burden of the struggle to end the oppression of women within the profession has been predominantly shouldered by women.

We argue that although empirical evidence does not necessarily support the overt sexism of men in social work, men have not actively and visibly contributed to the effort to end sexism. It is our contention that men in social work should be proactive in the effort to eliminate sexism in our profession and in society. Men in social work, by virtue of their professional status, training, and contact with the survivors and perpetrators of oppression, must take a leadership position locally, regionally, and nationally in supporting the feminist struggle to end the oppression of women.

Feminism, as we have mentioned, is consistent with social work values. Men who profess to be committed to social work cannot fulfill that commitment without taking responsibility for working to end the oppression of women. Moreover, men themselves will benefit from a feminist society that enables them to move beyond the destructive confines of the traditional male role into a healthier nonhierarchical, noncompetitive system of relationships. The problem for men is not that feminists have gone too far in challenging male privilege, but rather that they have not yet gone far enough in realizing their attempts to transform economic, social, and political structures.

Feminist Visions

If men in social work are to be a part of the realization of a feminist vision within social work and the larger society, they must be involved in developing a profeminist commitment. The term "profeminist" is used rather than "feminist" to connote that the commitment, although inspired by the vision of women, derives from the experience of men. Women have forged their identities as feminists and defined themselves apart from men. Respecting that process, the male authors of this chapter choose not to usurp the term "feminist" by claiming it for men. Yet we hope to convey our support and belief in feminist ideals by positively identifying ourselves as profeminist.

In this chapter, profeminist commitment will be examined in three ways. First, an analysis of men's response to the women's movement will reveal that male awareness of dysfunctional traditional sex roles has led men to develop reactionary as well as profeminist organizations. The difference between male liberation and profeminist ideology will be clarified. Second, profeminist men, whose consciousness includes a recognition of the oppression of women, have begun to identify key issues and critical assumptions that may serve as guidelines to the formulation of strategies for change. These key issues will be incorporated into a developing set of principles. Finally, action strategies for social work education and practice that are consistent with the principles will be offered.

Men and Feminism

The women's movement has raised men's consciousness about gender in two different, but not mutually exclusive, ways. Challenges to traditional sex roles by feminists have freed men to become more aware of the restrictions imposed by traditional male sex roles. In addition, consciousness of how men oppress women has grown from their relationships with women who confront their sexist behavior. This new consciousness about sex roles and the oppression of women has led men to organize themselves to address these issues.[10] On the one hand, men who have organized only around the restrictions of the male role have developed what can be characterized as the "male liberation" position. On the other hand, a profeminist position has been developed by those men whose consciousness has included an awareness of the oppression of women by men in our society. **63**

Profeminist Commitment Among Men

The critical differences between these two positions are explored below.

Male Liberation.   Negative aspects of male sex-role socialization, including competitiveness, emotional restrictions, estrangement from children and family life, and overemphasis on material success, have been explored in a growing body of literature.[11] This critique of the male role is widespread in the men's movement, and many men have begun to explore personal solutions for breaking out of stereotyped sex roles. The quest for these personal solutions has become the focus of popular attention and, predictably, has been lampooned in the media:

Q. What does the New Man do after work?
A. He cooks expertly, exercises relentlessly and cries whenever he feels like it.
Q. What is the New Man's favorite question?
A. What about *my* needs?[12]

Some men, however, have taken the critique of male roles a step further. A male liberation position has been developed that equates the restrictions of the male role with the oppression of women and argues that men as well as women need to be liberated. Some male liberation groups have focused on the need for "men's rights," such as equity in divorce and child custody laws. Choosing the few laws by which men are put at a seeming disadvantage, the men's rights position obscures the pervasive and systematic way women have been mistreated by the legal system. In our opinion, the male liberation position, by focusing on the discomfort of men, ignores institutional sexism and the privileges men accrue from their status in society.

Profeminist Men.   Others in the men's movement have criticized the emphasis on "male liberation" and have adopted a stance that directly reflects a feminist analysis. In this profeminist analysis, men are seen as oppressors benefiting from the domination of women. The negative aspects of male roles are addressed but are not equated with the systemic, pervasive oppression of women.[13]

Although they have not abandoned the struggle against traditional sex roles in their personal life, profeminist men have also promoted active participation in efforts to end the oppression of women. For example, men have organized child-care collectives to care for children at women's events, such as concerts and work-

64

Feminist Visions

shops, and at battered women's shelters. Other men's groups have formed to oppose violence against women in a variety of ways, including working directly with male perpetrators of violence. Many gay men, who are aware of the restrictions of male socialization and of heterosexist oppression, have been central in building a profeminist men's movement; profeminist groups have linked oppression based on gender to heterosexist oppression and have worked for gay and lesbian rights. Although membership in men's organizations is largely white and middle class, profeminist men's groups have adopted a political orientation that focuses on race and class issues.

To some extent, the male liberation and profeminist positions described above have been formalized on a national level in two organizations, the male liberation "Free Men" and the profeminist "National Organization of Changing Men (NOCM)."[14] Clearly, the commitment of the NOCM to work to end the oppression of women, people of color, and gays and lesbians is consonant with social work values, whereas male liberation groups that focus only on the discomfort of the oppressor are, in our opinion, reactionary. However, a challenge for men who support feminist ideals is not in deciding which organization to join, but rather in how to involve those men who feel angry or frustrated with, or threatened by, their individual experiences with women in a way that does not place the blame on women. A greater challenge is to convince men that it is worthwhile for them to struggle actively against the benefits that accrue to them from sexism, and to lead men to change the structures that oppress women, as well as gays, people of color, and other victims of discrimination in our society. It is our position that profeminism provides the soundest foundation for this effort.

Principles for a Profeminist Commitment

Issues central to the foundations of profeminist commitment among men in social work can be further clarified by identifying and defining basic profeminist principles that can guide understanding and action for social workers. The principles will clearly develop and change as experience increases and theory expands, but they represent the efforts of the authors to integrate feminist theory with our own experiences and key issues in the men's movement.

65

Profeminist Commitment Among Men

Develop a Historical, Contextual Understanding of Women's Experience.   A historical and contextual understanding of women's experience can lead men to understanding and action rather than to the confusion, alienation, and withdrawal that have often characterized men's reaction to the women's movement. Without this perspective, men are unable to understand the oppression of women.

Men in social work particularly need to develop an empathy with women's experience. For example, the National Coalition Against Domestic Violence (NCADV) conference in 1982 was attended by a number of men representing treatment programs for men who batter their partners.[15] The men were interested in attending some of the meetings on women's issues to enhance their understanding and offer input. At some of these meetings, however, concern about male presence was evident, and in some instances men were asked to leave. The initial reactions among the men included confusion, anger, and withdrawal. The men felt that they were there in a spirit of brotherhood and, therefore, they had expected a positive reaction to their presence. From a historical perspective, however, it became clear that no matter how well-intended these men were, men as a gender have for centuries denied women the opportunity to have the time and place to develop their own power base, solidify their self-definition, and name their oppressor. A profeminist commitment includes an awareness that men will not be responded to in an "ahistorical" manner simply because they have begun examining their own psyches and privileges with a feminist lens.

One way of obtaining an understanding of women's experience is by exploring feminist writing. In addition to the general theoretical writings from a feminist viewpoint that are available, feminist analyses have been applied to numerous issues and topics of interest to social work educators and practitioners. Fortunately, these works are not obscure and the materials are readily available. The exploration of feminist analyses is an ongoing process that cannot be accomplished in a short time. In addition, women's expression in other means of communication, such as art, music, and film, can provide powerful representations of women's experience and feminist visions.

Men Must Be Responsible for Themselves and for Other Men.
Many men have been influenced by the women's movement only out of self-interest. As women have changed, many men who

Feminist Visions

desire to maintain contact with women have made some progress by changing their vocabulary and eliminating blatantly sexist behavior, at least while in the presence of women. Blakely views this dependence on women for consciousness raising as a failure on the part of men to develop empathy for the totality of women's experience, resulting in a serious drain on the energy of women.[16] This dependence on women for consciousness raising amounts to continued oppression of women by men. By continuing to depend on women, men limit their ability to reach out to other men, beyond the narrowly defined ways dictated by traditional male roles.

What is required is for men to assume responsibility for their own part in sexist injustice, both individually and collectively. Actively pursuing the study of feminist writing is one step men can take in assuming personal responsibility. A further step is to become aware of and struggle against male privilege.

Redefine Masculinity.   Individually and collectively, men must examine what they gain and what they lose from the end of male domination. In a patriarchal society, men have tremendous power over women, but at the same time they depend on women for nurturance, domestic labor, and child care. Stoltenberg equates male identity with masculinity and remarks that "under patriarchy the cultural norm of male identity consists of power, prestige, privilege, and prerogative as over and against the gender class of women."[17]

Subsequently, the end of male privilege requires an active struggle against the prevailing cultural male identity. This raises a critical issue: Without conscious, uncompromising effort to confront and resist traditional male bonding, men will fall into a familiar pattern of relating that reinforces sexist consciousness rather than spurs them on to profeminist action. We are all familiar with the prototypical male bonding as reflected in locker room chatter. It is the seductiveness of this bonding that needs to be challenged, examined, and replaced with mutual confrontation and support based on the integrity of women and men.

Accept Women's Scrutiny without Making Women Responsible. Men who profess to organize against their own power must continually contend with the contradiction inherent in their effort. The contradiction in voluntarily and willingly working to end one's own power and the difficulty in developing empathy with **67** women's experience result in some women's being suspicious of a profeminist men's movement. Due to the propensity for male bonding, that is based on aggressiveness and feelings of superiority over women, men who get together for any reason, even if it is ostensibly to end their privilege, represent a potential for the further oppression of women.

Women's cautious scrutiny is healthy and vital to changing men. For example, men's groups are often dominated early on by two questions: Who has the power, and who might be gay? More recently, men's groups have been known to turn into forums for holier-than-thou "I am more profeminist than you are" exchanges; or groups may even evolve into a reaffirmation of masculinity as a defense against the feminist challenge. The scrutiny of women can help men avoid and correct these errors.

Two caveats must be stressed in relation to this principle of accepting women's scrutiny. First, encouraging and accepting women's scrutiny are not the same as expecting it. Second, the converse of this principle—women accepting men's scrutiny—is not in any way implied. Both of these issues are explored further in the discussion of the next principle.

Support the Efforts of Women without Interfering.   Men, individually and as a movement, must accept the need for women to define themselves and develop their own power base. The energies of men ought to be devoted to working for change within themselves and their movement, rather than to aligning with a particular faction or perspective within the women's movement. Men's efforts in any area must pay particular attention to how such efforts are perceived by women, or how they might confound or co-opt women's efforts.

For example, men's collectives and treatment programs for men who batter must be carefully coordinated with women's programs so that they do not usurp, duplicate, or provide services counterproductive to the women's programs. In a time of scarce resources, the funding priority must be placed on programs for victims, however strong the pressure may be to respond to the question, "What about the men?" Men's programs can be counterproductive if they obscure the societal roots of battering by focusing too narrowly on individuals.[18]

Struggle Against Racism and Classism.   A feminist analysis of the prevailing social order has challenged the numerous ways

Feminist Visions

in which the differences between groups of people are used as the basis for establishing, maintaining, and reinforcing artificial differences in social, economic, and political power. Paying attention to the empowerment of one group of people while neglecting the concerns of other groups ignores the basic interdependence of the oppression of these groups and ensures the continuation of an oppressive system. Ortiz noted that "a movement that clouds the realities of racism and class differences is doomed to being elitist, narrow, unrepresentative, and even oppressive."[19]

Men must be sensitive to the ways in which issues of race and class influence commitment to gender equality. It is a mistake to assume that men, regardless of race and class, have the same resources or responsibilities for promoting an end to male privilege. Sexual inequality, for example, between black men and women, has different cultural and historical antecedents than the sexual inequality that exists between white men and women.[20] As Staples notes:

> In the case of black men, their subordination as a racial minority has more than cancelled out their advantages as males in the larger society. Any understanding of their experience will have to come from an analysis of the complex problems they face as blacks and as men. Unlike white males, they have few privileges in this society except vis-à-vis black women. . . . [21]

Staples argues that although their lower position in society has prevented black men from suppressing black women in the same manner as white males, this "has not prevented black men from gaining ascendancy over women by virtue of their gender."[22] He argues that, in assigning priorities for black men in dealing with sexism and racism,

> the problems caused by the legacy of racism are paramount. Although many middle-class black males will have to concentrate on the changing role of women, black males of the working class must continue to confront the challenge of economic survival. It is questionable how much emphasis should be placed on re-orientating their concept of traditional sex roles when they, in many cases, have not been allowed equal access to those roles.[23]

The relationship between oppression based on gender and that based on race and class is indeed a complex one. Positing a hierarchy of oppression obscures the interdependence of oppres- **69** sion based on race, class, and power and analyzes the problem via a paradigm that violates a fundamental vision of feminism. Men who advocate feminism must attend to oppression based on race and class, as well as gender. As Staples concludes:

> The need is for both black and women's liberation. The issues of masculinity and of race are too interwoven to separate at this time. What is necessary is a serious effort by this society to eliminate both racism and sexism from our lives.[24]

Overcome Homophobia and Heterosexism. Patriarchy is a dual system of oppression that includes restrictive rules for relationships between men as well as the more visible and severe oppression of women by men. Heterosexism has been identified as the "cornerstone of male supremacy,"[25] which serves as "a central symbol for all rankings of masculinity, for the division on any grounds between males who are real men and have power and males who are not."[26] Men who deviate from the cultural norm of masculinity often receive the epithet of "queer," "fairy," or "faggot."

The sexual politics of male relationships supports the oppression of women and limits the ways that men can relate to each other. Masculinity under patriarchy dictates that men depend on women for nurturance and emotional support while limiting their relationships with other men to a structured hierarchy of competitive aggressiveness. Efforts to confront this dual system of oppression will be resisted with homophobia, which is fear of closeness to members of the same sex and fear of being labeled homosexual.

By removing the barriers of homophobia in their relationships to each other, men can begin to resist traditional male bonding. Men need to learn to care for each other, express feelings, and experience closeness. Developing profeminist consciousness, however, does not eliminate men's ambivalence toward other men, but rather makes conflict more acute. As men come to recognize the limitations and destructiveness in their relationships with other men, their desire to move beyond those limitations is increased. The need for a safe, supportive environment in which men can begin to explore these issues on a personal level can be met through men's groups. Active advocacy for the rights of gays and lesbians is also necessary. Successfully challenging homophobia is beneficial to heterosexual men, as it removes barriers to intimacy with other men. Although changing the

70

nature of men's relationships with other men will not in itself change men's domination of women, it may be a necessary component of that change. Pleck argues that "ultimately men cannot go any further in relating to women as equals than they have been able to go in relating to men as equals."[27]

Work Against Male Violence in All Its Forms.   Male violence includes, but is not limited to, the physical violence directed against women, children, and other men. If men are to address the problem of male violence successfully, the definition of violence must be broadened to include other forms of psychological and social violence that characterize domination and oppression. At the NCADV conference referred to earlier, one woman stated that if men stop other men from hitting their wives and children but do not stop their sexist oppression of others via attitudes and behaviors besides physical abuse, she would rather not waste her time and resources on programs for abusers.

In addition, it is important to acknowledge that male violence is a form of terrorism that serves to oppress all women. Programs that attempt to treat male perpetrators of violence must operate in such a way as to clarify rather than obscure the link between individual violence and systemic oppression. Men who want to work against rape, for example, must be aware of the less obvious oppressions of pornography, sexual harassment, and the sexual objectification of women. As the next principle posits, it is important that profeminist men actively confront how their own attitudes and behavior support violence, and not place all the blame for violence against women on the perpetrators of violent crime.

Do Not Set Up a False Dichotomy: Take Responsibility for Sexism.
Professing to be a feminist man does not change one's gender and the privileges that accrue from being male. Gender justice will not be achieved by setting up a false dichotomy between men who have achieved a "higher consciousness" and men who are "the problem." For example, if the problem of men who batter women is separated from male domination in all its forms, it becomes a problem of individual men who require treatment. Taking an exclusively individual approach to the problem avoids looking at society and how men obtain and maintain the right and privilege to dominate women. RAVEN (Rape and Violence End Now), a men's collective, in discussing violent men, made   **71**

Profeminist Commitment Among Men

the following connection between individual men and men's shared responsibilities:

> The individual man is not the enemy, nor is he insane. The system which socializes men to deny all emotion other than anger during stress; to seek refuge from the horrors of public life in our homes; and to blame women (and children) for our fears and insecurities, all must be struggled against by all men—in community with women.[28]

Act at the Individual, Interpersonal, and Organizational Levels. Men who are committed to working toward gender justice are obliged to challenge their past assumptions in light of a feminist perspective. Sexism in our society, from a feminist perspective, has been continuous over time and across settings and has been reinforced by patriarchal social structures. The overall goal for profeminist men is to change individual relationships and systemic relationships.

The problem of pornography provides an example of how men can work at all levels to contribute to a solution. At the individual level, men can become aware of and struggle against sexual objectification as part of their sexuality. Interpersonally, men may work against pornography in several ways. They may challenge the objectifying language or actions of other men. With their female or male partners, they can strive to build sexual relationships free from domination or objectification. At the organizational level, groups for men against pornography can provide public education about pornography and its relation to other kinds of victimization of women. Profeminist men can be particularly effective in speaking to traditional men's fraternal, business, or military groups. Men can join with women in direct protests against purveyors of pornography.

Attend to Process and Product. If men are to join in the effort to end patriarchal oppression, attention must be given to the processes by which that struggle is carried out. Men's groups, however sincere their intentions to end sexism, need to attend consciously to the extent to which competition and hierarchy, rather than cooperation and consensus, characterize their operations. As discussed earlier, it is all too easy for men to fall into traditional patterns of relating even when they are gathered to work against those patterns and to free themselves from sex-role

72

Feminist Visions

restrictions. For this reason, many men's groups have organized on a collective basis in an effort to avoid traditional hierarchical structures. In this way, process is also seen as product.

Profeminist Action in Social Work Education and Practice

Social work established a precedent among the major professions in making the first specific commitment to the goal of achieving equity for women.[29] As previously noted, however, the responsibility for achieving this goal has primarily been the burden of women. Men have tended to avoid confronting their own sexism and that of the profession.

Some examples of profeminist actions and guiding principles for carrying out those actions have already been discussed. Those examples and the ones that follow should not be viewed as a definitive plan of action for men in social work. The dynamics of oppression are highly complex, and there can be no simple recipe for change. Moreover, a feminist perspective, with its equal emphasis on process and outcome, its celebration of diversity, and its stress on the personal as political, sets the stage for change strategies that are at once personal and collective, creative and integrative, and that are addressed to multiple levels.

Assuming responsibility for themselves and other men is a key principle that can find expression in the personal as well as the professional lives of profeminist men in social work. Active participation in a men's group that emphasizes mutual support and confrontation facilitates this process. Groups formed specifically for men in social work could also become forums for exploring issues specific to profeminist commitment in our field.

On a direct level, men in social work can take responsibility for confronting other men's sexist behavior. Whether in the social work classroom, agency, or other setting, men need to speak up when their colleagues make overtly sexist remarks or are insensitive to women's issues, rather than wait for female colleagues to do the confronting. A confrontation need not be an aggressive denouncement but can take the form of a respectful educational encounter.[30] Men must risk holding each other accountable.

Men in social work can establish linkages with or work to organize profeminist men's centers in their communities. Many **73** communities already have such groups. Action groups have also been formed on the local, state, regional, and national levels around issues such as pornography, rape, and the Equal Rights Amendment. Men in social work can actively participate in and build coalitions with the women's movement, gay and lesbian rights groups, and people of color.

Feminism challenges men in social work educational settings to reexamine curriculum content, the dynamics of the classroom, and the structure of schools and the profession. This challenge can be extended to other male faculty and male students in several ways.

Male faculty can be encouraged to integrate feminist content and values into curriculum, instruction, and field placements. Informal study groups can be formed to study feminist literature, as an adjunct to established courses or to help male faculty to integrate feminist content into their courses. The small but developing profeminist literature can be explored in the same manner. Attending men's movement conferences and cultural events offers another way of becoming familiar with this material. Profeminist workshops and colloquia can increase the exposure of other men to these ideas, and consciousness raising and action groups can facilitate the formation of the energy required for organizational change efforts.

Classroom process as well as content is crucial to promoting profeminist commitment. The course itself can become a laboratory for feminist principles.[31] Gender and power issues reflected in classroom process can be opened up to examination by the class. Patriarchal teaching models that place the knowledge and power solely in the instructor's hand foster dependence, invalidate students' personal experience when they disagree with the instructor, and keep students in a passive role. A feminist teaching model acknowledges each student in the class as a potential teaching resource and validates the subjective, personal experience of students. Students can be encouraged to assume as much responsibility for their own education as possible through learning contracts and input into course planning. Cooperation rather than competition should be fostered. Vehicles for personal feelings, such as journals and small-group exercises, can be valuable tools for encouraging self-exploration and personal integration within the classroom.

Male students can be encouraged to consider field placements and career choices that involve them in profeminist work

74

Feminist Visions

with other men. If these placements do not currently exist, male faculty can advocate for them or work with male students in creating individual placements. Working to establish field placements for professional social work students in profeminist settings calls for special attention to process. Men's collectives, for example, may appreciate any expertise, energy, and commitment students can bring to their organization but may be sensitive to professional status issues. Indeed, grass-roots groups may be particularly critical of professionals or academics who are firmly entrenched in patriarchal systems of their own. Faculty and students should be willing to examine their own behavior and increase their sensitivity to issues of process in their relationships with organizations.

Men must join their female colleagues, whether in academic or practice settings, in working for equal pay, status, and job security for women. Men can work, along with women, to upgrade the status and career opportunities of direct practitioners—a task seen as critical for upgrading the status of women in the profession, because they tend to be concentrated in direct practice positions.[32]

In a novel approach to feminist implications for men in direct practice, Loewenstein summarizes the research on women as clients and seeks to dispel persistent myths about women. She also suggests that the most appropriate, perhaps only appropriate, professional role for men in direct practice is to work with other men who oppress women. Among the target groups Loewenstein identifies are men who batter, rapists, incest perpetrators, divorced men who fail to support their children, adolescent males involved in pregnancies, adolescents who abuse their elders physically, and employers who sexually harass their employees.[33]

Men who take on such direct service roles face unique difficulties. Male staff working with men who batter have reported that other staff members have displaced their anger at the perpetrators of violence and have directed it at the worker. Working with men who have been mandated by the court to seek service or who are not accustomed to seeking service may lead to worker burnout more rapidly than work with other clients. Supportive relationships with other men doing the same kind of work are critical.

Several implications for education arise out of a focus on men working in these areas. Men in direct service must be **75**

Profeminist Commitment Among Men

prepared adequately for work with "difficult" male clients if they are to take on this challenge. Innovative approaches are often required to accomplish the task of involving men in social work interventions. For example, Rappaport describes nontraditional strategies for involving men in family planning.[34] In addition, the involvement of social work researchers is crucial in developing the knowledge base necessary to guide successful work with male clients.

Children can be added to the list of target clients for men. Working with children eases the burden women have had to bear for child care and also increases children's exposure to men who are nurturing.

Although intervention methods may be stressed in direct practice classes, the link between individual male behavior, such as sexual abuse or desertion of children, and the broader context within which that behavior occurs must also be overtly addressed. For example, work with men who are violent toward women should not be limited to providing service delivery to individuals but should also include a public education component and advocacy efforts to influence court and police behavior. The work to influence the criminal justice system to be more responsive to female victims must also attempt to change racist and classist arrest and sentencing practices.

Final Thoughts

We have presented a set of principles to guide men in social work toward pursuing a profeminist commitment. We have attempted to integrate the extant literature with our personal experiences and have drawn heavily from our own work for examples of profeminist action. It is hoped that these initial guidelines will soon be enriched by the efforts of other men in social work.

Undoubtedly, the effort to transform the social order will not be completed in our lifetimes. Men in social work, however, can play a key role in the effort to build a feminist future. There is much for men to do and much for men to gain in the effort. If we look closely and courageously at what we have come to think of as privilege, we will see how it damages us; but we will not ignore, minimize, or excuse the more pervasive damage it does to others. As we work for change, we will find we have changed ourselves.

Feminist Visions

notes

Preparation of this chapter was supported in part by a postdoctoral fellowship awarded to Richard M. Tolman by the National Institute of Mental Health, National Research Service Award No. 1T32-MH17.152-01, from the Alcohol, Drug Abuse, and Mental Health Administration.

1. See, for example, Joan E. Cummings, "Sexism in Social Work: Some Thoughts on Strategy for Structural Change," *Catalyst*, 9 (1980), pp. 6–32; Mary Daly, "For and Against Us: Anti-Chauvinist Males and Women's Liberation," *Social Policy* (November–December 1973), pp. 32–34; and John Stoltenberg, "Toward Gender Justice," *Social Policy* (May–June 1975), pp. 35–39.

2. Diane Kravetz, "Sexism in a Woman's Profession," *Social Work*, 21 (November 1976), p. 421.

3. See Nan Van Den Bergh and Lynn B. Cooper's introduction to this volume for a clarification of the position that social work values are consistent with feminism.

4. See, for example, Diane Kravetz, "An Overview of Content on Women for the Social Work Curriculum," *Journal of Education for Social Work*, 18 (Spring 1982), pp. 42–49; Sharon Berlin and Kravetz, "Women as Victims: A Feminist Social Work Perspective," Guest Editorial, *Social Work*, 26 (November 1981), pp. 447–449; and David Fanshel, "Status Differentials: Men and Women in Social Work," *Social Work*, 21 (November 1976), pp. 448–454.

5. John F. Longres and Robert H. Bailey, "Men's Issues and Sexism: A Journal Review," *Social Work*, 24 (January 1979), pp. 26–32.

6. Ibid.

7. Arnold Kahn, "Reactions of Profeminist and Antifeminist Men to an Expert Woman," *Sex Roles*, 7 (August 1981), pp. 857–866.

8. See, for example, Robert Brannon, "Attitudes and the Prediction of Behavior," in B. Seidenberg and A. Snadowsky, eds., *Social Psychology: An Introduction* (New York: Free Press, 1976); and Clara Mayo and Marianne de France, *Evaluating Research in Social Psychology: A Guide for the Consumer* (Belmont, Calif.: Wadsworth Publishing Co., 1977), especially Chap. 9, "Attitude-Behavior Discrepancy: Prejudice and Racism."

9. Kahn, "Reactions of Profeminist and Antifeminist Men." Unexpected results in this study suggested that "so-called 'profeminist' men appear less interested in options for women than in redirecting them into nontraditional masculine areas" (p. 865).

10. See Joe Interrante, "Dancing Along the Precipice: The Men's Movement in the 80's," *Radical America*, 15 (December 1981), pp. 53–71.

11. See, for example, Joseph Pleck and Jack Sawyer, eds., *Men and Masculinity* (Englewood Cliffs, N.J.: Prentice-Hall, 1974); Robert A. **77**

Profeminist Commitment Among Men

Lewis and Pleck, "Men's Roles in the Family," special issue of *The Family Coordinator,* 28 (1979); Warren Farrell, *The Liberated Man* (New York: Random House, 1974); Jack Nichols, *Men's Liberation: A New Definition of Masculinity* (New York: Penguin Books, 1975); Herb Goldberg, *The Hazards of Being Male* (Plainview, N.Y.: Nash Publishing Corp., 1976); and Deborah David and Robert Brannon, eds., *The Forty-Nine Percent Majority: The Male Sex Role* (Reading: Mass.: Addison-Wesley Publishing Co., 1976).

12. "The New Man's Lament," *Newsweek,* July 16, 1984, p. 82.

13. For an account of the evolution from male liberation to an antisexist stance, see Jon Snodgrass, ed., *For Men Against Sexism: A Book of Readings* (Albion, Calif.: Times Change Press, 1977).

14. For a discussion of this division, see Robert Brannon, "Are the Free Men a Faction of Our Movement?" *M. Gentle Men for Gender Justice,* 7 (Winter 1981–1982), pp. 14–15.

15. Based on the personal experience of co-author John Brekke, who attended the conference in Milwaukee, Wis.

16. Mary Kay Blakely, "He's a Feminist, But . . .," *Ms.,* 11 (October 1982), pp. 44, 86.

17. Stoltenberg, "Toward Gender Justice."

18. For a detailed discussion of the issue of programs for men who batter, see Susan Schechter, *Women and Male Violence* (Boston: South End Press, 1982), particularly Chaps. 9 and 11.

19. Roxanne Dunbar Ortiz, "Toward a Democratic Women's Movement in the United States," in Evelyn Shapiro and Barry Shapiro, eds., *The Women Say; The Men Say* (New York: Dell Publishing Co., 1979), p. 238.

20. Gloria Joseph, "The Incompatible Menage à Trois: Marxism, Feminism, and Racism," in Lydia Sargent, ed., *Women and Revolution: A Discussion of the Unhappy Marriage of Marxism and Feminism* (Boston: South End Press, 1981), p. 94.

21. Robert Staples, "Masculinity and Race: The Dual Dilemma of Black Men," *Journal of Social Issues,* 34, No. 1 (1978), p. 169.

22. Ibid., p. 179.

23. Ibid., p. 181.

24. Ibid., p. 181.

25. Charlotte Bunch, "Not for Lesbians Only," in Shapiro and Shapiro, eds., *The Women Say,* p. 234.

26. Joseph Pleck, "Men's Power with Women, Other Men, and Society: A Men's Movement Analysis," in Shapiro and Shapiro, eds., *The Women Say,* p. 245.

27. Ibid.

28. *RAVEN's Flight,* 1 (June 1980), p. 3.

Feminist Visions

29. Nancy Coleman, *Toward Achieving Equity for Women in Social Work Education* (New York: Council on Social Work Education, 1981), p. 1.

30. For one approach to confronting other men's sexism, see Neil Callahan, "Men Dealing with Each Other's Sexist Patterns," *M. Gentle Men for Gender Justice,* 7 (Winter 1981–1982), p. 16.

31. For a discussion of feminist teaching principles, see Sharon B. Lord, "Teaching the Psychology of Women: Examination of a Teaching-Learning Model," *Psychology of Women Quarterly,* 7 (Fall 1982), pp. 70–80.

32. Catherine A. Faver, Mary Frank Fox, and Coleen Shannon, "The Educational Process and Job Equity for the Sexes in Social Work," *Journal of Education for Social Work,* 19 (Fall 1983), pp. 78–87.

33. Sophie Freud Loewenstein, "A Feminist Perspective," in A. Rosenblatt and D. Waldfogel, eds., *Handbook of Clinical Social Work* (San Francisco: Jossey-Bass, 1983), pp. 518–548.

34. Bruce Rappaport, "Helping Men Ask for Help," *M. Gentle Men for Gender Justice,* 7 (Winter 1981–1982), pp. 3–4, 25–27.

Profeminist Commitment Among Men

Joan M. Cummerton

a feminist perspective on research: what does it help us see?

i *t commonly happens that the choice of a problem is determined by the method instead of a method being determined by the problem. This means that thought is subjected to an invisible tyranny.*[1]

Social work research methods have been derived and adopted largely from the social sciences, particularly psychology and sociology. In the process, social work researchers have not only adopted the methods but implicitly accepted the assumptions underlying these methods.[2] Many social work educators and practitioners (or at least those who write about social work research methodology or critique social work research) seem oblivious to the "invisible tyranny" to which thought is subjected by the uncritical adoption of social science methodology. Method itself becomes more important than what one wants to investigate and, as Daly, a philosopher and theologian, pointed out, "under patriarchy, method has wiped out women's questions so totally that even women have not been able to hear and formulate our own questions to meet our own experience."[3] Writing in a different context, Heineman

summarized her thesis that "in a misguided attempt to be scientific, social work has adopted an outmoded overly restrictive paradigm of research. Methodological rather than substantive requirements determine the subject matter to be studied. As a result important questions and valuable data go unresearched."[4]

If the profession's commitment to social justice, particularly justice for all women, is to be realized, it is imperative that we practitioner/researchers move beyond current efforts to correct sexist biases in research. We must become increasingly aware of the androcentric, patriarchal nature of research models and methods. We must consider alternative means of increasing our knowledge and understanding of the people we claim to serve and the institutionalized arrangements through which services are delivered. The purpose of this chapter, then, is twofold: first, to describe, compare, and contrast three different paradigms of social work research—patriarchal or traditional, nonsexist, and feminist; second, to discuss some of the theoretical, practical, and ethical issues that arise in the course of doing research when the social work practitioner/researcher adopts a feminist research perspective.

The Traditional, or Patriarchal, Research Paradigm

Most familiar to social workers is the traditional, or patriarchal, model of research. Generations of social workers have learned to equate this paradigm with "good" science. It was and still is seen by many as *the way* rather than *a way* to knowledge and understanding. This model assumes that the use of certain data-gathering techniques will produce objective results. For example, the use of tape recorders, videotapes, and trained human observers who are not involved in planning the research or in implementing the treatment plans is often assumed to yield value-neutral data about social interactions. Practitioners' records are looked at as subjective reports of practice, possibly useful in supplementing more "objective" data.

This model also assumes that observed and theoretical entities can and should be sharply distinguished.[5] Kogan, for example, asserted that "the research worker shuttles between the real world and the world of concepts. The real world provides his empirical evidence, the world of concepts a scheme or map for 'making sense' out of a portion of the real world which he is seeking to account for, explain, or predict."[6] In this model of social work research, "data which are assumed to be 'empirical' **81** or 'objective,' that is, thought both to mirror reality and to appear similar to all normal people, straightforwardly 'ground' theoretical concepts in reality."[7] Consequently, a theoretical research is said to be both possible and desirable.

Bloom and Black, in an article on "Evaluating One's Own Effectiveness and Efficiency," discussed the possibility of a theory-free measurement procedure.[8] Wood, in her study of social work outcome research, viewed practitioners who bring a preexisting theoretical orientation to their work as unethical.[9] While censuring practitioners for forcing data into preconceived theoretical orientations, she paid no attention to the effects on research and practice of unquestioning adherence to a rigid research methodology.

Still another important assumption of the traditional patriarchal model is that good science involves prediction. Polansky, Mullen, and Blenkner are among those who have strongly advocated the goal of prediction for social work research.[10] In 1950, Blenkner asserted that without prediction and experimental manipulation, "nothing is really established, except that one has done a more or less adequate job of describing one's sample."[11] Writing more recently, Polansky asserted that "[t]he whole aim of research in the profession is to improve our feeble ability to predict the course of events."[12]

We find, then, that the prevailing paradigm for research in social work posits a hierarchy of research designs. Experimental designs with their concomitant requirements for experimental manipulation, control groups, and randomization are at the top; quasi-experimental designs are somewhat less acceptable; correlational designs are further down the hierarchy; and exploratory designs lie at the bottom. The experimental design is used normatively, a standard against which all other methodologies are measured, rather than selectively, to answer those questions for which it would be most appropriate. The pervasiveness of this position is exemplified in the following suggestion by Reid:

> In short, testability should be made an important
> criterion in determining what social workers should do.
> Practitioners have always taken the position that the
> requirements of science should be adapted to existing
> forms of practice, no matter how difficult it might be to
> apply scientific methods to the study and improvement
> of that practice. The author is suggesting that this
> position be reversed and that service models be adapted
> to scientific requirements wherever feasible.[13]

Feminist Visions

Among the other assumptions that are often subsumed under those previously discussed or implicit in the paradigm are (1) the expectation that research should produce generalizations capable of explaining or predicting large segments of "reality," (2) the assumption that research findings obtained from white men are normative and can be generalized to other populations, (3) the conception of research as a rational, logical, coherent, and orderly process, (4) the assumption that the units of study should be predefined, operationalized concepts, (5) the expectation that the researcher can and should remain completely detached from the subjects in the study, (6) the assumption that the relationship between the researcher and the subjects is a hierarchical one, with the researcher clearly in control of the "objects" of research, (7) the assumption that topics or questions for study should be selected for their potential contribution to theory, and (8) the assumption that the criteria to be used in judging the validity of a study include the statistical significance of the results and the ability to replicate the study and obtain the same results.

To summarize, objectivity, predictability, generalizability, logic, rationality, order, and control are usually attributed to the traditional, patriarchal research paradigm. It is clearly the norm to which all research efforts are expected to conform and in relation to which they are compared and judged.[14]

The Nonsexist Perspective

Nonsexist research can be seen as the result of a growing recognition of the sexist bias inherent in the traditional, patriarchal research paradigm. Scholars in psychology, sociology, and, to a lesser extent, social work have begun to recognize the multitude of ways in which the nonconscious ideologies that this society holds about women are incorporated into the research they perform. A major assumption of this perspective is that sexist biases are antithetical to obtaining useful data about social phenomena.[15]

Sexist biases have been found to influence the way research problems are formulated, the way variables are conceptualized, and the questions that are considered for research. Gottlieb identified several ways in which stereotyped views of women can affect the formulation of problems.[16] Women are usually viewed in their family roles, with little or no attention paid to their work 83 roles; women are frequently studied in the context of their reproductive life, with a focus on the negative aspects of menstruation and menopause. Little research has been done on women's roles in economic, political, or religious life. Although considerable research has been done on criminals and drug addicts, little attention has been given to female addicts or felons. Study variables often have reflected behaviors expected of men and women, that is studies of passive traits in women and of aggressiveness, decision making, leadership, and achievement in men.

The nonsexist perspective also is concerned with the influence of sexism on sampling. A frequent practice has been to study only males but to generalize the results to all individuals. Kohlberg, who carried out important and fundamental work in moral development in the late 1960s, developed, with Kromer, a six-stage model of moral thinking that was viewed as the definitive word in human moral development.[17] At no time did he indicate that his subjects were all male. In the 1970s, Gilligan, a colleague of Kohlberg's at Harvard University, discovered that women's moral reasoning is different from that of men.[18] Therefore, Kohlberg's stages did not fit. In 1981, four years after Gilligan published her research in the *Harvard Educational Review*, Kohlberg published *The Philosophy of Moral Development*.[19] The book jacket extolled his "Six Universal Stages." Gilligan's work was treated in one paragraph and dismissed as a possible alternative variation of Stage Six. The gender implications of Gilligan's work were not acknowledged, and the limitations they present for the "universal stages" were never discussed.[20]

In other studies, sexist bias is evident in the choice of women for the samples. Sexuality, menopause, and depression have been studied utilizing clinical rather than normal samples. Married women were eliminated from the sample in a study of retirement on the assumption that their husbands' retirement experience was more important.[21]

In addition, sexist bias is found in the choice of variables to be measured and in data collection procedures. Instruments have been constructed that bias the direction of findings; for example, masculinity-femininity scales are used that build on stereotyped sex roles and assume mutually exclusive opposite ends of a continuum as expected behavior for men and women. Sex-typed measurements are evident in standardized personality and vocational tests. Often, tests have few items with reference points grounded in women's experience. Studies with mixed or

84

Feminist Visions

all female subjects conducted by male interviewers fail to test for the effect of the sex of the interviewer, despite literature showing the importance of this variable.

Finally, the nonsexist perspective directs attention to biases in the analysis and interpretation of research results. Among the ways in which biases are reflected in this phase of the research process are (1) the failure to test for significant difference between men and women, (2) the neglect or elimination of data on women when they are found to be different from the data on men, and (3) the attribution of findings of sex differences to innateness only rather than to the impact of both biology and socialization.

The purpose, then, of a nonsexist perspective is to eliminate sexist biases wherever they may be found in the research process, to ensure that questions and issues of interest to men and women can and will be studied, and to ensure that the results of research are fairly interpreted and alternative explanations are offered when appropriate. In no way does this perspective challenge the logical, empiricist assumptions and world view of the traditional, patriarchal perspective.

Over the past decade, female scholars have produced a large body of knowledge about women in psychology, sociology, and related fields. Much of this research, however, although free from obvious sexist biases, has duplicated the traditional, patriarchal model described earlier. Knowledge about women is added on to knowledge about men. This add-on approach assumes that the environment gives off the same signals to men and women, that it has the same impact on men's and women's lives, and that the answers it elicits from women are comparable to the answers it elicits from men. The nonsexist perspective can be seen as representing an equal rights philosophy that ignores that not only was our past man made, but so is our present.

A Feminist Perspective

A feminist perspective is one in which women's experiences, ideas, and needs are valued in their own right. Put another way, androcentricity—man as the norm—ceases to be the only recognized frame of reference for human beings. Women's experiences are seen as constituting a different view of "reality"—an entirely different "ontology" or way of making sense of the world.[22] Women's place in the social structure is clearly different from that of men;

therefore, it is reasonable to assume that women will perceive "reality" differently.[23] "Feminist consciousness" is the expression frequently used to refer to the awareness of women's unique view of social reality. It makes available to everyone the previously untapped reservoir of knowledge about what it is to be a woman, what the social world looks like to women, and how that world is constructed and negotiated by women.

A feminist research perspective differs from the patriarchal perspective in that there is a clear recognition that the results of research are neither value-free nor objective. The artificial dichotomy of objective-subjective that is characteristic of the logical-empiricist tradition often is replaced by a dialectical relationship between the researcher and participants, which Westkott labeled "intersubjectivity."[24] Whenever possible, feminist methodology allows and encourages such "intersubjectivity," permitting the researcher to compare her work with her own experiences as a woman and as a scientist.[25] This work can then be shared with the research particpants, who may add their views to the research, which, in turn, might change it.

The questions the researcher asks the participants grow out of her concerns and experiences and are influenced by the concerns of the participants. The answers she may discover emerge not only from the way the participants confirm and expand her experiences, but from the ways they oppose or remain silent about them. Thus, "the intersubjectivity of meaning takes the form of a dialogue from which knowledge is an unpredictable emergent rather than a controlled outcome."[26]

Related to the concept of "intersubjectivity" is the feminist concern for valuing both process and product. To the degree possible, research participants negotiate the extent of their involvement in the research process.[27] They may be involved in formulating the problem or question to be studied, providing data, reviewing findings and their interpretation, suggesting alternative explanations, disseminating findings, or using findings to improve the quality of life for themselves or for other women. The involvement of participants in various phases of the research process in no way denies the expertise of the researcher in such technical skills as the construction of questionnaires and the interpretation of statistical tests. The feminist perspective, then, suggests a sharing of power throughout the research, replacing the researcher-subject dichotomy characteristic of patriarchal models.

86   In the introduction to this book, Van Den Bergh and

Feminist Visions

Cooper noted that the feminist principle "The personal is political" "demonstrates an interconnectedness between individual activities and societal structures...[and] suggests that institutional change can be effected by personal, social, and political action."[28] If this principle is to be taken seriously, then the presence of both the personal and the political in research must be not only acknowledged but reported in the results.[29] The involvement, perceptions, feelings, and values of the researcher are an integral part of the research process and create part of the context for other participants. Stanley and Wise challenged us to recognize the personal in the research process:

> Whether we like it or not, researchers remain human beings complete with the usual human assembly of feelings, failings, and moods. All of these things influence how we feel and understand what is going on. Our consciousness is always the medium through which research occurs: there is no method or technique of doing research other than through the medium of the researcher.[30]

Thus, reports of research done within a feminist perspective would include a description of the researcher's involvement, value stance, and experience related to the problem or issue. In addition, researchers would share how they know what they do about the research situation and the people in it.

Research in a feminist perspective is clearly political in that its ultimate goal is to improve the quality of life for women and for other oppressed populations.[31] Research *for* women rather than research *on* women remains a major theme in this perspective.[32]

Methods that allow for women to study women in an interactive dialectical relationship without the artificial dichotomy between object and subject or between researcher and researched will end the exploitation of women as research objects. In a feminist perspective, women are at the center of the study. They are neither compared to nor measured against "normative" (male) standards. What is valued is the experience of women and socially significant problems which often are but two sides of the same coin, as exemplified in the Stanley and Wise study of obscene phone callers.[33] (During a seven-week period in 1976, Stanley and Wise, a British sociologist and social worker, respectively, received 286 telephone calls, 105 of which were defined by them as obscene. These calls were linked to their involvement in the gay rights movement and the use of their home telephone **87** to provide information and advice and for referrals of isolated gay people to gay groups. Their decision to research these calls was a means of coping with a constant assault on them and a means of documenting systematically one aspect of the larger societal problem of violence toward women.) In addition, the findings of research would be expected to have substantive significance to the participants and, in many instances, might be part of the data used to change governmental or agency policies to benefit the participants.

Table 1 (pp. 90–93) compares the three perspectives in relation to the major phases of the research process, the nature of the relationship between the researcher and the researched, and the ways in which the research may be used.

Issues Related to a Feminist Research Perspective

Whenever a feminist perspective on research is discussed, a number of issues arise. Some are concerned with what can be called "boundary issues," or setting limits on the what, who, and how of translating feminist ideology into research practice. Others might be labeled "ethical issues" and are concerned with protecting the rights of all parties in the research enterprise.

Boundary Issues. Should feminist research concentrate exclusively on women's experiences? One would expect that much feminist research would focus on the gaps in knowledge about women and about women's experiences as givers and receivers of most of the social services offered in this country. However, there is a danger in concentrating exclusively on women's experiences. Feminist research should be concerned with all aspects of social reality and all participants in it.[34] Any analysis of the oppression of women must involve research on the part played by men and by the interaction of women and men in it. Similarly, analyses of oppression based on race, sexual preference, age, or any other basis of discrimination must look at both the oppressor and the oppressed and the interaction between them.

Feminists who have critiqued traditional social science assumptions and methods have argued that no one person or set of persons has the right to impose definitions of reality on others. Therefore, feminist researchers must avoid doing the same thing. To insist that feminist research focus exclusively on women's expe-

88

Feminist Visions

rience is to continue to maintain the false dichotomies and artificial separations that have prevented us from gaining an integral, holistic understanding of any phenomenon being studied.

Does feminist research require the use of particular research techniques or methods? A number of feminists seem to associate feminist research with qualitative methods because such methods seem more compatible with feminist values.[35] This association can lead to another artificial separation and false dichotomy. Neither qualitative nor quantitative methods are inherently feminist. It is how the particular tools are used that determines whether the process and product are feminist. For example, Pearce, a social worker and sociologist, used quantitative methods to analyze U.S. Department of Labor data; she discovered that if current trends continue, by the year 2000 the only poor people in this country will be women and children.[36] Conversely, researchers holding traditional, patriarchal values could use qualitative methods (such as ethnographic interviewing) to show that women who remain in battering relationships are suffering from "learned helplessness."

Can men be feminist researchers? Feminists differ in their responses to this question, partly, no doubt because of their different views of feminism. For me, this is an empirical question. There is evidence that some men, including many social workers, are seriously concerned and involved with improving the status and opportunities available to oppressed groups, including women. There is also evidence that some "liberal" social workers of both sexes take a paternalistic view of oppressed groups and seek to *do for* them. These people, of whatever sex, are not capable of conducting feminist research because their values and subsequent behavior indicate an inability to share a research undertaking with other participants. Some men are becoming increasingly aware of the ways in which they are oppressed, with such oppression having its origins in color, class, age, disablement, or sexual preference. To the extent that male social workers are aware of both their own oppression and the privileges that they enjoy because of their sex, they are able to participate constructively in feminist research endeavors.

No man, however sensitive, aware, and socially conscious, can bring the perspective or viewpoint to the significance, meaning, and possible implications of the data that can be brought by a feminist. It is the unique perspective that feminists bring from their *lived experience* in this or other societies that I see as **89**

Table 1
Traditional/Patriarchal, Nonsexist, and Feminist Research Perspectives

	Research Perspective		
Research Dimension	Traditional/ Patriarchal	Nonsexist	Feminist
Statement of the Problem			
Role of theory	Crucial as determinant of research design	Same as in the traditional/patriarchal perspective	Emerges from implementation of the research
Theory bias	Theory developed primarily on males or from a male bias	Rejects obviously male-biased theory and stereotyped views of men and women	Theory grounded in feminist ideology; must be validated in participants' experiences
Role of hypothesis	Hypothesis testing; deductive	Hypothesis testing; deductive	Often hypothesis generating; inductive
Choice of topic or question for study	Past research and leading theories; what is currently being funded or published in leading journals —selected for potential scholarly contribution, sometimes socially significant	What is currently being funded or published in leading journals— selected for potential scholarly contribution, sometimes socially significant	Researcher attempts to fill in gaps in the research on women or the oppressed population; involves personal experiences and concerns of participants and researcher; checks with participants to determine how the research can further participants' group; socially significant problem sometimes related to issues discussed in the scholarly literature
Units of study	Predefined operationalized concepts noted as hypotheses	Same as in the traditional/patriarchal perspective	Often studies natural events encased in their ongoing contexts
Characteristics of the Researcher			
Role	Expert who may hide behind professional role; often controls and manipulates the situation; conceals purposes and processes of research conditions of responses, so participants are more likely to conform to researchers' expectations; low trust between researcher and participant	Same as in the traditional/patriarchal perspective	Expert on research process only; informs participants of the purposes and processes of research; allows for wide range of participant responses; develops trust with participants

Table 1
(Continued)

Research Dimension	Research Perspective		
	Traditional/ Patriarchal	Nonsexist	Feminist
Values	Male oriented; ostensibly "value free"—a stance that may conceal a bias for the status quo	Male oriented or humanistic; does not pretend to be value free; tries to minimize own values; builds in safeguards to prevent intrusion of own biases	Female oriented, articulates own values; attempts to understand how own values may affect research outcome
Responsibility to participants	Minimal—complies with ethical guidelines of "informed consent" and no harm to participants; concern for welfare of participants does not extend beyond the research period	Same as in the traditional/patriarchal perspective	Concern for participants goes beyond formal compliance with guidelines—concern for long-term impact on participants' life; uses research to promote growth in participants' behavior, when feasible; attempts to further participants' interests
Interaction between researcher and participant	Limited—attempts to minimize all but controlled interactions	Same as in the traditional/patriarchal perspective	Encourages the development of a relationship between the researcher and participants
Characteristics of the Participants			
Role	Often passive—naive respondents	Same as in the traditional/patriarchal perspective	Active collaborator—expert on own perceptions and experiences; is involved in all stages of the research
Values	Little concern for participants' values and interests unless they are the focus of the study	Same as in the traditional/patriarchal perspective	Participants' values and interests are sought and incorporated into the research
Responsibility to the researcher	Participants are expected to follow the researcher's instructions and to produce responses	Same as in the traditional/patriarchal perspective	Participants allowed to negotiate their level of involvement in research and may renegotiate as the research proceeds
Methodology			
Methods preferred	Quantitative—laboratory or standardized situations or tests and questionnaires	Quantitative	Qualitative—field research interviews; personal documents (letters, diaries, autobiographies); quantitative when essential to context or to questions asked

Table 1
(Continued)

	Research Perspective		
Research Dimension	Traditional/ Patriarchal	Nonsexist	Feminist
Control groups	Often uses control groups, but they are not appropriate to sex bias	Often uses control groups that are appropriate to controlling for sex bias	Seldom uses control groups; often conducts in-depth study of subgroup; not concerned with comparisons between sexes
Type of data	Reports of attitudes and actions through questionnaires, interviews, and archives	Same as in the traditional/patriarchal perspective	Feelings, behavior, thoughts, insights, actions, as witnessed or experienced
Size of N	Based on the power of the test or the number of participants needed to obtain statistically significant differences between groups	Same as in the traditional/patriarchal perspective	Based on the number of participants necessary to identify the range and similarities of experience
Stimulus materials or situations used in study	Appeal to the interest of white men	Appeal to the interest of men and women	Appeal to the interest of the persons being studied—women, ethnic groups, the aged, etc.
Attention given to situational or social factors	Tends to ignore social or situational factors; psychological studies focus on individual, intrapsychic dynamics	Same as in the traditional/patriarchal perspective	Tends to emphasize social or situational determinants of behavior; focuses on interaction between individual and social/situational environment
Criteria of validity	Proof, evidence, statistical significance; study must be replicable and yield the same results to have valid findings	Same as in the traditional/patriarchal perspective	Completeness, plausibility, illustrativeness, understanding, responsiveness to readers or participants' experience
Analysis of the Data			
Type preferred	Predominantly quantitative analysis determined a priori; if qualitative techniques are used, researcher may apologize for lack of "scientific rigor"	Same as in the traditional/patriarchal perspective	Types of analysis are determined by the data; analysis is decided a posteriori
Findings sought	Differences between groups	Same as in the traditional/patriarchal perspective	Similarities and the range of experience of the participants
Attention to sex differences	Most studies use male subjects only; if a study includes both men and women, there is a tendency not to analyze for sex differences	An equal number of men and women, analyzed for sex differences	Many studies use female participants only; if a study includes men and women, the subjects are analyzed for sex differences

Table 1
(Continued)

Research Dimension	Research Perspective		
	Traditional/ Patriarchal	Nonsexist	Feminist
Interpretation of Sex Differences			
Biases	Interprets differences to conform with sexual stereotypes; differences frequently are interpreted as positive for men and negative for women	Questions sexual stereotypes; generally views differences in terms of socialization and social roles	Interprets differences in terms of power and oppression; looks at the adaptive aspects of differences
	Studies where no differences are found are usually not reported		
Generalization of findings	Generalizes male norm to "people"; thus the male becomes the standard; does not seek input from participants	Generalizes male norms to male and female norms to female	Does not generalize beyond the group studied
Use of Research			
Publication	Often primary purpose of research; values only data that confirm hypotheses; negative results seldom reported; little or no credit given to participants	Attempts to publish negative results regarding sex differences; may report disconfirmation of a major theory; little credit given to participants	Publication is not always the most important use of data; the more unexpected the findings, the more they are valued; credit given to participants for their contribution
Social action and policy	Little concern for the policy implications of results; when used, often furthers goal of maintaining status quo	Limited concern for policy implications, sometimes used to liberalize social policy; may inadvertently perpetuate status quo	Often has a political focus designed with social change in mind— to further the interests of participants and the population to which they belong
Professional implications	Application would have a negative impact on women's growth and development	Limited application; adds to scientific understanding of women	Applications are likely to promote women's growth and development; advances scientific understanding of women
Heuristic value of research	Tests finding against a priori hypotheses; generates little new information	Same as in the traditional/patriarchal perspective	Generates new concepts, meanings, and information; attempts to construct theory and hypotheses from the data collected

93 / Feminist Perspective on Research

the primary differentiation between feminists and what have come to be called "profeminist men."

In a similar vein, I would argue that when the research is focused on some aspect of the lives of women of color, lesbians, the elderly, or the incarcerated, members of that particular group must be involved in all phases of the research, particularly in making sense of the findings. When the researchers are not themselves members of the group studied, it would be advisable to include both the researchers' and the participants' interpretations of findings in any report of the research.

Ethical Issues. A comparison among sexist, nonsexist, and feminist paradigms shows different relationships between researchers and participants. Both sexist and nonsexist paradigms require researchers to obtain the informed consent of participants and to do no harm to them. The feminist approach requires researchers to obtain the approval of a subset of the group, which should ensure that the research is not exploitative and that it is likely to be beneficial to the participants or members of their group. It is a move from "Leave the subjects no worse than you found them" to "Leave the participants better off than you found them."

For participants to be "better off," the objectives of the research project should indicate how the research aims to further the interests of the group studied. The improvement can be in any area: social, political, economic, psychological, biological, and so forth. Such a guideline clearly limits the areas in which a feminist approach can be used. For example, one might genuinely seek the participation of wife batterers in a study but could not align oneself with any need of the participants that would further the battering. Clearly, a feminist approach is limited to situations in which it is possible to develop a collaborative relationship between the researchers and the participants.

A collaborative relationship between the researcher and the participants could increase the possibility that the results of a study would be used to bring about change rather than collect dust on a shelf. For example, I have found that collaborative relationships between researchers and agency staff members in program evaluation studies have made it more likely that suggestions for change will be implemented.

The feminist paradigm also calls for an interpretation of the findings by the researcher *and* the participants and for the views of each to be acknowledged in any formal presentation of results.

Feminist Visions

This joint interpretation should lessen the likelihood that the researcher will use theory in stereotyped or prejudicial ways. In essence, the feminist paradigm has additional built-in protections for participants from misunderstanding and misinterpretations, which seems necessary in doing research about all oppressed groups.

Who owns the data? In traditional models of research, there is seldom any question about ownership of the data. Participants share their truths after having given their informed consent, and the researcher has ownership and control of the data. In a feminist model, control may be shared between participants and the researcher. In some instances, a third party—a sponsor—may also want a say in the control and use of data. Whether the particular research involves two or three parties, it seems essential that contractual arrangements be negotiated among all the parties at the initiation of the research and that such arrangements be open to renegotiation at any time during the project.

Implications of a Feminist Perspective

The Researcher as an Agent of Change. Use of a feminist perspective moves the researcher into the role of change agent. Initially the researcher would be guided by the concerns and questions of the subgroup to be studied. She or he would not be investigating women as "objects" and pursuing academic questions but, rather, using the findings of the research to influence or change the lives of those studied and of other members of the group. This role seems compatible with the interest of most social workers in service delivery and social change. Conceivably, adaptation of a feminist perspective would help bridge the gap between research and practice, leading to more true practitioner-researchers.

Feminist research *always* has a political focus. It is designed with social change in mind—to further the interests of the participants and the population to which they belong. In no way need we be apologetic for this political purpose. Is it too visionary to think that as feminist research influences social work more and more, it can be useful in moving us from a reactive to a more proactive, change-oriented profession?

Generating Concepts vs. Hypothesis Testing. Much feminist research focuses on generating new concepts, meanings, and in- **95** formation rather than on testing existing theory, partly because of the paucity of knowledge about many aspects of women's experiences. That many feminists do not begin their research with clearly and precisely defined conceptual and operational definitions of the phenomena to be studied is troubling to many who have been trained and ingrained in traditional research methodology. Those who would engage in research from a feminist perspective should anticipate challenges from the largely patriarchal world and be prepared to address such concerns without compromising the feminist perspective of the project. The current state of knowledge about the phenomena being studied rather than some traditionally valued approach should provide the criteria for the type of research that is being proposed and that is being funded.

Societal Sanction and Support. Many feminist research projects focus on substantive areas that are of little interest to the dominant white male heterosexual power structure and consequently are not likely to receive much financial support from institutional structures that are controlled by this group. Increased financial support for feminist-oriented research seems unlikely in the current political climate. Therefore, redoubled efforts at networking among feminist researchers in and outside of social work seems essential. Social work faculty members, practitioners, and students will need to piggyback on one another's efforts as well as collaborate with one another to overcome some of the restrictions imposed by limited financial support.

Traditionally, much of the leadership in research and many social work researchers have come from the ranks of academia. As more feminist-oriented research is produced in schools of social work, will faculty members suffer the same punishment as their colleagues in the other social sciences and in the humanities? Will tenure be denied or competent women not be promoted because their research is judged insignificant or too political? To what extent are social work faculty members being discriminated against if they engage in less traditional research efforts or make their results known in other than prestigious journals? Will promotion and tenure committees in schools of social work value efforts to bring about social change with groups of oppressed research participants equally with publication?

Can you envision what might be different about social work education and practice if a feminist perspective were to

Feminist Visions

become more pervasive? Students and practitioners no longer alienated by research but actively involved in both research and practice, and not making fine distinctions between them? Research, practice, and social action or social change as one unified effort? Empowerment of oppressed groups and of ourselves occurring simultaneously? An increased understanding of the phenomena being studied? Far fewer pieces of research cranked out to meet a publish-or-perish dictum? Genuine recognition and valuing of the *multiple* sources of knowledge and understanding? More excited, energized, and knowledgeable faculty, students, and practitioners?

Conclusion

Feminist research has been conceptualized here as being process oriented, allowing participants to define themselves and their experiences, focusing on the growth of researchers and participants, and leading to action and social change. As more researchers of both sexes adopt or are influenced by a feminist perspective, one may expect to see a major cultural transformation in social science and social work research methodology. This transformation was aptly described by Capra, an eminent professor of physics at the University of California at Berkeley:

> The first and perhaps most profound transition is due to the slow and reluctant but inevitable decline in patriarchy. . . . It is the one system which until recently had never in recorded history been openly challenged, and whose doctrines were so universally accepted that they seemed to be laws of nature, indeed, they were usually presented as such. Today, however, the disintegration of patriarchy is in sight. The feminist movement is one of the strongest cultural currents of our time and will have a profound effect on our further evolution.[37]

notes

1. Mary Daly, *Beyond God the Father* (Boston: Beacon Press, 1973), pp. 11–12.

2. Linda Rosenman and Roy Ruchdeschel, "Catch 1234B: Integrating Material on Women into the Social Work Research Cur- **97**

riculum," *Journal of Education for Social Work,* 17 (Spring 1981), pp. 5-11; and Martha Brunswick Heineman, "The Obsolete Scientific Imperative in Social Work Research," *Social Service Review,* 55 (September 1981), pp. 371-397.

3. Daly, *Beyond God the Father,* p. 12.

4. Heineman, "The Obsolete Scientific Imperative," p. 371.

5. Harris Goldstein, "Criteria for Evaluating Research," *Social Casework,* 43 (November 1962), p. 476.

6. Leonard J. Kogan, "Principles of Measurement," in Norman Polansky, ed., *Social Work Research* (Chicago: University of Chicago Press, 1960), p. 90.

7. Heineman, "The Obsolete Scientific Imperative," p. 373.

8. Martin Bloom and Stephen Black, "Evaluating One's Own Effectiveness and Efficiency," *Social Work,* 22 (March 1977), p. 130.

9. Katherine Wood, "Casework Effectiveness: A New Look at the Research Evidence," *Social Work,* 23 (November 1978), p. 451.

10. Norman Polansky, "Introduction: Social and Historical Context," in *Social Work Research* (rev. ed.; Chicago: University of Chicago Press, 1975), p. 2; Edward Mullen, "The Evaluation of Social Work Progress," Occasional Paper No. 1 (Chicago: Jane Addams College of Social Work, 1979), pp. 24-25; and Margaret Blenkner, "Obstacles to Evaluative Research in Casework: Part II," *Social Casework,* 31 (March 1950), p. 99.

11. Blenkner, "Obstacles to Evaluative Research in Casework," p. 99.

12. Polansky, *Social Work Research,* p. 2.

13. William J. Reid, "Social Work for Social Problems," *Social Work,* 22 (September 1977), p. 378.

14. Feminists are neither the first nor the sole critics of the traditional model of research. Socialists, phenomenologists, and others have challenged many of the assumptions underlying this model. A summary of these critiques is beyond the scope of this article. Interested readers are referred to such works as Thomas Kuhn, *The Structure of Scientific Revolutions* (Chicago: University of Chicago Press, 1962); Alfred Schultz, "The Problem of Rationality in the Social World," in *Collected Papers,* Vol. 2 (The Hague, The Netherlands: Martinus Nijhoff, 1964); Paul Feyerabend, *Against Method* (London, England: Humanitarian Press, 1975); and George Psathus, ed., *Phenomenological Sociology* (New York: John Wiley & Sons, 1973).

15. Naomi Gottlieb, "Issues in Non-Sexist Research," paper presented at the Annual Program Meeting of the Council on Social Work Education, Louisville, Kentucky, 1981; Irene H. Frieze et al., *Women and Sex Roles: A Social Psychological Perspective* (New York: W. W. Norton & Co., 1978), chaps. 1 and 2; Joan Huber, "Review Essay: Sociology," *Signs: Journal of Women in Culture and Society,* 1

Feminist Visions

(Spring 1976), pp. 685–697; and Mary Brown Parlee, "Review Essay: Psychology," *Signs: Journal of Women in Culture and Society,* 1 (Autumn 1975), pp. 119–138.

16. Gottlieb, "Issues in Non-Sexist Research."

17. Lawrence Kohlberg and Richard Kromer, "Continuities and Discontinuities in Childhood and Adult Moral Development," *Human Development,* 12 (1969), pp. 93–120.

18. Carol Gilligan, "In a Different Voice: Women's Conception of the Self and of Morality," *Harvard Educational Review,* 47 (1977), pp. 481–517. For a fuller exposition of Gilligan's work, see Gilligan, *In a Different Voice* (Cambridge, Mass.: Harvard University Press, 1982).

19. Lawrence Kohlberg, *The Philosophy of Moral Development: Essays in Moral Development,* Vol. 1 (New York: Harper & Row, 1981).

20. Elizabeth Dodson Gray, *Patriarchy as a Conceptual Trap* (Wellesley, Mass.: Roundtable Press, 1982), pp. 52–56.

21. As described in Gottlieb, "Issues in Non-Sexist Research."

22. Liz Stanley and Sue Wise, *Breaking Out: Feminist Consciousness and Feminist Research* (London: Routledge & Kegan Paul, 1983), p. 117; Dorothy Smith, "Women's Perspective as a Radical Critique of Sociology," *Sociological Inquiry,* 44 (1977), pp. 7–13; and Marcia Westkott, "Feminist Criticism of Social Sciences," *Harvard Educational Review,* 49 (November 1979), pp. 422–430.

23. Philosophers of science and others differ as to whether "reality" exists or is the creation of people. The position taken here is that there is no one social reality for all people. Reality does not exist "out there." Rather, we perceive reality through the lens of our social formulations.

24. Westkott, "Feminist Criticism of Social Sciences," p. 426.

25. Feminists differ about whether men can do feminist research. This issue is discussed later in the chapter.

26. Westkott, "Feminist Criticism of Social Sciences," p. 426.

27. Obviously, the degree of participation will vary and may be impossible if the study participants are rapists, wife batterers, and so forth.

28. See p. 9.

29. Reports of research usually present the process as an orderly, coherent, and logically organized series of steps. Research neophytes often believe the descriptions of research to be a reasonable representation of reality. When the experience fails to correspond to the textbook descriptions, they often question their adequacy as researchers rather than the descriptions.

30. Stanley and Wise, *Breaking Out,* p. 157.

31. Frequently, critics challenge a feminist perspective, claiming that it is biased. Feminists in general will acknowledge their values "up **99**

front" in research and in other aspects of social work practice. Others who claim to be neutral usually are unwilling to admit that traditional research models value the existing patriarchal and hierarchical social structure.

32. Renate Duelli Klein, "How to Do What You Want to Do: Thoughts about Feminist Methodology," pp. 90–96, and Maria Mies, "Toward a Methodology for Feminist Research," pp. 128–131, in Gloria Bowles and Klein, eds., *Theories of Women's Studies* (London, England: Routledge & Kegan Paul, 1983); and Westkott, "Feminist Criticism of Social Sciences," p. 428.

33. Liz Stanley and Sue Wise, "Feminist Research, Feminist Consciousness and the Experiences of Sexism," *Women's Studies International Quarterly,* 2 (1979), pp. 359–374.

34. See Arlene K. Daniels, "Feminist Perspectives in Sociological Research," in Marcia Millman and Rosabeth Kanter, eds., *Another Voice: Feminist Perspectives on Social Life and Social Science* (Garden City, N.Y.: Doubleday & Co., 1974), for cogent arguments on why feminist research should have a particular focus on women.

35. See Shulamit Reinharz, *On Becoming a Social Scientist* (San Francisco: Jossey-Bass, 1979); Evelyn Fox-Keller, "Feminist Critique of Science: A Forward or Backward Move?" *Fundamenta Scientiae,* 1, No. 3 (1980), pp. 341–346; and Charlene Depner, "Toward the Further Development of Feminist Psychology," paper presented at the mid-winter conference of the Association for Women in Psychology, Boston, 1981. For a thoughtful analysis of both the limits and the value of quantitative methods, see Toby Epstein Jayaratne, "The Value of Quantitative Methodology for Feminist Research," in Bowles and Klein, eds. *Theories of Women's Studies,* pp. 140–161.

36. Study by Diana Pearce, cited by Marti Bombyk in "Reclaiming Our Profession Through Feminist Research: Some Methodological Issues in the Feminist Practice Project," paper presented at the Symposium on Women's Issues, Annual Program Meeting of the Council on Social Work Education, Washington, D.C., February 1985.

37. Fritjof Capra, *The Turning Point: Science, Society, and the Rising Culture* (New York: Simon & Schuster, 1982), p. 29.

Diane Kravetz

women and mental health

the integration of feminist scholarship on women and mental health into the knowledge base of social work is crucial for social workers' understanding of the social and psychological problems of women. The information and insights resulting from this work provide prerequisite knowledge for social workers' understanding of the cultural and social context of women's psychological distress, counter prevailing cultural myths about women, and increase our understanding of the nature of female experience and female oppression. Social workers have long understood the relationships between private troubles and public issues and the importance of the transactions between individuals and the social environment. Feminist literature provides the knowledge base through which social workers can understand the nature of those relationships and transactions for women. In addition, this literature documents the influence of sexism on the theory and research that have traditionally provided the foundations for social work research, education, and practice and provides social work with the theoretical and empirical base for developing nonsexist and feminist interventions for women.

This chapter presents a representative overview of the work by feminist scholars that examines the relationships among sexual inequality, female subordination, and women's mental health. The overview includes literature concerning (1) the influence of gender inequality and traditional gender roles on women's mental health, (2) the influence of sexism on traditional theory and research in the area of women and mental health, (3) the influence of sexual stereotypes and sex bias on practitioners' attitudes about and behavior toward female clients, and (4) feminist approaches to clinical intervention.

Psychological Development and Female Subordination

In the field of psychology, feminist scholars have gained new knowledge about the nature of female development and sex differences. Much of this work challenges traditional assumptions about biologically based "female" traits and personality characteristics. The extent to which cultural values about women have a profound and negative effect on women's psychological development is becoming increasingly clear.

The prevailing cultural ideology defines "male" characteristics, activities, and achievements as superior to and more worthwhile than "female" ones. In support of these cultural assumptions, girls are socialized to develop personal characteristics and assume social roles that are consistent with their devalued status. Girls are socialized toward dependence, submissiveness, and achievement through others by way of marriage and child rearing.[1]

The women's movement has had a dramatic impact on the behaviors, roles, and opportunities of women. Women are becoming increasingly autonomous, psychologically and economically. However, although there is evidence of gender-role changes for women of every class,[2] in general, women continue to assume major responsibility for child care and homemaking, and all institutional arenas continue to be pervaded by androcentric values and discriminatory policies and practices.

Social myths of equality in conjunction with idealized images of motherhood and female privilege create ambivalence and anxiety for those women who seek to achieve through autonomous and nontraditional efforts. Women are socialized to value "female" qualities and achievements but they also understand that these same features are socially defined as less important than those that are "male." Also, women encounter severe social sanctions for not conforming to traditional definitions of the "female." Achieving women are judged more harshly than men, are considered unfeminine, and are perceived and treated as deviants.[3] Single women and child-free women also suffer social ostracism and suspicion.[4]

In addition to investigating how female development is affected by traditional gender-role socialization and societal responses to women who deviate from traditional roles and behaviors, feminist psychologists have challenged traditional models and methods of inquiry. Sex bias has been identified in every aspect of the research process, including the conceptualization of problems, measurement procedures, the presentation of findings, interpretations, and conclusions.[5] For example, research on male subjects dominates the psychological literature, and there is a greater likelihood that generalizations will be made to all human beings when the subjects are males than when they are females. The alternate and frequent pattern is not to identify the sex of the subjects.[6]

Research on sex differences has been a major target of feminist criticism. It has been suggested that a primary function of such research is to support the status quo by providing "objective" evidence to explain and justify women's subordinate social status.[7] In her review of the psychological study of women during the functionalist era (from the latter half of the 19th century to the first third of the 20th century), Shields observed:

> For centuries the mode of Eve's creation and her
> greater guilt for the fall from grace had been credited
> as the cause of woman's imperfect nature, but this was
> not an adequate explanation in a scientific age. Thus,
> science sought explanations for female inferiority that
> were more in keeping with contemporary scientific
> philosophy. . . .
>
> . . . . .
>
> That science played handmaiden to social values cannot
> be denied.[8]

Recent considerations of sex differences have revealed that there are only four areas in which relatively consistent differences can be demonstrated.[9] Studies have indicated superiority for females in the area of verbal ability, superiority for males on measures of visual-spatial and mathematical ability, and greater physical aggressiveness by males. Also, some work has suggested that **103** males are more active, more competitive, and more dominant, whereas females are less assertive, more dependent, and more compliant.

Feminist psychologists place interpretation of these results within a sociocultural, as opposed to a biological, framework. They stress that these observed differences closely correspond to cultural conceptions of appropriate female and male behavior. Given differences in female and male socialization by parents, teachers, and the media, it is not possible to determine the extent to which biological predisposition may contribute to differences, especially considering that most differences do not become evident until adolescence. In addition, the behavior of females and males with respect to these traits forms two overlapping distributions with only a minority of females or males at the extremes. Because there are women and men who are high and low on every trait and because statistical differences do not predict the behavior and abilities of any one individual, it is particularly oppressive to have research on sex differences become additional justification for discriminatory policies and practices.

Also, feminist scholars have criticized research on sex differences for its emphasis on traits because such a perspective fails to acknowledge the extent to which situational variables influence behavior. The problem of understanding sex differences is further compounded by the fact that the same behavior exhibited by males versus females is likely to be perceived differently by the performers themselves and to receive different social responses and interpretations.

Much of the current literature on the psychology of women is based on studies of white middle-class heterosexual females. Less attention has been given to the experiences of women of color, lesbians, and working-class women. Our understanding of women as an oppressed group, however, must take into account the divergent as well as the common aspects of female oppression, recognizing that many women are victims of racism, classism, and heterosexism as well.

For women of all classes, sexual inequality undermines their psychological development and personal achievements. However, for working-class women, economic deprivation and dependence also are primary issues. Their economic status has a devastating effect on their expectations, freedom of choice, and options for change.[10] Working-class women enter the labor force primarily because of economic necessity, and their employment in low-

Feminist Visions

status, low-paying jobs does not significantly alter traditional gender roles in their families.

Black, Hispanic, Asian American, and Native American women represent four distinct cultural groups, each having specific and different problems, issues, and concerns. In each of these groups, moreover, women's experience differs by class and, for some groups, by nationality or tribe. Some generalizations can be made, however. The experiences of males and females differ significantly, in every cultural group, with women in each group having problems related to gender inequality in their own culture and in the dominant culture. Also, for minority women, issues related to gender must be understood in the context of the overwhelming influence of racism and economic deprivation on their lives.

Racism has placed extraordinary burdens on blacks, including inferior housing, education, and health care; high rates of unemployment and limited job opportunities; and racial violence. Nonetheless, black women have managed to create and maintain strong family and community networks; they place a high value on women's education and participation in the labor force.

The intersection of myths about gender and myths about race is most evident in the notion of the black matriarch. The perceived inner strength, independence, and power of black women have been reinterpreted to conform to patriarchal definitions of the stable family and appropriate female roles. Instead of recognizing the central role of social and ecoomic factors in black female-headed households, researchers and commentators have viewed black women as domineering, as emasculating, and as promoting pathology in the black family.[11] Reviewing the empirical literature on black employment and black families, Harrison concluded that black women do not dominate the black community and that black matriarchy is a myth.[12]

Because of their long-standing participation in the paid labor force, black women are less tied to stereotypical female roles and behaviors, view work as compatible with family roles, and have more egalitarian marital relationships. Also, black women, in general, have positive self-concepts.[13] As noted by Smith, "Despite the evidence that black girls and women are faced with the prospects of being devalued by both blacks and the general white society in favor of white women, black females have been able to maintain a positive sense of self against what appear to be overwhelming odds."[14]

105

Women and Mental Health

Patriarchal family, community, and religious systems have a pervasive effect on the lives of Hispanic women. The *machismo* norm promotes female passivity and frequent childbearing and discourages education and employment for women.[15] Powerlessness is reinforced for those Hispanic women who work, for they are often isolated by language barriers and exploited as migrant farm laborers. As with white women, male dominance has debilitating consequences for Hispanic women. For example, Mexican American females have lower self-esteem, are less competitive, and have lower academic achievement than Mexican American males.[16]

Traditionally, Asian American women have also held compliant and submissive roles in their families and communities and in the work place. Like other women of color, Asian American women in the work force are concentrated in low-status and low-paying jobs, even though they tend to have more education than blacks, Hispanics, or whites. In recent years, Asian American women have assumed more authority in their families, are increasingly questioning the traditional roles of Asian women in their ethnic communities, and are becoming more assertive as students and as workers.[17]

For most Native American women, oppression stems from racism, poverty, and the sexism of white culture. Native Americans are the most economically depressed and least acculturated minority, and Native American women earn less than and are less acculturated than Native American men. Native American women have had poor access to education, and those in the labor force are in service, clerical, and operative jobs. Although Native American culture is not patriarchal, Native American women's prestige and influence have decreased as a result of federal policies and practices that have given decision-making power and other rights (minimal as they were) only to Native American men.[18] Being in the center of family life, Native American women deal with all the stresses of their families, such as poor living conditions, educational problems, and poor health, including high rates of infant mortality and alcoholism.[19]

For lesbian women, oppression stems from sexism and heterosexism, the latter being a belief system that values heterosexuality as superior to and more natural than homosexuality. Misconceptions about the prejudice toward lesbians are extensions of cultural myths and biases concerning traditional female roles and female sexuality. Lesbianism is defined by a lifestyle and a subculture

Feminist Visions

in which women function relatively independently of men. Thus, lesbianism challenges cultural mandates that women seek personal fulfillment and economic security through heterosexual bonding. Heterosexism is, then, a major aspect of male-dominated culture, for it functions to maintain traditional power relationships between women and men. Homophobia, including the fear of being labeled homosexual, serves to keep both women and men within the confines of traditional gender roles.

There are numerous cultural myths about lesbian women, including the myths that lesbians are man haters, that they always assume "butch-femme" roles, that they are sick, and that they are child abusers. All these assertions have been shown to be cultural stereotypes and false.[20] Studies have suggested that lesbians are a diverse group of women "in personality, family constellation, and developmental experiences, and categorizing them as a group becomes as meaninglesss as categorizing all heterosexual women."[21] As victims of heterosexism, lesbians share some problems, including the stresses associated with "coming out" and difficulties stemming from discrimination in housing, employment, and child custody. In other important ways, lesbian and nonlesbian women are similar; both groups are likely to be mothers and have similar psychological profiles. In comparison with nonlesbians, however, lesbians are more inner directed, assertive, and self-sufficient and have greater job satisfaction.[22]

Mental Health Consequences of Female Subordination

The dysfunctional consequences for women of gender inequality have been discussed extensively in the psychological and clinical literature. There is consensus that stereotypical notions of "femininity" and "masculinity" have a restrictive and debilitating effect on female development. Confining social roles and limited options in education and employment further reinforce women's sense of powerlessness and personal devaluation. It is becoming increasingly apparent, too, that large numbers of women are victims of physical, psychological, and sexual abuse, often from members of their own families. Feminist scholarship on women and mental health has identified all these factors as influencing women's mental health problems.

There is consistent and extensive evidence that more women —both white women and women of color—than men receive ser- **107** vices from private mental health hospitals, community mental health centers, inpatient units of general hospitals, and outpatient psychiatric facilities.[23] Epidemiological data also reveal that, compared with men, women have higher rates of neurotic disorders; women have a higher prevalence of anxiety, depression, mental impairment, manic-depression, nervousness, unhappiness, loneliness, worry, and phobias.[24] In sum, women experience more neurotic symptomatology than men and are more likely to be in treatment.

The relationship beween gender inequality and women's psychological problems is most clearly evidenced in the differences in rates of depression of women and men. For whites as well as for racial minorities, women have higher rates of depression than do men.[25] Men have higher rates of personality disorders. Inasmuch as depression involves feelings of inadequacy, helplessness, and passivity and personality disorders involve antisocial and aggressive behaviors, it appears that women and men develop psychological disorders that are exaggerated versions of traditional gender roles.

Because sex differences in rates of depression occur in nonclinical populations, and there is no evidence that women are more willing than are men to report symptoms, current discussions conclude that the reported sex differences are real, not an artifact. Furthermore, although social mythology associates high levels of psychological distress with menstrual cycles, childbirth, and menopause, there is little evidence to support biological explanations.[26] Only in the postpartum period is there evidence linking hormonal shifts to psychological disorders, especially depression. However, in addition to endocrine changes, there are significant social and emotional factors involved in childbirth that contribute to women's psychological distress. In any case, postpartum depression cannot account for the high rates of depression among women as a group.

Several factors have been identified as influencing women's greater susceptibility to depression, including their subordinate social status, female socialization, and traditional gender-role divisions in the family. Institutionalized sexism limits women's perceived and real options and results in "legal and economic helplessness, dependency on others, chronically low self-esteem, low aspiration, and, ultimately, clinical depression."[27] In addition, it has been proposed that women have "learned helplessness"; they have learned that goal-directed, competent behavior

Feminist Visions

is not expected of them and will not be rewarded with support, encouragement, equal pay, or equal rights. On the basis of their extensive review of research on female development and socialization, Radloff and Monroe found substantial evidence "that females are more likely to learn 'helplessness' (by lack of reinforcement of instrumental actions) than males."[28] To the extent that helplessness contributes to depression, this sex difference could help explain the excess depression experienced by women.[29]

Numerous studies point to women's traditional marital role as a primary factor in their higher rates of depression. Except in the case of unemployed men, married women are at greater risk for depression than are married men; single men, however, are at greater risk than are single women.[30] For both sexes, rates of depression for divorced, separated, and widowed persons are higher than are those for married persons. However, some studies have found that divorced or separated women are more depressed and more poorly adjusted than are divorced or separated men.[31] The differences in rates of depression among married women and men have been generally viewed as strong evidence for a sociocultural explanation of the high rates of depression among women.

The roles of wife and mother have been widely discussed as primary sources of women's problems.[32] Marriage and children (especially young children) adversely affect the mental health of women—married women with paid employment as well as married full-time homemakers.[33] The institutions of marriage and the family have a debilitating effect owing to women's loss of autonomy; the low social value of wife and mother roles; and the unstructured, invisible, and isolating roles of housewife and mother.

Other social factors also increase women's vulnerability to distress and disorder. Women heading families without partners have a particularly high rate of utilization of mental health facilities.[34] Also, for both sexes, the lower the income, the higher the incidence of depression.[35] Thus, at most risk are low-income, poorly educated women who head single-parent families.[36]

Racism exacerbates female oppression and compounds women's feelings of helplessness and hopelessness. In addition to problems created by white ethnocentrism and discrimination based on race and sex, minority women experience substantial stress as they attempt to reconcile their ethnic values and traditions with the demands of white society. Many are caught between **109** their desires to assimilate into American society and to preserve their ethnic heritage.

Finally, family violence is a widespread social problem, with women and female children in traditional patriarchal families being most at risk for sexual abuse and other forms of violence.[37] Victims of family violence are economically dependent; they receive little assistance from family, friends, and the police; and they find few remedies through the criminal justice, legal, and social service systems. Thus, wife abuse is another source of married women's sense of helplessness, isolation, and depression.

The Mental Health System and Female Subordination

A central concern of feminists has been the extent to which the mental health system reinforces and exacerbates women's powerlessness. Traditional psychotherapy is denounced as an adjustment-oriented system, helping women to understand, accept, and adjust to sexist roles and norms. The criticisms of feminists have been given substantial support by analyses of clinical theories and by empirical investigations of sexual stereotypes and sex bias in clinical attitudes and practices.

There are numerous critical analyses of androcentric theories of feminine personality, particularly those of Freud, Deutsch, Jung, and Erikson.[38] Feminist critiques have revealed the extent to which this literature (1) uncritically mirrors social myths and stereotypes about women, (2) uses the experience of men as the standard against which the experience of women is judged, (3) values "male" behaviors and roles over "female" ones, and (4) uses female biology to explain women's feelings and behavior.

Freud's notions of penis envy and female oedipal conflict provide clear examples of how male experience becomes elevated to the level of an ideal and "femaleness" is defined as the regrettable absence of "maleness." Similarly, Freud has been criticized for his phallocentric view of female sexuality, a view that prescribes orgasm by vaginal stimulation as the indicator of normality and defines clitoral orgasm as psychosexually "immature" and "perverse." As Deckard noted: "That his [Freud's] theories could have been and, in many quarters, still are taken seriously illustrates the incredible misogyny prevalent in Western society."[39]

Erikson's work is another example of theory that defines

women in terms of their relationship to men. For Erikson, a woman's identity is complete when she "relinquishes the care received from the paternal family in order to commit herself to the love of a stranger and to the care to be given to his and her offspring."[40] Erikson's emphasis on biological determinism is evident in his view that women's "productive inner space" dictates their behavior and that women's reproductive role is the primary determinant of their identity.

Feminist critiques of such clinical theories of personality stress the central role of cultural determinism instead of biological determinism. For example, on the basis of her extensive review of the literature on the Freudian theory of female development, Sherman concluded: "There is little evidence of castration anxiety in women or of widespread anatomical envy. . . there is pervasive evidence of differential sex status positions and preference for the higher male sex-role status."[41] The work of Masters and Johnson laid to rest Freudian views linking mature female sexuality with vaginal orgasm.[42] Also, current feminist scholarship on motherhood convincingly has challenged the concept of a "maternal instinct" and examines motherhood as a social institution—one that does not uniformly promote personal growth and fulfillment for women.[43]

Studies of clinicians' attitudes about and behavior toward female clients confirm the pervasive effects of sex bias and stereotyping. One nationwide survey identified four areas in which sex bias is evident in psychotherapy: (1) in the fostering of traditional gender roles, (2) in the adherence to biased expectations and devaluating concepts of women, (3) in the sexist application of psychoanalytic concepts, and (4) in responding to women as sex objects.[44]

A classic study by Broverman and her colleagues found that clinicians' judgments of the traits of healthy women and healthy men paralleled sexual stereotypes. Furthermore, concepts of health for an adult, sex unspecified, and for a man did not differ; concepts of health for a woman differed significantly from those for a healthy adult.[45] These results are commonly viewed as demonstrating a double standard of mental health for women and men among mental health professionals. Since the study by Broverman et al., there has been substantial additional evidence that clinicians and clinicians-in-training hold conservative and stereotypical attitudes about women and men.[46]

Evidence of sexism in the mental health system can be seen **111** in other areas as well. For example, Sherman, Koufacos, and Kenworthy found that therapists were poorly informed about the current research on the psychology of women, especially in the areas of female sexuality, menstruation, pregnancy, childbirth, and menopause.[47] In addition, much of the traditional clinical literature on topics such as agoraphobia, hysteria, alcohol and drug abuse, obesity, and anorexia has been found to reflect sex bias and to include distortions and inaccuracies about women. In each of these areas, feminist scholarship has provided new information and new perspectives.[48] There is also increasing evidence of sexual abuse of female clients by male therapists.[49] Furthermore, it remains true that women are the primary users of mental health services—services that are financially controlled, administered, and delivered primarily by men.

Investigators who have examined issues of race and psychotherapy have focused primarily on therapy with minority clients, sex unspecified. As Collier noted, underutilization of mental health services by ethnic minorities can be attributed to the inaccessibility of agencies, the cost of services, the lack of bilingual counselors, and the class and cultural stereotypes and biases of counselors.[50] Ethnocentrism leads counselors to interpret all differences as deficits.[51] Practitioners know little about the cultural heritages of minorities and are especially ignorant of the unique aspects of women's lives in their own cultural groups. Also, they often fail to understand the extent to which the economic status of minority women determines their psychological and social well-being.

Given societal myths, stereotypes, and prejudices about Native American, Asian American, black, and Hispanic women, it is likely that minority women encounter considerable ignorance and bias in psychotherapy.[52] There is, however, an emerging body of literature on the history, culture, and social problems of minority women directed toward providing basic information and guidance for mental health practitioners.[53]

As noted in several recent reviews of the clinical research on lesbianism, lesbianism has generally been viewed as psychopathological—an arrest of normal sexual development, an outgrowth of poor human relationships, narcissistic, self-centered, and emotionally immature. In contrast, current research consistently demonstrates that lesbian women are at least as healthy as nonlesbian women.[54]

Inasmuch as most Americans disapprove of homosexual relationships and are homophobic,[55] it is not surprising that hetero-sexist bias is evident among psychotherapists as well.[56] Also, because the research on homosexuality has focused predominantly on gay men, it is unlikely that therapists are knowledgeable about the unique experiences of lesbians and the nature of the lesbian subculture.[57] Only recently has there been literature describing the nature of lesbian relationships; the special problems of lesbian daughters, lesbian mothers, and minority lesbians; and the implications of this information for psychotherapy with lesbians.[58]

Clinical literature on women and mental health has begun to reflect an awareness that the female experience differs by class, race, and sexual orientation. There is also growing recognition that generalizations cannot be made for all minority women, all lesbians, or all poor women. Although there is growing sensitivity to the white middle-class heterosexual bias in the literature on women and mental health, research has only begun to identify and examine how gender-race-class interactions affect the incidence and prevalence of mental health problems, service-utilization patterns, and treatment. Because successful therapeutic outcomes require therapists' empathic understanding, positive regard, and openness, it is likely that therapists' biases and ignorance concerning issues of gender, class, race, and sexual orientation limit their potential usefulness for and effectiveness with many women, especially poor, lesbian, and minority women.

Feminist Approaches to Clinical Intervention

On the basis of their analysis of the relationships between gender inequality and women's mental health and on an understanding of sex bias in traditional psychotherapy, feminists have defined and developed nonsexist and feminist approaches to psychotherapy with women. In nonsexist practice with women, therapists are aware of the effects of sexism on their beliefs, values, expectations, and behavior. A nonsexist therapist is knowledgeable about the current research on gender roles and the psychology of women and is aware of the differences in the socialization and life experiences of women and men. In nonsexist therapy, women's personal problems are evaluated in terms of existing gender roles and discriminatory practices, and goals are not based on culturally prescribed behaviors. Alternate lifestyles, lesbianism, role reversals, and other behaviors that do not meet **113** cultural expectations are not viewed as pathological or deviant. Also, the awareness that women's lack of social power can generate passivity and dependence leads nonsexist therapists to encourage female clients to be assertive, autonomous, and self-directed in their personal lives and their therapy.[59]

Principles of feminist therapy include, but go beyond, the elements of nonsexist therapy. In nonsexist therapy, the focus of treatment is individual change and the modification of individual behavior. In feminist therapy, a feminist critique of society and social institutions is a primary ingredient.

Feminist therapy is based on the belief that gender inequality is the underlying problem for women and that economic and psychological autonomy are essential factors for women's mental health and psychological well-being. The development of feminist therapy reflects the conviction that personal and sociopolitical change are inextricably linked. Within the context of this political perspective, feminist therapists combine the nonoppressive aspects of humanistic, psychodynamic, and behavioral therapies with feminist principles and strategies.

Rawlings and Carter listed the following as the central values of feminist therapy:

> 1) The inferior status of women is due to their having less political and economic power than men.... Feminists all agree that the basic problem is the power differential between males and females. However, they disagree on which social factors account for the power difference. Feminist therapists emphasize different personal-political issues in therapy, depending on which feminist philosophy they identify with most strongly;
> 2) A feminist therapist does not value an upper- or middle-class client more than a working-class client;
> 3) The primary source of women's pathology is social, not personal: external, not internal;
> 4) The focus on environmental stress as a major source of pathology is not used as an avenue of escape from individual responsibility;
> 5) Feminist therapy is opposed to personal adjustment to social conditions; the goal is social and political change;
> 6) Other women are not the enemy. Without isolation from one another and without the need to compete for men in order to survive economically, women trust and feel close to other women;

114

Feminist Visions

7) Men are not the enemy either. . . . However, since men benefit more from sexism than women do and since most men are loath to give up their position of privilege, women cannot count on help from men in changing the social role system. Women will have to liberate themselves;

8) Women must be economically and psychologically autonomous. Economic autonomy is a value which always needs to be considered in relationship to hard reality. . . . (it) will be difficult to implement for some women;

9) Relationships of friendship, love, and marriage should be equal in personal power; and

10) Major differences between "appropriate" sex-role behaviors must disappear.[60]

In addition, a feminist approach acknowledges that racism, class bias, and heterosexism are major sources of women's personal problems and psychological distress. To help women change the oppressive aspects of their lives, feminist therapists recognize that they must eliminate classism, racism, and heterosexism in their therapy. Feminists stress their responsibility to be knowledgeable about how clients' experiences, interactive styles, problems, and goals are related to their group memberships.

Feminist approaches to therapy are based on androgyny as a model of mental health. Derived from the Greek (*andro* — man; *gyne* — woman), the concept of androgyny affirms the possible integration and balance of "feminine" and "masculine" characteristics in an individual. As a standard of mental health, androgyny reinforces the notion that the behavior of women and men should be based on the full range of human traits; it helps clients move toward and accept their unique blend of attitudes, behaviors, and feelings, increasing their potential for self-actualization and self-fulfillment.[61]

In feminist therapy, women are encouraged to develop the independence and assertiveness that have previously been defined as "male." In addition, feminists value and validate aspects of women's socialization that, although devalued in the male-dominated culture, are central to a woman-centered value system. Nurturance, sensitivity to the needs of others, expressiveness, and noncompetitiveness are considered important female contributions to society.

To eliminate the oppressive aspects of therapy, feminist **115**

Women and Mental Health

therapists stress the feminist principles of self-help and the sharing of resources, power, and responsibility with clients. Therapeutic strategies are selected to maximize these principles, including discretionary and appropriate use of self-disclosure by the therapist, viewing the client as a consumer who is expected to take an active part in setting goals and in evaluating outcome, making the therapists' values explicit, the formation of an egalitarian therapist-client relationship, providing a realistic role model, and emphasizing the clients' strengths and assets.[62]

The expertise of feminist therapists is shared with the client; it is not used to dominate, manipulate, or mystify. Demystification of the therapy process includes avoidance of jargon and diagnostic tests, whenever possible, and giving clients complete access to their records. These strategies are designed to minimize dependence of clients on the therapist, to increase the likelihood that clients will feel free to reject the values and approaches of the therapist, and to demonstrate concretely the belief that women are capable of being autonomous and should be in control of their lives. A humanist approach to therapy shares many of these beliefs and practices. However, it does not take into account that women's individual change efforts are constrained and restricted by the powerlessness of women as a group.

Feminist therapists believe that it is growth producing for women to understand the influence of social factors on their personal lives and therefore incorporate gender-role analysis into therapy. As Greenspan explained:

> It is vital that women in therapy develop a strong consciousness of the social roots of female emotional pain....Without such a consciousness, it is impossible for the female client to claim an authentic sense of her own power, both individually and along with others....Ultimately, the goal is to help a woman see how her own power as an individual is inextricably bound to the collective power of women as a group.[63]

Gender-role analysis encourages women to evaluate the ways in which social roles and norms and structural realities limit female autonomy and choice. Gender-role analysis is also a process through which women come to understand how, by internalizing cultural values about women, they become co-conspirators in their own oppression.

All-women groups are frequently used in feminist therapy. These groups deemphasize the authority of the therapist and help

Feminist Visions

group members share and understand the experiences that have influenced them as women. Most important, these groups facilitate the respect and trust of women for one another and help women develop a sense of solidarity with other women as a group.

Finally, feminist therapists view themselves as social activists and encourage their clients to participate in social action on their own behalf as well. As Sturdivant explained:

> While it is true that each individual woman must define for herself how she can contribute to society and how she can participate in alleviating injustices that affect all women, there is an implicit assumption that some sort of action is necessary and expected as a treatment goal.[64]

Also, it is therapeutic for women to engage in social actions designed to change the conditions at work and in their community that most directly have a negative effect on their own lives.

Although direct participation in social action is a desirable outcome of feminist therapy, it should be recognized that many of the changes in women's personal attitudes and behavior that result from feminist therapy are in opposition to established social roles and norms concerning women. When the nature of personal change conflicts with the dominant values of society, personal change becomes political and holds broad social implications. Psychological change, behavioral role-related change, and change in political analysis all have significant implications for broad-based social change.

Because the emergence and development of feminist therapy are relatively recent, there has been little empirical investigation of its processes and outcomes. Marecek, Kravetz, and Finn found that women who identified themselves as members of the women's movement evaluated feminist therapy as more helpful than traditional therapy, whereas nonmembers rated feminist and traditional therapies as equally helpful.[65] Johnson found that women entering traditional and feminist therapies did not differ in their level of pretherapy stress or target complaints. Also, there were no differences in their self-reported improvement after therapy and with their satisfaction with the therapy experience, although clients in feminist therapy were treated in groups by female therapists for an average of four months and clients in traditional therapy were seen individually by male therapists for an average of ten months. Clients in feminist therapy reported that the **117** helpful factors in their therapy included (1) seeing therapists as competent women, (2) knowing that, as women, therapists have shared the female experience, and (3) discovering that other women are central in one's life and are helpful.[66]

Some empirical data provide indirect but supportive evidence of the benefits of feminist therapy. Feminist therapy, especially when done with all-women groups, incorporates many of the principles and processes of consciousness-raising groups. Studies have found that the outcomes of consciousness-raising groups include (1) increased self-awareness, self-respect, and self-esteem, (2) increased awareness of the effects of traditional gender roles and sexism, (3) increased awareness of a commonality with other women, (4) improved relationships and a sense of solidarity with other women, (5) development of a sociopolitical analysis of female experience and the nature of female oppression, (6) changes in interpersonal relationships and roles, and (7) participation in work and community activities to change the social circumstances of women.[67] It is likely that the benefits of feminist therapy include, but are not limited to, the benefits of consciousness-raising groups for women.

Further, Gilbert reviewed a range of studies that affirmed the importance of many of the key components of feminist therapy, such as (1) informing clients of the nature of therapy, (2) not taking the position of expert, (3) enhancing the autonomy of clients in therapy, (4) serving as a positive role model, and (5) facilitating the expression of anger. In addition, there is evidence that helping women to develop a sociopolitical analysis of women's issues and a feminist identity may be beneficial for their mental health. Numerous studies have indicated that feminists, compared with nonfeminists, more strongly value autonomy and independence, have higher self-esteem, and are more self-accepting and self-actualized.[68] It also appears that all-women groups are especially beneficial for women.[69]

Some feminists believe that women should be in therapy only with female therapists. Female therapists serve as role models for their clients and can avoid the female-male interactive strategies that reinforce women's passivity. Being female increases the therapist's ability to empathize with her clients and to understand and share experiences related to being female in a male-dominated society.

Rawlings and Carter acknowledged that male therapists cannot serve as role models for women. However, they concluded

Feminist Visions

that a nonsexist or profeminist man who is knowledgeable about women's problems is qualified to treat women and is clearly preferable to a sexist female therapist. They discussed four circumstances in which men should not treat women:

> 1) A man should not do therapy with an all-female group...(it) sets up precisely the situation which women traditionally have learned is the only appropriate one in which to compete—competition for male attention.... Unless women learn competition in other areas is acceptable and that competition for male attention is self-defeating, they will not be able to form close emotional ties with other women, one of the essential ingredients for feminist therapy...(having a man lead an all-female group) makes it difficult for women to learn to look to themselves for their own answers;
>
> 2) Men who have vestiges of guilt about the enforced subservience of women or who have rescue fantasies about women should not do therapy with dependent women whose husbands mistreat them... neither may realize that she has simply replaced the husband upon whom she was dependent with her male therapist;
>
> 3) Men should not do therapy with women who are hostile to men; and
>
> 4) Men should not do therapy with women who relate to men primarily in a seductive manner....When these women develop close relationships with other women and increase their self-esteem, they no longer need to resort to seductiveness in order to feel safe and powerful.[70]

Rawlings and Carter further suggested that it is preferable that a male therapist not treat a woman in the crisis of divorce, "when she is tremendously vulnerable to intense transference feelings," and that men do not treat extremely dependent, inhibited women who equate femininity with passivity and docility; these women would benefit more from a female therapist "who can model assertiveness and strength in the context of positive feminine qualities."[71]

Feminist approaches to therapy are defined primarily by the knowledge base, values, and methods of practitioners—not by their sex. When profeminist men work with female clients, they incorporate a feminist perspective, including an awareness that there are limitations on their ability to understand and empathize with women's concerns and experiences. Two such limitations are **119** their inability to serve as role models and their reinforcement, at some level, of the view that women are dependent on male authority. Awareness of these limitations enables a profeminist therapist to evaluate whether he is an appropriate therapist for a particular client or problem. If transfer to a nonsexist or feminist woman therapist is preferable but impossible, he must then develop ways to deal with and minimize the effects of these limitations.

The various elements of nonsexist and feminist approaches to therapy define the range of knowledge, values, and interventions that are incorporated by feminist therapists with both feminist and nonfeminist clients. The critical advantage for women in having a feminist therapist is that a feminist therapist has the ability to conduct both nonsexist and feminist therapy, depending on which is most appropriate for the client throughout the therapeutic process. Feminist therapists use a feminist perspective and knowledge base to assess the experiences and problems of their clients; to make judgments about the biological, psychological, and social factors that have influenced the clients' problems; and to select therapeutic strategies to help clients reach their goals. They incorporate their knowledge of female oppression and gender-role socialization in the same manner that they incorporate their knowledge of all other aspects of their clients' problems and situations: selectively and sensitively. On the basis of their knowledge and experience, feminist therapists can move along a continuum of nonsexist-to-feminist strategies and interventions, depending on the values, needs, problems, and goals of their clients.

Conclusion

Feminist scholarship concerning women and mental health serves several important functions as part of the knowledge base of social work. First, feminist theory and research provide the framework for understanding the relationships between gender inequality and women's mental health problems. This work details a perspective through which social workers can analyze and evaluate how the cultural ideology about women shapes women's reality and maintains women's oppression.

Second, feminist critiques document the influence of sexism on the established mental health literature that has been well integrated into social work courses on human growth and develop-

Feminist Visions

ment, marriage and the family, mental health, psychopathology, and casework. In addition, feminist scholarship provides knowledge about women and women's lives in areas that have previously been overlooked, ignored, or assumed to be unimportant and thus not part of social work knowledge. Feminist scholarship has provided the foundations for new models of mental health and clinical interventions designed specifically for the needs of female clients—work that is particularly applicable to and useful for social work practice.

Third, feminist scholarship provides models of the analytical and empirical processes through which knowledge about women is reassessed, reconceptualized, reconstructed, and expanded. The application and incorporation of these emerging approaches to knowledge building greatly facilitate the development of substantive and nonsexist social work knowledge about women. This work provides the basis for building a practice-oriented scholarship about women, for designing social work courses to prepare students for nonsexist practice, and for developing nonsexist practice models and methods. It also provides the foundation for the development of feminist approaches to social welfare policies and services and to social work practice.

Feminist approaches to understanding and dealing with women's mental health problems can be usefully applied to work with members of other oppressed groups as well. A feminist perspective highlights how workers and clients alike benefit from understanding the multifaceted ways in which institutionalized inequality creates psychological distress and disorders. A feminist perspective defines the linkages between personal and social change and provides strategies and methods for empowering the oppressed to make meaningful changes in their lives.

As a profession, social work has long been committed to the values of human dignity, personal autonomy, and self-realization. Social work ethics obligate professional social workers to base their practice on available knowledge and to eliminate discrimination. Social workers cannot meet these responsibilities if they are operating in accordance with a biased, inaccurate, and incomplete knowledge base regarding women. Through understanding the relationships between female subordination and women's mental health problems and through becoming knowledgeable about feminist scholarship on women's lives and concerns, social workers can design, evaluate, and implement meaningful mental health services, programs, and interventions for women. **121**

notes

1. Jean Baker Miller, *Toward a New Psychology of Women* (Boston: Beacon Press, 1976); Virginia E. O'Leary, ed., *Toward Understanding Women* (Monterey, Calif.: Brooks/Cole Publishing Co., 1977); and Juanita H. Williams, *Psychology of Women: Behavior in a Biosocial Context* (New York: W. W. Norton & Co., 1977).

2. Jean Lipman-Blumen, *Gender Roles and Power* (Englewood Cliffs, N.J.: Prentice-Hall, 1984).

3. O'Leary, ed., *Toward Understanding Women*; and Rhoda K. Unger, *Female and Male: Psychological Perspectives* (New York: Harper & Row, 1979).

4. Margaret Adams, *Single Blessedness: Observations on the Single Status in Married Society* (New York: Basic Books, 1976); and Jessie Bernard, *The Future of Motherhood* (New York: Dial Press, 1974).

5. Kathleen E. Grady, "Sex Bias in Research Design," *Psychology of Women Quarterly*, 5 (Summer 1981), pp. 628–636; Mary Brown Parlee, "Review Essay: Psychology," *Signs: Journal of Women in Culture and Society*, 1 (Autumn 1975), pp. 119–138; Carolyn Sherif, "Bias in Psychology," in Julia Sherman and Evelyn Beck, eds., *The Prism of Sex: Essays in the Sociology of Knowledge* (Madison: University of Wisconsin Press, 1979), pp. 93–133; and Reesa M. Vaughter, "Review Essay: Psychology," *Signs: Journal of Women in Culture and Society*, 2 (Autumn 1976), pp. 120–146.

6. Wendy McKenna and Suzanne J. Kessler, "Experimental Design as a Source of Sex Bias in Social Psychology," *Sex Roles*, 3 (April 1977), pp. 117–128.

7. Kathleen E. Grady, "Androgyny Reconsidered," in Juanita H. Williams, ed., *Psychology of Women: Selected Readings* (New York: W. W. Norton & Co., 1979), pp. 172–177.

8. Stephanie A. Shields, "Functionalism, Darwinism, and the Psychology of Women: A Study in Social Myth," *American Psychologist*, 30 (July 1975), pp. 740 and 753.

9. Eleanor E. Maccoby and Carol N. Jacklin, *The Psychology of Sex Differences* (Stanford, Calif.: Stanford University Press, 1974).

10. Helen S. Farmer, "Career Counseling Implications for the Lower Social Class and Women," *Personnel and Guidance Journal*, 56 (April 1978), pp. 467–471; and Nancy Seifer, *Absent from the Majority: Working Class Women in America* (New York: National Project on Ethnic America of the American Jewish Committee, 1973).

11. Daniel Patrick Moynihan, *The Negro Family* (Washington, D.C.: U.S. Department of Labor, 1965).

12. Algea O. Harrison, "Black Women," in O'Leary, ed., *Toward Understanding Women*, pp. 132–146.

13. Harrison, "Black Women"; Saundra Rice Murray, "Who Is That

Feminist Visions

Person? Images and Roles of Black Women," in Sue Cox, ed., *Female Psychology: The Emerging Self* (2nd ed.; New York: St. Martin's Press, 1981), pp. 113–123; and La Frances Rodgers-Rose, ed., *The Black Woman* (Beverly Hills, Calif.: Sage Publications, 1980).

14. Elsie J. Smith, "The Black Female Adolescent: A Review of the Educational, Career, and Psychological Literature," *Psychology of Women Quarterly*, 6 (Spring 1982), p. 281.

15. Elizabeth M. Almquist and Juanita L. Wehrle-Einhorn, "The Doubly Disadvantaged: Minority Women in the Labor Force," in Ann H. Stromberg and Shirley Harkess, eds., *Women Working: Theories and Facts in Perspective* (Palo Alto, Calif.: Mayfield Publishing Co., 1978), pp. 63–88.

16. Maria Nieto Senour, "Psychology of the Chicana," in Cox, ed., *Female Psychology*, 2nd ed., pp. 136–148.

17. Irene Fujitomi and Diane Wong, "The New Asian-American Woman," in Sue Cox, ed., *Female Psychology: The Emerging Self* (1st ed.; Chicago: Science Research Associates, 1976), pp. 236–248; Reiko Homma True, "The Profile of Asian American Women," in Cox, ed., *Female Psychology*, 2nd ed., pp. 124–135.

18. Almquist and Wehrle-Einhorn, "The Doubly Disadvantaged"; and Shirley Hill Witt, "Native Women Today: Sexism and the Indian Woman," in Cox, ed., *Female Psychology*, 1st ed., pp. 249–259.

19. Helen V. Collier, *Counseling Women: A Guide for Therapists* (New York: Free Press, 1982); Shirley Hill Witt, "The Two Worlds of Native Women," in Cox, ed., *Female Psychology*, 2nd ed., pp. 149–155.

20. Sandra J. Potter and Trudy E. Darty, "Social Work and the Invisible Minority: An Exploration of Lesbianism," *Social Work*, 26 (May 1981), pp. 187–192.

21. Sophie Freud Loewenstein, "Understanding Lesbian Women," *Social Casework: The Journal of Contemporary Social Work*, 61 (January 1980), p. 31.

22. Potter and Darty, "Social Work and the Invisible Minority"; Barbara Sang, "Lesbian Research: A Critical Evaluation," in Ginny Vida, ed., *Our Right to Love* (Englewood Cliffs, N.J.: Prentice-Hall, 1978), pp. 80–93.

23. Nancy Felipe Russo and Suzanne Barbara Sobel, "Sex Differences in the Utilization of Mental Health Facilities," *Professional Psychology*, 12 (February 1981), pp. 7–19.

24. Noreen Goldman and Renee Ravid, "Community Surveys: Sex Differences in Mental Illness," in Marcia Guttentag, Susan Salasin, and Deborah Belle, eds., *The Mental Health of Women* (New York: Academic Press, 1980), pp. 31–55.

25. Russo and Sobel, "Sex Differences in the Utilization of Mental Health Facilities."

26. Gerald L. Klerman and Myrna M. Weissman, "Depressions Among Women: Their Nature and Causes," in Guttentag et al., *The Mental Health of Women*, pp. 57–92.

27. Ibid., p. 79.

28. Lenore Radloff and Megan K. Monroe, "Sex Differences in Help-lessness—With Implications for Depression," in L. Sunny Hansen and Rita S. Rapoza, eds., *Career Development and Counseling of Women* (Springfield, Ill.: Charles C Thomas, 1978), p. 206.

29. Ibid., pp. 199–221.

30. Deborah Belle, "Who Uses Mental Health Facilities?"in Guttentag et al., *The Mental Health of Women*, pp. 1–20; Walter R. Gove, "The Relationship Between Sex Roles, Marital Status, and Mental Illness," *Social Forces*, 51 (September 1972), pp. 34–44; and Russo and Sobel, "Sex Differences in the Utilization of Mental Health Facilities."

31. Lenore Radloff, "Sex Differences in Depression: The Effects of Occupation and Marital Status," *Sex Roles*, 1 (September 1975), pp. 249–265; and Radloff, "Risk Factors for Depression," in Guttentag et al., *The Mental Health of Women*, pp. 93–109.

32. Walter R. Gove, "Sex Differences in the Epidemiology of Mental Disorder: Evidence and Explanations," in Edith S. Gomberg and Violet Franks, eds., *Gender and Disordered Behavior* (New York: Brunner/Mazel, 1979), pp. 23–68.

33. Radloff, "Sex Differences in Depression."

34. Belle, "Who Uses Mental Health Facilities?"

35. Bruce P. Dohrenwend and Barbara Snell Dohrenwend, *Social Status and Psychological Disorder: A Causal Inquiry* (New York: John Wiley & Sons, 1969); and Radloff, "Sex Differences in Depression."

36. Goldman and Ravid, "Community Surveys"; and Radloff, "Risk Factors."

37. Sandra Butler, *Conspiracy of Silence: The Trauma of Incest* (San Francisco: New Glide, 1978); R. Emerson Dobash and Russell Dobash, *Violence Against Wives: A Case Against the Patriarchy* (New York: Free Press, 1979); Del Martin, *Battered Wives* (San Francisco: Glide, 1976); and Murray Straus, Richard Gelles, and Suzanne Steinmetz, *Behind Closed Doors: Violence in the American Family* (Garden City, N.Y.: Doubleday Anchor Books, 1980).

38. Jean Baker Miller, *Psychoanalysis and Women* (Baltimore: Penguin, 1973); Julia Sherman, *On the Psychology of Women* (Springfield, Ill.: Charles C Thomas, 1971); and Williams, *Psychology of Women: Behavior in a Biosocial Context*.

39. Barbara S. Deckard, *The Women's Movement: Political, Socioeconomic, and Psychological Issues* (New York: Harper & Row, 1975), p. 18.

40. Erik Erikson, *Identity: Youth and Crisis* (New York: W. W. Norton & Co., 1968), p. 265.

41. Sherman, *On the Psychology of Women*, p. 67.

124

Feminist Visions

42. William H. Masters and Virginia E. Johnson, *Human Sexual Response* (Boston: Little, Brown & Co., 1966).

43. Bernard, *Future of Motherhood;* Adrienne Rich, *Of Woman Born* (New York: W. W. Norton & Co., 1976); and Nancy Felipe Russo, "The Motherhood Mandate," *Journal of Social Issues,* 32 (Summer 1976).

44. "Report of the Task Force on Sex Bias and Sex-Role Stereotyping in Psychotherapeutic Practice," *American Psychologist,* 30 (December 1975), pp. 1169–1175.

45. Inge K. Broverman et al., "Sex-Role Stereotypes and Clinical Judgments of Mental Health," *Journal of Consulting and Clinical Psychology,* 34 (February 1970), pp. 1–7.

46. Julia Sherman, "Therapist Attitudes and Sex-Role Stereotyping," in Annette M. Brodsky and Rachel Hare-Mustin, eds., *Women and Psychotherapy* (New York: Guilford Press, 1980), pp. 35–66.

47. Julia Sherman, Corinne Koufacos, and Joy Anne Kenworthy, "Therapists: Their Attitudes and Information about Women," *Psychology of Women Quarterly,* 2 (Summer 1978), pp. 299–313.

48. Pauline B. Bart and Diana H. Scully, "The Politics of Hysteria: The Case of the Wandering Womb," in Gomberg and Franks, eds., *Gender and Disordered Behavior,* pp. 354–380; Marlene Boskind-Lodahl, "Cinderella's Stepsisters: A Feminist Perspective on Anorexia Nervosa and Bulimia," *Signs: Journal of Women in Culture and Society,* 2 (Winter 1976), pp. 342–356; Hilde Bruch, *The Golden Cage: The Enigma of Anorexia Nervosa* (New York: Vintage, 1978); Dianne L. Chambless and Alan J. Goldstein, "Anxieties: Agoraphobia and Hysteria," in Brodsky and Hare-Mustin, eds., *Women and Psychotherapy,* pp. 113–134; Gomberg, "Problems with Alcohol and Other Drugs," in Gomberg and Franks, eds., *Gender and Disordered Behavior,* pp. 204–240; Susie Orbach, *Fat Is a Feminist Issue* (New York: Paddington, 1978); and Marion Sandmaier, *The Invisible Alcoholics: Women and Alcohol Abuse in America* (New York: McGraw-Hill Book Co., 1980).

49. Virginia Davidson, "Psychiatry's Problem With No Name: Therapist-Patient Sex," *American Journal of Psychoanalysis,* 37 (Spring 1977), pp. 43–50; and Jean C. Holroyd and Annette M. Brodsky, "Psychologists' Attitudes and Practices Regarding Erotic and Nonerotic Physical Contact with Patients," *American Psychologist,* 32 (October 1977), pp. 843–849.

50. Collier, *Counseling Women.*

51. Elsie J. Smith, "Counseling Black Individuals: Some Stereotypes," *Personnel and Guidance Journal,* 55 (March 1977), pp. 390–396.

52. Esteban L. Olmedo and Delores L. Parron, "Mental Health of Minority Women: Some Special Issues," *Professional Psychology,* 12 (February 1981), pp. 103–111; Doris Y. Wilkinson, "Minority Women: Social-Cultural Issues," in Brodsky and Hare-Mustin, eds., *Women and Psychotherapy,* pp. 285–304.

53. Nancy Ayala-Vazquez, "The Guidance and Counseling of Hispanic Females," *Journal of Non-White Concerns in Personnel and Guidance*, 7 (April 1979), pp. 114–21; Collier, *Counseling Women*; Elaine J. Copeland, "Oppressed Conditions and the Mental Health Needs of Low-Income Black Women: Barriers to Services, Strategies for Change," *Women and Therapy*, 1 (Spring 1982), pp. 13–26; Doris Jefferies Ford, "Counseling for the Strengths of the Black Woman," in Lenore Harmon et al., eds., *Counseling Women* (Monterey, Calif.: Brooks/Cole Publishing Co., 1978), pp. 186–192; Guadalupe Gibson, "Hispanic Women: Stress and Mental Health Issues," *Women and Therapy*, 2 (Summer-Fall 1983), pp. 113–133; and Wynne Hanson, "The Urban Indian Woman and Her Family," *Social Casework: The Journal of Contemporary Social Work*, 61 (October 1980), pp. 476–483.

54. Loewenstein, "Understanding Lesbian Women"; Potter and Darty, "Social Work and the Invisible Minority"; and Sang, "Lesbian Research."

55. Eugene E. Levitt and Albert D. Klassen, "Public Attitudes Toward Homosexuality," *Journal of Homosexuality*, 1 (Fall 1974), pp. 29–43; and Kenneth L. Nyberg and Jon P. Alston, "Analysis of Public Attitudes Toward Homosexual Behavior," *Journal of Homosexuality*, 2 (Winter 1976–1977), pp. 99–107.

56. Ellen M. Garfinkle and Stephen Morin, "Psychologists' Attitudes Toward Homosexual Psychotherapy Clients," *Journal of Social Issues*, 34 (Summer 1978), pp. 101–112; Harold Lief, "Sexual Survey: Current Thinking on Homosexuality," *Medical Aspects of Human Sexuality*, 11 (November 1977), pp. 110–111; and Eugene P. May, "Counselors', Psychologists', and Homosexuals' Philosophies of Human Nature and Attitudes Toward Homosexual Behavior," *Homosexual Counseling Journal*, 1 (January 1974), pp. 3–25.

57 Stephen Morin, "Heterosexual Bias in Psychological Research on Lesbianism and Male Homosexuality," *American Psychologist*, 32 (August 1977), pp. 629–637.

58. Virginia R. Brooks, *Minority Stress and Lesbian Women* (Lexington, Mass.: Lexington Books, 1981); Diana D. Dulaney and James Kelley, "Improving Services to Gay and Lesbian Clients," *Social Work*, 27 (March 1982), pp. 178–183; Josette Escamilla–Mondanaro, "Lesbians and Therapy," in Edna I. Rawlings and Dianne K. Carter, eds., *Psychotherapy for Women* (Springfield, Ill.: Charles C Thomas, 1977), pp. 256–265; Loewenstein, "Understanding Lesbian Women"; Del Martin and Phyllis Lyon, *Lesbian/Woman* (New York: Bantam Books, 1977); Potter and Darty, "Social Work and the Invisible Minority"; Dorothy Riddle and Barbara Sang, "Psychotherapy with Lesbians," *Journal of Social Issues*, 34 (Summer 1978), pp. 84–97; and Sang, "Psychotherapy with Lesbians: Some Observations and Tentative Generalizations," in Rawlings and Carter, eds., *Psychotherapy for Women*, pp. 266–275.

59. Jeanne Marecek and Diane Kravetz, "Women and Health: A Review of Feminist Change Efforts," *Psychiatry*, 40 (November 1977), pp. 323-329; and Edna I. Rawlings and Dianne K. Carter, "Feminist and Nonsexist Psychotherapy," in Rawlings and Carter, eds., *Psychotherapy for Women*, pp. 49-76.

60. Reprinted from Edna I. Rawlings and Dianne K. Carter, "Feminist and Nonsexist Psychotherapy," in Rawlings and Carter, eds., *Psychotherapy for Women* (Springfield, Ill.: Charles C Thomas, 1977), pp. 54-57. Courtesy of Charles C Thomas, Publisher, Springfield, Ill.

61. Sandra L. Bem, "Probing the Promise of Androgyny," in Alexandra G. Kaplan and Joan P. Bean, eds., *Beyond Sex-Role Stereotypes* (Boston: Little, Brown & Co., 1976), pp. 48-62; Lucia Albino Gilbert, "Toward Mental Health: The Benefits of Psychological Androgyny," *Professional Psychology*, 12 (February 1981), pp. 29-38; Alexandra G. Kaplan, "Androgyny as a Model of Mental Health for Women: From Theory to Therapy," in Kaplan and Bean, eds., *Beyond Sex-Role Stereotypes*, pp. 352-362; and Alexandra G. Kaplan, ed., "Psychological Androgyny: Further Considerations," in special issue, *Psychology of Women Quarterly*, 3 (Spring 1979).

62. Nechama Liss-Levinson, "AWP Feminist Therapy Roster: Therapist Criteria, Past Use and Future Suggestions." Unpublished paper, Association for Women in Psychology, 1976.

63. Miriam Greenspan, *A New Approach to Women and Therapy* (New York: McGraw-Hill Book Co., 1983), p. 247.

64. Susan Sturdivant, *Therapy with Women: A Feminist Philosophy of Treatment* (New York: Springer Publishing Co., 1980), p. 172.

65. Jeanne Marecek, Diane Kravetz, and Stephen E. Finn, "A Comparison of Women Who Enter Feminist Therapy and Women Who Enter Traditional Therapy," *Journal of Consulting and Clinical Psychology*, 47 (August 1979), pp. 734-742.

66. Marilyn Johnson, "An Approach to Feminist Therapy," *Psychotherapy: Theory, Research and Practice*, 13 (Spring 1976), pp. 72-76.

67. Diane Kravetz, "Consiousness-Raising and Self-Help," in Brodsky and Hare-Mustin, eds., *Women and Psychotherapy*, pp. 267-283.

68. Lucia Albino Gilbert, "Feminist Therapy," in Brodsky and Hare-Mustin, eds., *Women and Psychotherapy*, pp. 245-265.

69. Elizabeth Aries, "Interaction Patterns and Themes of Male, Female and Mixed Groups," *Small Group Behavior*, 7 (February 1976), pp. 7-18; Charlene J. Carlock and Patricia Y. Martin, "Sex Composition and the Intensive Group Experience," *Social Work*, 22 (January 1977), pp. 27-33; and Lilly J. Schubert Walker, "Are Women's Groups Different?" *Psychotherapy: Theory, Research, and Practice*, 18 (Summer 1981), pp. 240-245.

70. Rawlings and Carter, "Feminist and Nonsexist Psychotherapy," pp. 71-73.

71. Ibid., pp. 73-74.

127

Roslyn H. Chernesky

a new
model of
supervision

Supervision holds a central position in social work, and, despite significant changes over the years in social work practice, in the profession, in education, and in society, supervision is fundamentally the same as it was when it emerged a century ago. Therefore, it is not surprising that supervision has been the subject of extensive criticism. During the 1950s and 1960s, supervision was accused of creating a wide range of problems considered to be dysfunctional to workers, to the delivery of services, and to the profession. It was blamed for encouraging dependence among professional social workers, discouraging innovation and experimentation, and contributing to the semiprofessional status of social work. A number of possible solutions were considered, such as separating the conflicting supervisory functions, simplifying the job of the supervisor, and replacing the traditional pattern of individual supervision with group approaches.

The feminist concern with social work supervision today thus joins a rich history of criticism. This article examines some of the problems with supervision and shows that the issues feminists raise are not so different from those addressed by the pro-

128

fession 20 and 30 years ago. Feminists oppose traditional social work supervision on ideological grounds because it is incongruent with feminist principles and values. Consequently, feminists are committed to developing a new model of supervision—one that is consistent with a feminist perspective. It is to be hoped that they will offer a viable alternative, even though none has yet successfully replaced nor seriously challenged the traditional model.

Social Work Supervision

Supervision in social work is a peculiar institution, and an understanding of it is important to appreciate the criticism it draws. Social work supervision incorporates the traditional definition and meaning of "supervise":

> to coordinate, direct, and inspect continuously and at first hand the accomplishment of: oversee with the powers of direction and decision the implementation of one's own or another's intentions.[1]

In addition to the administrative aspect that is implicit in this general definition, three other functions distinguish social work supervision: the educational, the supportive, and the professionalization. Rather than engaging in a debate about how many functions there actually are or which function is primary, I will briefly review the four commonly accepted functions to convey the complexity of social work supervision.

Administrative Function.   Supervision is an administrative job; the supervisor helps the agency carry out its purposes as effectively as possible. The ultimate objective of supervision, according to Williamson, is "to implement agency purposes and plans, and continually deepen the quality of the service through which the agency seeks to express its purposes."[2]

It is helpful to use the specific job responsibilities of the supervisor suggested by Scherz to understand why the supervisor is an arm of administration. Scherz identified three responsibilities:

> 1. ...(a) knowing how effective the caseworker's service is, (b) assisting the caseworker to give service according to the standards of the agency, and (c) assisting the caseworkers to develop further skill in giving effective service...developing ideas and content which

129

will influence the standards of casework practice in the agency.

. . . . .

2. . . .facilitating the work of the casework staff through using agency procedures and routines in such a way that smooth flow of service is assured.

. . . . .

3. . . .evaluating the casework staff in accordance with agency classification requirements and for making appropriate recommendations in relation to salary changes, promotions, separations, and so on.[3]

Stiles offered three additional administrative responsibilities:

Through [the supervisor] the administrator is ensured a steady flow of data about the changing needs of the community, the attitudes of the community toward the agency, and interagency relations.

. . . . .

[The supervisor communicates] information to the worker about the purpose of the program. . .is able to detect variations in procedures and to assist the workers in developing a consistent, yet flexible, application of agency policy.

. . . . .

The supervisor also promotes the creative participation of the workers in the administrative process: he [or she] encourages them to examine the effects of policy on their daily practice, to contribute their ideas about revisions, and to help bring about changes that are needed.[4]

Finally, the supervisor as administrator is responsible for maintaining a stable and integrated agency. The supervisor helps to strengthen and reinforce the workers' identification with the purposes of the agency, department, and programs; to develop and maintain effective and efficient work groups; and to link workers and work units with other units across vertical and horizontal levels.

Educational Function. Supervision also is an educational job. Austin noted that "the central responsibility of supervision. . .is teaching, that is, participating in the professional education of students and in the professional development of agency staff members."[5] In his 1973 study of almost 400 social workers, Kadushin found that "supervisees regarded 'teaching the case-

Feminist Visions

work aspects of the job—the knowledge, skills, and attitudes that the supervisee needs for effective job performance'—as the most important function of supervision."[6]

As an educator, the supervisor has four responsibilities:

1. To teach specific content related to the theory and technical skills of and information necessary for effective practice.

2. To create the climate in which learning can take place.

3. To help workers handle the wide range of potentially emotionally charged content.

4. To help workers develop insight and self-awareness.[7]

The importance of the last is stressed by Kadushin:

> Since the worker's personality and behavior are significant determinants of what happens in the worker-client interaction, the supervisee herself, her attitudes, feelings, and behavior become a necessary and inevitable subject of educational supervision. The aim is to develop a greater measure of self-awareness in the worker so that she can act in a deliberate, disciplined, consciously directed manner in the worker-client interaction so as to be optimally helpful to the client.[8]

Supportive Function. The third function is the provision of support to workers. Kadushin claimed that the purpose of supportive supervision

> is to reduce anxiety, allay guilt, increase self-esteem, enhance the worker's capacity for adaptation to the demands of the work situation, and her psychic energy for more adequate job performance. By increasing the supervisees' feelings of emotional well-being, the supervisor increases their emotional fitness to offer more effective service.[9]

The importance of supportive or therapeutic supervision grows out of the high degree of stress and tension associated with the nature of social work practice. Wasserman studied the frustration experienced by workers from constraints that did not allow them to use the values, knowledge, and skills that their training had prepared them to use, as well as the exhaustion they felt from facing critical human situations day after day with insufficient resources.[10] Problems brought by clients can be upsetting and clients' attitudes and behaviors can confront workers with their own negative feelings, create anxiety, and interfere with practice. Workers may be unrealistic in what they expect **131** to accomplish and thus feel they are failures. They may be torn between competing roles or loyalties. Work conditions can be stressful. Thus, many stressors can contribute to what today is called burnout and these can be reduced via supervision.

Professionalization Function.   The fourth function of supervision is to serve as a vehicle for the continued socialization of the worker into the ways of the profession. The goal is to help the worker behave in accordance with professional norms as a matter of personal, public, and professional conscience. Although the socialization process begins in social work education, it requires ongoing reinforcement if social workers are to remain in the profession and fulfill their potential as professional leaders. Workers can easily become disenchanted with the profession, question their decision to enter the field, and seek alternatives.[11] Maintaining a commitment to the profession can be difficult when agencies try to win the workers' loyalty. Identification with organizational goals and identification with the profession need not conflict; however, the two often do.[12] It also has been suggested that it may be more difficult for women workers to achieve professional commitment because their family roles will have greater importance for them than their work roles.[13]

Supervisor-Worker Relationship

Although an examination of the functions of social work supervision and the roles of the supervisor is useful, it is not sufficient to understand fully the problems associated with supervision. A knowledge of the supervisory relationship is critical.

Traditional social work supervision takes place in an individual, one-to-one conference. The supervisor and worker meet, on a regularly scheduled basis, an average of three to four times a month for an hour to an hour and a half each time. The content of the conference is based on records of interviews with clients written and submitted by the worker. Through this case-discussion method, the worker explains what she or he has been doing, discusses problems in case management, advocates for the needs of clients, and seeks guidance concerning specific problems.

The distinguishing characteristics of this relationship follow:

■ No formal time limit is placed on the duration of supervision. There is no ending point signifying that the worker is

132

Feminist Visions

nized as a competent and autonomous professional, responsible for and capable of providing effective service to clients. Workers are therefore expected to remain indefinitely under supervision, obligated to report regularly in a prescribed manner rather than confer as they think necessary.[14] Wax suggested that in reality supervision often "just peters out....The worker functions with greater independence, but both parties are anxious and guilty about their evasion of the agency's intention that the worker be supervised."[15]

- No differentiation is made in the kind of supervision necessary to respond to differences in workers, especially the less experienced and more experienced workers.[16]

- No limit is placed on what may or may not be brought up in supervision. As Toren noted, the relationship is diffuse insofar as the workers' personal problems may be probed and discussed and their feelings, conflicts, or projections examined and handled.[17] As Levy stated, only workers are expected to expose themselves and place themselves in vulnerable positions in which revelations can be misused or used inappropriately.[18]

- Although the worker is theoretically responsible for decisions about a case, the supervisor ultimately is accountable to the agency's higher administration. If differences in professional judgment arise, the supervisor's point of view invariably will predominate. As Levy pointed out, the insecure or uncertain worker is not in a position to challenge the supervisor's greater knowledge or expertise, or information that only the supervisor may have access to, nor can the worker take a chance that she or he will be accused of being unable to accept supervision.[19]

- The supervisor-worker relationship is not an egalitarian one, although workers often perceive it as such. Kadushin found that 60 percent of the supervisees and 30 percent of the supervisors in his study viewed the relationship as that of "colleague-collaborator."[20] The relationship is a hierarchical arrangement, with supervisors holding legitimate authority, that is, administratively assigned and sanctioned authority. Supervisors are in a position to reward and punish; the worker is accountable to the supervisor. Inherent in this position is the supervisor's jurisdiction over the worker's job because of the right to evaluate performance. The supervisor can influence hiring, firing, promotion, salary increases, work assignments, references, and the content of the worker's personal file. Levy explained that because the worker's status and movement, if not the job itself, are contingent on the supervisor's approval, the more the worker needs the job and the less mobile she or **133** he is, the more dependent the worker will feel and will be.[21]

- The supervisor's strategic location in the organization between workers and the higher administration allows the supervisor, according to Levy, to represent and interpret "the supervisee to those in higher authority and in turn determines whether and how the agency will be represented and interpreted to the supervisee."[22] How workers are viewed in an agency—if, for example, they are thought of as having management potential, if they are visible to administration, if they believe the agency appreciates their work and cares about their future—all are conveyed through and by their supervisor.

- The combination of the administrative function and the educational function in one position is based on an assumption that the organization's expectations and the profession's expectations are likely to be the same. However, demands made on workers for administrative purposes may conflict with professional ethics as well as the interests of clients. The supervisor can obtain compliance from the worker in her or his administrative role or can support the worker's noncompliance in her or his professional role. In either case, the worker must rely on the supervisor's preference to resolve the conflict.

- The supervisor-worker relationship provokes anxiety and produces tension. In 1953, Babcock first described the many anxieties that resulted from the supervisory process. Workers reported feeling depreciated; they feared evaluation and writing required case records.[23] Scherz noted that anxiety was a normal response, as were feelings of pressure and resentment, when supervisors controlled or protected workers and removed the responsibility that belonged to them.[24] Kadushin, in discussing why workers are likely to initiate games in supervision, explained that they were reacting to the anxiety brought about by social work supervision's focus on changing their behavior and, perhaps, personality.[25] And Berl made the point that the supervisory role, which prescribes both equality and inequality between professional colleagues, invites tension.[26]

Problems with Social Work Supervision

The distinguishing characteristics of social work supervision are the sources of its problems as well. Since Austin's evaluation of supervision appeared in 1956, a litany of criticism has followed in the social work literature.[27] The following represents a sampling of

Feminist Visions

the accusations. Supervision, it has been said, weakens the assimilation of knowledge and internalization of standards; limits professional contacts in agencies; fosters dependence in workers—indeed, overdependence; hampers the workers' achievement of professional maturity; inhibits workers' full use of their knowledge, their assumption of responsibility, and their ambition to function more independently; inhibits workers from trying new ideas; creates chronic feelings of inadequacy; produces anxiety; encourages infantile hostile fantasies; discourages innovation and experimental action; prevents workers from feeling the satisfaction that comes from taking responsibility for a task at hand; leads to dissatisfaction with work; weakens workers' ability to function in multidisciplinary settings where egalitarian relationships among professionals are important; prevents the work situation from producing leaders; and constricts professional experience. Thus, social work supervision creates the very kind of workers that the profession hoped *not* to produce. As Perlmutter noted,

> supervision was formalized as the vehicle for the development of professionalism, but in reality it served the opposite function. It encouraged and perpetuated dependence and prevented the acceptance of social work as a full-fledged profession both internally and externally.[28]

Feminist Critique

Although feminists, as an identified group, have not joined in expressing opposition to social work supervision, clearly they would be among its most vociferous critics. At the heart of traditional social work supervision is the patriarchal model of power expressed as a hierarchy, with those higher up on the pyramid controlling and dominating their subordinates. Workers and supervisors are separated, if not divided. This structure is considered essential for effective organizational functioning. Claims that the model is also valuable for workers ignore or cover up the fact that workers are invariably seen and treated as subservient and are denied the opportunity to have full control over their work lives.

A review of the assumptions on which traditional social work supervision is based illustrates the ideological problems for feminists. Those assumptions are as follows:

■ Workers require external, organizational controls to do their work and to do it well.

135

- If workers were not monitored on a regular basis, they would not comply with organizational mandates.
- The commitment and the internalized standards and norms of workers are not adequate to ensure the effective performance of workers.
- Workers cannot be trusted to take responsibility for the work they perform.
- Workers require protection, support, and overseeing to perform their work.
- Workers always need to learn and to be taught for their professional and personal growth and well-being and thus can never be independent, autonomous practitioners.
- Only superiors and authority figures have the knowledge, expertise, or experience to teach.
- Workers cannot and should not express concerns, problems, or discontent directly to the higher administration but only indirectly through supervisors.
- Authority must preside in a hierarchical arrangement; those who do must be separated from those who manage.
- Workers are less capable than are administrators of deciding how to implement policies—when, how, and by whom tasks should be performed.
- Only through a personal relationship between a supervisor and supervisees is it possible to supervise and control workers.

The pervasiveness of traditional supervision in social work is especially troublesome for feminists. In social work, the supervisees are *professionals* who expect to practice with a high degree of autonomy. There is sufficient evidence that close supervision of professionals is inappropriate; it decreases independence and makes workers feel stifled, anxious, and infantilized.[29]

A number of reasons have been posited to explain why social work continues the traditional one-to-one model of supervision. They include the nature of social work's organizational auspices, the functions performed, the circumstances of its historical emergence, and the societal mandate and expectations. However, Kadushin probably was most insightful in his suggestion that "perhaps the most telling reason is the fact that social work is a women's profession."[30] It is apparent that when the predominant gender of the work force is female, the use of supervision to keep workers dependent and submissive is more likely.

136

Feminist Visions

Alternatives to Traditional Social Work Supervision

As dissatisfaction with traditional social work supervision mounted, alternatives were called for by an increasing number of practitioners and educators. It is useful to review the alternatives proposed and to understand the outcome to appreciate the task facing feminists.

Challenges to the traditional model have had two seemingly different thrusts. One approach favors a realignment of supervisory functions and seeks to separate the administrative and educational functions so that they would no longer be concentrated in one supervisory role. The second approach seeks to restructure the one-to-one model to allow greater expression of workers' needs, experiences, and training. An elaboration of each of these approaches follow.

Realignment of Supervisory Functions.   Austin first proposed in 1956 what was then a radical solution—the separation of the administrative and teaching functions and their assignment to two different positions in the agency.[31] The teaching function was conceived of as solely a staff-development function, located in a position outside the hierarchical authority ladder. The administrative tasks would then be lodged in another position, one with organizational authority. A worker would thus be responsible to two supervisors—one for education and one for administration. Even though the arrangement could be cumbersome and require greater attention to coordination and communication than might otherwise be necessary, much of the tension and anxiety inherent in the tutorial model would be alleviated. Scherz commented that, in experimenting with this approach, "caseworkers have expressed satisfaction with the clearer definition of job responsibility and a feeling of relief that evaluations are used solely for administrative implementation of salary scales."[32] Devis claimed that when the U.S. Army Medical Service used the model of separate functions, no objections, dissatisfaction, or staff turnover occurred that were attributed to the supervisory model.[33]

The attractive aspects of this approach include the dilution of power held by any one supervisor over workers and the recognition that no one person can teach everything well even if that person is at a higher level in the hierarchy. Frequently, the educational supervisor is renamed "mentor" or "preceptor," thus neutralizing an emotionally charged term and redefining **137**

A New Model of Supervision

the educational function heretofore associated with and held by the supervisor.

Structural Models. In recognition that no one supervisory model can meet the needs of all staff under all conditions, alternative structures that respond to differences among staff were offered. Watson proposed six options: the tutorial, case consultation, the supervisory group, peer group supervision, tandem supervision, and the team.[34]

Case consultation is a variation of the tutorial model in which certain workers, usually designated by the agency as consultants, are available to be used when workers wish to seek their opinion. The worker is not obligated to seek a consultant nor bound by the consultant's opinion. It is left to the practitioner to determine if she or he could benefit from another point of view and if and when new ideas should be adopted. The model provides the opportunity for workers to review with experienced colleagues case-related concerns and thus be exposed to differences in thinking in a collegial atmosphere without fear of being evaluated. According to Leader, it is intended to give practitioners more responsibility for their own professional activity and further dilute the one-to-one supervisory relationship.[35] The model is especially appropriate in programs and agencies in which certain workers, regardless of their hierarchical position, may be considered experts in fields such as substance abuse or sexual victimization. Because case consultation is an alternative only to the educational function of supervision, it requires that the administrative functions be carried out by someone other than the consultant.

Tandem supervision is an infrequently used form of case consultation in which two workers choose to be consultants to each other because they respect each other's skills and opinions. Discussions about cases help the worker who is assigned the cases to decide on how to handle them. Eventually, because the two workers become familiar with each other's cases and styles, decisions tend to become more collaborative, although workers are not accountable for each other's performance.

Group supervision is, in many ways, an extension of the tutorial model, albeit somewhat more efficient. It is by far the most popular alternative that has been tried, described, and advocated.[36] In this model, a group of designated workers with the same supervisor meet regularly to discuss cases for which they need direct help and to build knowledge and skills. Workers are

138

Feminist Visions

accountable to the supervisor, who evaluates them on a one-to-one basis. Just as the group can be used for teaching purposes, it can also be used for administrative purposes. Meetings are used to discuss agency or staff concerns, to inform staff of new policies and procedures, or to consider changes in programs. In effect, group supervision supplements individual supervision, and it is the combination of the two rather than replacement of the tutorial model by the group that is recommended.

In peer group supervision or peer group consultation, as described by Appleby et al. and Fizdale, there is no designated supervisor, and all the members of the group participate as equals.[37] Meeting on a regular basis, the peer group determines its agenda by mutual agreement and selects a group leader or moderator for the discussion. As in the case consultation model, the worker is free to accept or reject the ideas of group members. Case accountability and worker evaluations are not the responsibility of the group but must be assumed by administrators outside the peer group.

A variation of peer group supervision is the team. The task of the team is to arrive at decisions through the group process. The decisions made are binding on all members, and the team as a whole is accountable for each decision, regardless of which member carries it out. The team retains some responsibility for seeing that members perform tasks accordingly and for upholding standards. Team members may jointly participate in the evaluations of workers.

Clearly these efforts to restructure the traditional model would improve the supervisory process. Although they all retain the role of the supervisor, they broaden the concept of supervision, demonstrating that it can take place in a structure other than a hierarchy—that is, among equals—and other than on a one-to-one basis. But all these models deal only with the educational function of supervision. Although the teaching-learning aspect is altered, the administrative-authority component is left intact. Supervision thus remains a method of controlling professional behavior.

Despite the interest in solving the problems associated with traditional supervision and the proliferation of articles in which alternatives are discussed, none of the ideas has received the full support of the profession. Change among agencies struggling with the tutorial model has been slow. The social work profession has not assumed leadership in this respect. Clearly, the one-to-one **139**

A New Model of Supervision

model proved to be too entrenched to be toppled over. Moreover, the discussions and suggestions never seriously questioned, much less threatened, the prevailing notion that supervision of professional social workers is necessary to the well-being of the agency, the clients, or the workers. Instead, by focusing on restructuring supervision as a way of encouraging greater autonomy and maturity in workers, the profession has been able to avoid the real issue—that is: "Why supervision?"

Although not all feminists would agree, I contend that supervision is, in itself, the problem; it is not just a matter of how it is carried out. The alternatives offered are really no more than efforts to make supervision more palatable and, perhaps, more just, but the basic assumptions of supervision remain—and it is these assumptions that are in opposition to a feminist vision. The overall issue for social work feminists to consider is similar to that posed by feminists in general: will acceptance of reform mean the danger of accepting the existing structure and ultimately preventing fundamental change in the situation in the future?

A Feminist Alternative

Some feminists argue that supervision as it is now known is neither necessary nor desirable because "superior domination through hierarchical patterns of authority is not essential to the achievement of important goals but in fact is restrictive of the growth of the group and its members."[38] Others claim that practitioners should be given the power delegated to supervisors and be allowed to carry out the functions performed by supervisors.

It is proposed here that the feminist agenda for an alternative to traditional supervision should be based on the following assumptions:

- Individual workers have the capacity to be self-directing, self-disciplined, and self-regulating.
- Workers can be expected to assume responsibility for the quality of their work and need not abdicate personal responsibility to the authority of superiors.
- Authority need not reside in a hierarchical arrangement but can be diffused among a membership.
- Leadership (supervisory and administrative) roles can be assumed by all members of an organization just as workers' roles can be assumed by all.

140

Feminist Visions

- Expertise is not positively correlated with hierarchical position; individuals at all organizational levels can teach, advise, consult, and learn.

- Supervision is not the only method of monitoring performance and bringing about desired actions; impersonal mechanisms such as performance records, continuous training, high visibility of work, and a high level of horizontal communication and feedback can be effective substitutes.

- Personal growth and professional development need not depend on a teacher-pupil relationship.

- A fluid, temporary structure in which the process is as important as the task can be efficient and effective for organizations.

An alternative model, as described by Martin, is a reorganization in which self-managing units are established and supervision is performed without supervisors.[39] The units or collectivities, whether they are work groups or teams, must be autonomous, that is, given the responsibility and the authority to manage their own work. They would be expected to plan work, assign cases, arrange for the coverage of services, discuss cases with special problems and share ideas about treatment approaches, design quality assurance mechanisms, review and evaluate work, regulate and discipline members, and adopt procedures to facilitate the work of individuals and the coordination of activities within the collectivity as well as with other organizational bodies. In other words, the alternative model would enable the purposes for which supervision exists to be fulfilled without the necessity of superior domination through hierarchical patterns of authority. It would also eliminate the false dichotomy between workers and supervisors. It would require a fundamental change in the way we think about organizations and the way members of organizations behave.

The model proposed here is not original to feminists because it draws liberally on proposals for peer group supervision, participatory management, matrix organizational designs, and quality control circles. The model takes into account that autonomous work groups have been tried with successful results in settings other than social work and human service organizations.[40] Published analyses of collectivist organizations that deliberately reject hierarchical arrangements and strive to realize feminist principles have been especially influential.[41] The peer group model used at the Arthur Lehman Counseling Service (ALCS) is an example of a successful alternative to traditional supervisory practice. **141**

A New Model of Supervision

The ALCS was a family service agency founded in 1954 to demonstrate that it was possible to reach upper- and middle-income groups and to extend casework counseling to them. The belief on which the ALCS was established was that hiring highly experienced staff, each of whom had direct professional account-ability for the quality of service given to clients, as well as pro-moting team relationships, warranted the elimination of tradi-tional supervision. This experiment demonstrated that, in the absence of a traditional supervisory structure, "mature practi-tioners can be relied upon to carry out their professional role and accountability for the quality of their service to clients— perhaps even more because they experience directly what is involved when full responsibility is vested in them."[42]

This model differed from the previously noted feminist pro-posal in that responsibility for ensuring the consistency of policies and programs, as well as adherence to policies and procedures, the evaluation of the performance of practitioners, and the moni-toring of trends on which to base changes in programs and plan-ning, remained an administrative function. The peer group was thus only independent and autonomous in relation to its accoun-tability for the quality of practice; it did not take on administra-tive tasks heretofore located in hierarchical positions of authority.

Similarly, recent experiences with the establishment of pro-fessional review organizations and utilization review committees in hospital social work departments have demonstrated that peer groups positively influence the quality of services rendered to clients and that they influence workers' attitudes and behaviors in the direction of group norms. Chernesky and Young described their experience in developing a peer review system in a hospital social work department. As workers became more involved in the system and assumed greater responsibility for coordinating re-views, providing feedback to colleagues, and educating workers about peer review, they became more committed to the system and its effectiveness.[43]

Kahle proposed a unit organization structure, similar to the model suggested here, that replaces the traditional supervisor-supervisee relationship. The unit serves as a forum for discuss-ing procedural problems and developing policies and programs. The supervisor becomes the unit administrator, responsible to the administration and to the unit, and is an equal participant in the group process of the unit. This "pyramidal-collegial system," according to Kahle, "retains the basic managerial con-

142

Feminist Visions

trol of the pyramidal system but allows the freedom and two-way communication of the collegial system."[44]

In one of the few such discussions of participatory government in social work, Hirsch and Shulman proposed a model of governance in which the administration and staff share administrative responsibility and decision making. When there is clarity about what are the appropriate as well as inappropriate areas for joint undertakings, neither the role of the director nor the viability of the department or agency is undermined. This model replaces the traditional role of the supervisor as the one who determined policies and practices affecting the lives of workers and contributes to a breaking down of the division between supervisors and workers.[45]

Matrix organizations, a variation on task-oriented teams established to carry out projects, also capture much of the flavor of the feminist alternative. In contrast to traditional organizations with one chain of command and authority based on hierarchical position, matrix designs bring together all personnel appropriate to a project regardless of their function, specialization, or hierarchical position. These individuals work together as equals. Authority in the matrix is lodged with the individual or individuals who, because of their expertise or technical skills to accomplish the task, are put in charge of the work of all on the project, regardless of their position or level in the organization. As Argyris noted:

> The pyramidal structure acquires its form from the fact that as one goes up the administrative ladder (1) power and control increase, (2) the availability of information increases, (3) the degree of flexibility to act increases, (4) the scope of the decisions made and the responsibilities involved increase. *Implicit in the matrix organization are almost opposite tendencies* [italics added].[46]

Proponents of matrix models see many advantages to this structure; it is especially useful for handling problems that call for quick, creative, and flexible responses. The dangers cited are those that feminists would be pleased to have.[47] For example, matrix organizations make it difficult to foster supervisor-subordinate relations, to establish clear authority relationships, and to prevent decisions from becoming group decisions. It is important to note that the matrix model is basically a short-term temporary arrangement for work on specific projects; it is not seen or used as a permanent organizational structure. Matrices coexist with traditional hierarchical forms.

143

A New Model of Supervision

Quality circles are an increasingly popular organizational structure in which small groups of workers volunteer to meet regularly, on agency time, to identify the causes of on-the-job problems and to propose solutions to management. In a carefully structured group, led by their immediate supervisor, the members use advanced problem-solving techniques, in which they have been trained, to reach solutions. As Middleman noted, the concept is powerfully marketed for "reestablishing the dignity of the employees and their work, treating them as adults with minds as well as hands . . ., an approach offering more than a sense of participation or problem discussion, in a 'bull session' atmosphere."[48] Their popularity, first in Japan and now in the United States, has grown from the realization that when employees have the opportunity to use their creative abilities and to care about their jobs, their interest and pride increase, which leads not only to greater quality and productivity but to improved job performance and satisfaction. Quality circles are a management tool that is based on a participatory approach to involving and motivating workers and solving organizational problems.[49]

Conclusion

Although the vision of supervision from the feminist perspective is not yet fully articulated, its basic elements are clear. Its goal is not the creation of dependence in workers, but the emergence of autonomous, self-directing, and self-regulating workers. Direct supervision as a means of monitoring and controlling the performance of workers is replaced by indirect mechanisms such as group norms and peer approval that appeal to individuals' commitment and motivation to do well and to develop and grow personally as well as professionally. Rather than the traditional domination of workers through supervision, alternative forms of organizational structure and patterns of leadership are designed that do not separate workers and managers and that create ongoing channels for horizontal communication and feedback. Finally, workers, in addition to their practice in the service of clients, also engage in problem solving, decision making, and management of tasks and activities that affect their practice and their work lives.

Even if the feminist model were clearly conceptualized, it is far from being implemented, given the societal pressures toward bureaucratic styles of organization. Furthermore, workers are not

144

Feminist Visions

necessarily ready to abandon the supervisory model they have known and to accept the additional tasks and responsibilities inherent in the proposed alternative approach. Therefore, it will not be sufficient just to envision a model. Feminists also will need to envision a strategy for implementing and institutionalizing this alternative model.

notes

1. *Webster's Third New International Dictionary* (Springfield, Mass.: G. & C. Merriam Co., 1961), p. 2296.

2. Margaret Williamson, *Supervision: New Patterns and Processes* (New York: Association Press, 1961), p. 21.

3. Frances H. Scherz, "A Concept of Supervision Based on Definitions of Job Responsibility," *Social Casework*, 39 (October 1958), pp. 437 and 439.

4. Evelyn Stiles, "Supervision in Perspective," *Social Casework*, 44 (January 1963), p. 20.

5. Lucille N. Austin, "Basic Principles of Supervision," *Social Casework*, 33 (December 1952), p. 411.

6. Alfred Kadushin, "Supervisor-Supervisee: A Survey," *Social Work*, 19 (May 1974), p. 293.

7. Fred Berl, "The Content and Method of Supervisory Teaching," *Social Casework*, 44 (November 1963), pp. 516–532; Mary C. Hester, "Educational Process in Supervision," *Social Casework*, 32 (June 1951), pp. 242–251; and Norma D. Levine, "Educational Components of Supervision in a Family Agency," *Social Casework*, 31 (June 1950), pp. 245–250.

8. Alfred Kadushin, *Supervision in Social Work* (New York: Columbia University Press, 1976), p. 152.

9. Ibid., p. 233.

10. Harry Wasserman, "Early Careers of Professional Social Workers in a Public Child Welfare Agency," *Social Work*, 15 (July 1970), pp. 93–101.

11. See, for example, Alice Kelvin, "Life After Social Work," *Ms.* (April 1984), pp. 54–58.

12. See, for example, Wilbur A. Finch, Jr., "Social Workers Versus Bureaucracy," *Social Work*, 21 (September 1976), pp. 370–375; and W. R. Scott, "Professional Employees in a Bureaucratic Structure," in Amitai Etzioni, ed., *The Semi-Professions and Their Organizations* (New York: Free Press, 1969), pp. 82–140.

13. Janet S. Chafetz, "Women in Social Work," *Social Work,* 17 (September 1972), pp. 12–18; William J. Reid, "Social Work and Motherhood: Competitors for Womenpower," *Personnel Information,* 10 (January 1967), pp. 1, 44–47; and John E. Tropman, "The Married Professional Social Worker," *Journal of Marriage and the Family,* 30 (November 1968), pp. 661–665.

14. Nina Toren, *Social Work: The Case of a Semi-Profession* (Beverly Hills, Calif.: Sage Publications, 1972), p. 75.

15. John Wax, "Time-Limited Supervision," *Social Work,* 8 (July 1963), p. 37.

16. Kenneth W. Watson, "Differential Supervision," *Social Work,* 18 (November 1973), pp. 80–88.

17. Toren, *Social Work,* p. 75.

18. Charles S. Levy, "The Ethics of Supervision," *Social Work,* 18 (March 1973), p. 17.

19. Ibid.

20. Kadushin, "Supervisor-Supervisee," p. 290.

21. Levy, "The Ethics of Supervision," p. 18.

22. Ibid., p. 16.

23. Charlotte G. Babcock, "Social Work as Work," *Social Casework,* 34 (December 1953), pp. 415–422.

24. Scherz, "A Concept of Supervision Based on Definitions of Job Responsibility."

25. Alfred Kadushin, "Games People Play in Supervision," *Social Work,* 13 (July 1968), pp. 23–32.

26. Fred Berl, "An Attempt to Construct a Conceptual Framework for Supervision," *Social Casework,* 41 (July 1960), pp. 339–346.

27. Lucille N. Austin, "An Evaluation of Supervision," *Social Casework,* 37 (October 1956), pp. 375–382.

28. Felice Perlmutter, "Barometer of Professional Change," in Florence W. Kaslow and Associates, *Issues in Human Services* (San Francisco: Jossey-Bass, 1972), p. 17.

29. R. C. Day and R. L. Hamblin, "Some Effects of Close and Punitive Styles of Supervision," in G. D. Bell, ed., *Organizations and Human Behavior: A Book of Readings* (Englewood Cliffs, N.J.: Prentice-Hall, 1967), pp. 172–182.

30. Kadushin, *Supervision in Social Work,* p. 36.

31. Austin, "An Evaluation of Supervision."

32. Scherz, "A Concept of Supervision Based on Definitions of Job Responsibility," p. 443.

33. Donald A. Devis, "Teaching and Administrative Functions in Supervision," *Social Work,* 10 (April 1965), pp. 83–89.

Feminist Visions

34. Watson, "Differential Supervision."

35. Arthur L. Leader, "A New Program of Case Consultation," *Social Casework*, 45 (February 1964), pp. 86–89.

36. Paul A. Abels, "On the Nature of Supervision: The Medium Is the Group," *Child Welfare*, 49 (June 1970), pp. 304–311; Tsuneko K. Apaka, Sidney Hirsch, and Sylvia Kleidman, "Establishing Group Supervision in a Hospital Social Work Department," *Social Work*, 12 (October 1967), pp. 54–60; George S. Getzel, Jack R. Goldberg, and Robert Salmon, "Supervising in Groups as a Model for Today," *Social Casework*, 52 (March 1971), pp. 154–163; Jadwiga Judd, Regina E. Kohn, and Gerda L. Schulman, "Group Supervision: A Vehicle for Professional Development," *Social Work*, 7 (January 1962), pp. 96–102; and Florence W. Kaslow, "Group Supervision," in Kaslow and Associates, *Issues in Human Services*, pp. 115–141.

37. J. J. Appleby et al., "A Group Method of Supervision," *Social Work*, 3 (July 1958), pp. 18–22; and Ruth Fizdale, "Peer Group Supervision," *Social Casework*, 39 (October 1958), pp. 443–450.

38. Robert B. Denhardt and Jan Perkins, "The Coming Death of Administrative Man," *Public Administration Review*, 38 (July–August 1976), p. 382.

39. Shan Martin, *Managing Without Managers* (Beverly Hills, Calif.: Sage Publications, 1983).

40. Thomas G. Cummings and Edmond S. Molloy, *Improving Productivity and the Quality of Work Life* (New York: Praeger Publishers, 1977), pp. 21–49.

41. Denhardt and Perkins, "The Coming Death of Administrative Man," pp. 379–384; and Joyce Rothschild-Whitt, "The Collectivist Organization: An Alternative to Rational-Bureaucratic Models," *American Sociological Review*, 44 (August 1979), pp. 509–527.

42. Ruth Fizdale, *Social Agency Structure and Accountability* (Fair Lawn, N.J.: R. E. Burdick, 1974), p. 132.

43. Roslyn H. Chernesky and Alma T. Young, "Developing a Peer Review System," in Helen Rehr, ed., *Professional Accountability for Social Work Practice* (New York: Prodist, 1979), pp. 74–91.

44. Joseph H. Kahle, "Structuring and Administering a Modern Voluntary Agency," *Social Work*, 14 (October 1969), p. 22.

45. Sidney Hirsch and Lawrence C. Shulman, "Participatory Governance: A Model for Shared Decision Making," *Social Work in Health Care*, 1 (Summer 1976), pp. 280–293.

46. Chris Argyris, "Today's Problems with Tomorrow's Organizations," in R. E. Hill and B. J. White, eds., *Matrix Organization and Project Management* (Ann Arbor, Mich.: University of Michigan Press, 1979), p. 23.

47. Theodore Walden, "The Matrix Organization: An Alternative to Bureaucracy," *Administration in Social Work*, 5 (Spring 1981), pp. **147**

A New Model of Supervision

31–42; and K. R. Wedel, "Matrix Designs for Human Service Organizations," *Administration in Mental Health,* 4 (Fall 1976), pp. 36–42.

48. Ruth Middleman, "The Quality Circle: Fad, Fix, Fiction?" *Administration in Social Work,* 8 (Spring 1984), p. 36.

49. Ralph Barra, *Putting Quality Circles to Work* (New York: McGraw-Hill Book Co., 1983), p. xii.

148

Susan Meyers Chandler

the hidden feminist agenda in social development

the profession of social work has historically been committed to a process of social change that aims to ensure adequate provisions and opportunities for the needy, the vulnerable, the oppressed, and the underprivileged.[1] And while social workers were hard at work developing a professional reputation as caseworkers who assist *individuals* to cope with stresses within their environment, a small cadre of them, starting with such great women leaders as Jane Addams, Florence Kelley, and Lillian Wald were also working to identify and reform the *structural* forces that maintain and perpetuate that stressful environment.[2] Many nineteenth-century social workers saw the need to bring about the type of change that involved focusing on the social, structural, and institutional elements of stress, such as unemployment, poverty, and discrimination, and removing them from the environment. The settlement house workers of the early 1900s struggled not only to help families integrate successfully into their new environments but to bring about changes in their communities. These social reformers accurately saw the limitations and frustrations that resulted from the **149**

role expectations that were assigned to women in traditional family life. The early reform efforts related to child welfare, day care, and employment pointed up the problems women faced daily, yet much of the analysis of the problem remained "clinical" and individualistic. Little social work activity was organized around examining the problems of women as a *class* of people subjected to prejudice, oppression, and discrimination.

Freud's psychoanalytic theories strongly influenced the development of social work's direct practice interventions. Although Freud created complex theories of "human" development, he remained unable to figure out the answer to his famous question, "What do women want?" Professional social work sometimes seems equally baffled.

It was not until the civil rights and equal opportunity legislation of the Great Society's reforms were under way in the 1960s that social workers once again were pushed into the realization that social problems could not be adequately diminished through clinical interventions alone.[3] Macro analyses that examine the institutional and structural causes of social problems such as unemployment, poverty, family violence, sexism, and racism are essential if social workers are fully to understand human concerns and oppression.

For example, it is important to examine the potential systemic factors that may be associated with the findings that women experience more depression than men,[4] that women are paradoxically institutionalized more frequently than men[5] and overrepresented among the homeless, that married women are less mentally healthy than are married men (and, incidentally, than are single women),[6] and that women have graced the poverty statistics with the increasing "feminization of poverty"—and that women of color have the worst statistics in all these categories. Research has clearly substantiated that women, as a group, are institutionally and structurally discriminated against, are vulnerable, and are oppressed. New forms of social work practice are necessary to develop and implement strategies of social change that will eliminate barriers to equal opportunity, achieve social justice, and ensure equitable social policies that enhance rather than impede self-actualization and opportunity for all citizens.

Social work has a rich literature on social change strategies aimed at achieving equal opportunities for all citizens.[7] Social workers, subscribing to a philosophy called *social development,* are

150 trying to bring about systematic improvement of the quality of life

Feminist Visions

through the development of social policies and programs, renewed institutional approaches, and the development of resources.[8] A goal of social development is to foster the emergence and implementation of a social structure in which all citizens are entitled to equal social, economic, and political rights and equal access to status, roles, prerogatives, and responsibilities, regardless of gender, race, age, sexual orientation, or disability.

Principles of social development include cooperation, participatory planning and decision making, distributive justice, advocacy, and nondiscrimination. Dennis Falk, in 1981, surveyed social development experts in social work and found that participation, respect for human dignity, humanism, nondiscrimination, and global awareness were ranked by these experts as the top five social development values.[9] Feminism also upholds these broad values and principles. The recent activism of feminists to curb nuclear proliferation is an example of feminism's global awareness and breadth of concern.

In 1966, with the birth of the National Organization for Women (NOW), the contemporary women's movement began to articulate its concern for bringing women into full participation in the mainstream of American society and ensuring that women obtain all privileges and responsibilities in true equal partnership with men. The goals of the contemporary women's movement correspond with the approach articulated by social development experts. Yet in the profession of social work there seems to be a lack of interest in the development of a feminist agenda; a disinterest in the gender gap that separates men and women economically, politically, and socially; and little enthusiasm to work on solving the real problems that face 51 percent of the U.S. population—women.

This chapter examines several components of a social development perspective and compares them with a feminist perspective. The similarities include the value of participation, respect for the dignity and worth of human beings, and institutional equity. The author attempts to show that a social developmental perspective contains many feminist precepts, although they are sometimes hidden in social work. The principles of social work and those of feminist ideology also are similar, the only difference being that feminists insist on applying theirs. Specific attention is given to the distinction between role change and role equity,[10] and, using these concepts, suggestions for a social work action agenda will be offered.

Feminist Agenda in Social Development

Participation and the Social Development Perspective

The social development perspective embraces the value of participation in the community and has developed strategies to ensure the participation of the citizens to be affected by change in planning and policy development activities. The mid-1960s saw the implementation of the concept "maximum feasible participation," which was a legislative mandate to ensure that disenfranchised people were actively and meaningfully involved in the participatory aspects of planning at the community level (at least whenever federal funds from the Office of Economic Opportunity were to be used). The logic of maximum feasible participation was to enable greater citizen participation in civic affairs, political decision making, and democratic activities in the community. Social development currently strives to develop new leadership from the disenfranchised and works toward achieving a broad cross section of the community with which to plan and utilize resources. An important social work and social development value is that planning should not be done *to* people, but *with* them—that people should be actively recruited into the planning process and participate in all levels of discussion and decision making about the changes that affect them.

Participation and the Feminist Perspective

Participation from a feminist perspective is viewed similarly. Contemporary feminist organizations, such as NOW and the National Women's Political Caucus, have sought legal and social equality for women through efforts designed to help qualified women participate fully in the local and national political system and, in particular, to attain positions of political power. Leadership training was the expressed goal of the National Women's Education Fund, founded in 1972; the main objective was to prepare women for participation in party politics and government service. Yet many feminists quickly became concerned about encouraging participation in a political structure that was, in their view, inherently hierarchical, authoritarian, and elitist. Many were unwilling to participate in or create bureaucracies that epitomized the "male establishment." Ideologically, some feminist theorists wanted to rethink the traditional notions of power. They began to redefine and reconceptualize the meaning of power and to

Feminist Visions

develop models focusing on *empowering* rather than *overpowering.*

Traditionally, power has been viewed in terms of the haves and the have-nots, with the strategies of social change focused on the have-nots organizing and developing enough political power to take resources away from the haves.[11] A feminist reinterpretation of power expands the concept beyond and away from one's ability to dominate, control, and influence other persons toward one's ability to become empowered to achieve one's aspirations.[12] The achievement of one's aspirations occurs noncoercively, collaboratively, and collectively and results in true participation, with the strengths of all participants maximized and liberated.

Feminists have begun successfully to replace traditional, bureaucratic, organizational structures with new types of interactional ones.[13] Nonauthoritarian leadership models are emerging that encourage people at all levels to contribute to the level of their capacity. These innovations are replacing the "rules" of meetings with less impersonal procedures and sanctioning the expression of personal feelings in place of the traditional task-oriented and task-structured organizational protocols. As Freeman recognized, however, without leaders, organizations are subject to the "tyranny of structurelessness."[14] Thus, new models that facilitate the group's goals and the full and active participation of the membership are needed.

Social Work's Record on Participation

Although the profession of social work is over two-thirds female, the leadership structure (agency executives, deans of schools of social work, and professors) is predominantly male, as well as white. Despite its history of articulating a concern for the powerless, the disadvantaged, and the oppressed, social work has only recently begun to whisper about the systematic discrimination against women in our society and our profession. Not only are women frequently denied equal access to the opportunity structures of our society, but they are stigmatized with definitions of inferiority in the very roles and activities that society assigns to them.

In social work, the field of clinical or direct practice, which is predominantly female, has traditionally focused on the uniqueness of each individual, while being cognizant of common human needs. The profession is respectful of a practitioner's intuitions, **153** experiences, and understanding, and the conscious use of self is a basic construct in social work intervention. Yet, since more men have entered and taken control of the profession, this approach has been called to task.

Today, social work journals publish mainly in the male voice.[15] Davis discussed the suppression of the female voice in social work as she charted the shift from relationship building to contracting, from intuitive knowledge to empirically based practice, and from process to a near-obsession with outcome research. Women authors are underrepresented in the "prestigious" journals of social work,[16] and articles about women and women's issues are not plentiful, even though the majority of social workers and their clientele are women. The social work literature is still written primarily by men about men, and the participation of women in the field remains mostly hidden.[17]

Salary inequities have been documented widely[18], and the differentials remain even when education and work experience are held constant.[19] Women work actively in the social work profession, but have not been able to realize their potential, accomplish their aspirations, and refocus the field into a more human and feminist profession.

Human Dignity, Worth, and the Social Development Perspective

Respecting the dignity and worth of all human beings is a deeply held value among social workers and inherent in the philosophy of social development. To ensure that all clients are treated with dignity and respect and to communicate a sense to all client systems that they are worthy of esteem are principles basic to all social work practice. And yet, does the profession respect equally the worth of all its clients, male and female?

Social work values frequently parallel the commonly held, central values in the United States. Williams attempted to identify the major values in American culture.[20] He found that achievement and success are most frequently defined in terms of the accumulation of money in the operation of one's business or profession. Money and position are the symbols of success and personal worth. "What do you do?" is often a friendly greeting, but it really means, "Where do you work, at what position, and with what salary?"

Feminist Visions

Griffith contended that American economic policy is biased heavily toward those who work outside the home and clearly presumes that women are secondary earners.[21] The Internal Revenue Service, the social security system, most health insurance and pension plans, and the public welfare system all assume that married women work to "supplement" their husbands' salaries for those "little luxuries" in life that the women want. That most women work to survive and support themselves and their families seems to be ignored in the development of economic policy. U.S. economic policy does not treat a female wage earner equally with a male wage earner, even if a woman's work record is equal, for example, to her husband's. Single women, however, are sometimes better protected than are married women, reinforcing the notion that a husband will provide for his wife and a wife should remain dependent on her husband for security and status. Yet, with almost 50 percent of the first marriages in this country ending in divorce, a woman is waging a poor bet if she expects her economic security to be ensured with a wedding vow.

Pearce's term, "the feminization of poverty," is a chilling reminder that poverty has become a women's issue.[22] Pearce asserted that the price women are paying for achieving economic independence from their spouses by participation in the labor force (often accompanied by divorce) has been their pauperization and dependence on welfare. Over 67 percent of those over age 16 in poverty in the United States are women, over 70 percent of the aged poor are women, and over half of all poor families are female headed, although female-headed families represent only 14 percent of the population. These statistics are even more tragic for women of color. Families headed by black men are 2½ times more likely to be poor than are families headed by white men. But families headed by white women run more than four times the risk of being poor than do those headed by white men, and for families headed by black women, the risk is almost nine times greater. The sex of the family head now outweighs race as a predictor of poverty in this country.[23]

It is by now commonly known that women in all occupations, professions, and jobs receive less pay for comparable work than do men; that, on the average, women only earn 59 cents to the dollar of comparably employed men; and that occupational segregation keeps 60 percent of all working women in only ten occupations—high-stress, low-paying jobs. Moreover, women often fill the ranks of the "permanent temporary" workers, that **155**

Feminist Agenda in Social Development

is, employees without benefits, security, or potential. President Reagan has been successful in undercutting the crucial affirmative action policies of the last 20 years. The Equal Employment Opportunity Commission, which has the responsibility of ending discrimination against women, blacks, and other minorities, has a budget that is one-seventh as large as that of the U.S. Weather Bureau.

With these economic policies, how is social work respecting the dignity and worth of its clients? Are we social workers tacitly accepting the huge class, race, and sexual divide that is engulfing our nation? Are we supporting and maintaining social policies that assist those who do and have done well? As Titmuss so eloquently pointed out, the social welfare system really supports the middle class and has never had any intention of bringing about an economic redistribution of resources.[24] The "tip of the iceberg" is the public welfare system, but the bulk of the welfare state is the iceberg itself, heavy with occupational and fiscal policies that support the already fortunate—the "deserving" wealthy and the "worried well." The increase of private practice among social workers seems to indicate that much of the profession is ready to serve middle-class clients and give the poor away to the "nonprofessionals." Social development, however, speaks of creating and renewing institutions, developing resources to ensure equity, and obtaining equal opportunities for all citizens. If this is truly the agenda for social development, then the following types of policy options should be actively supported and fought for by social work:

- The Equal Rights Amendment and all federal policies that support equality of opportunity.

- A children's allowance that provides an adequate amount of money to *all* families (whether headed by a single parent or a couple, poor or not) for the cost of bringing up children. The United States is still the only modern industrialized nation without such a family support policy.

- Subsidized child care that is adequate, of high quality, and available. Before-school and after-school child care must also be provided, and a national family policy must be developed that addresses the broad concern of child care for working parents.

- Maternity and paternity leaves that permit families to spend time with their newborn infants without loss of seniority or fear of losing their jobs.

156　　　- Payments for homemaking tasks that recognize the homemaker's role in the economic livelihood of the family. Homemaking must be calculated into the social security system so that women who have done years of unpaid domestic work do not instantly become impoverished displaced homemakers if they get divorced or become widows.

■ Employment policies that guarantee a job for all who want to work and encourage flextime, job sharing, and other innovative work practices that respect the realities of working parents.

These are the issues that social development should be exploring in social work. These policy options clearly flow from the social development agenda when analyzed in relation to feminist concerns. They are clearly in alignment with a feminist agenda that strives to improve the position of women and other oppressed groups in order for them to gain human respect and dignity.

The Feminist Perspective

Feminist ideology is similar to the social development perspective but expanded in certain key areas. There is an underlying consensus among feminists that "barriers to the realization of...full and unique human potential can and must be challenged and changed."[25] The International Federation of Social Workers' Policy on Human Rights sets forth the basic rights of women as members of the human race. It states, in part:

> Every person is born free and equal and has the right of self determination within the limits of the same rights of others....Everyone is entitled to their rights and freedom without distinction as to birth, sex, sexual orientation, race, color, language, national or social origin, property, intellect, ideology, political opinion or other condition.[26]

This goal may seem lofty and unattainable in view of the conservative political sweep witnessed in the 1984 U.S. elections. Earlier efforts by women that resulted in improved legislative and administrative policies include the Equal Credit Opportunity Act, the Equal Pay Act, the Pregnancy Disability Act, Title IX of the Educational Amendments of 1972, and the Affirmative Action Executive Orders. These efforts clearly were important first steps in achieving equity for women through public policies. Recently, feminists have successfully taken leadership to bring about insti- **157**

Feminist Agenda in Social Development

tutional renewal and social change in the areas of reproductive rights, health care, and the delivery of mental health services. Institutional renewal, in the true sense of developing alternative, more responsive institutions to meet the newly felt needs of individuals or groups, has been achieved through the development of many feminist services, including the following: (1) women's health centers that are oriented to participatory health care and focused on women's special health concerns, (2) new humanistic, consumer-focused approaches to birthing that offer a variety of childbirth experiences, with the mother's wishes as the primary determinant, and (3) feminist mental health strategies that return dignity and respect to those who seek psychotherapy or counseling.

Feminist concerns clearly parallel the concerns of social development. Feminists have been successful as a political force in bringing about some significant political and social changes over the past 20 years. The record for social development is as yet unassessed. In what areas have policies and structures been most amenable to social change? And in what areas is it likely that social work will be able to bring about the types of change that social development experts desire? If there is information that we can learn from examining the patterns of the last decade, perhaps we will be more successful in achieving the egalitarian goals both feminists and social development experts seek. These issues will be addressed in the concluding section of this chapter.

Personal Change vs. Institutional Equity

The profession of social work seems to have divided itself into two components, both attempting to achieve the same goal. One component strives to intervene with an individual's intrapsychic or interpersonal problems and assist him or her to find new strategies of coping or changing. Another component attempts to examine the systems that negatively impinge on individuals and intervene by altering, changing, or restructuring those systems, institutions, and environments that may directly or indirectly prevent individual, group, or community self-actualization. This polarization may be conceptualized as a commitment to personal change versus a commitment to institutional equity.

Social work students are expected to be familiar with several intervention strategies and generic social work practice but may concentrate their educational and practicum experiences on one.

158

Feminist Visions

The profession seems to be willing and able to incorporate both individual (case) advocacy and system (class) advocacy within its code of ethics, and the polarization does not seem to have the negative effect of dividing or weakening it.

However, if we examine closely the areas for which social work has truly advocated, it is apparent that the individualistic, personal-change strategies have been paramount in the literature, practice wisdom, and commitments of social work. A brief historical review of the recent major federal legislation involving the development of "social casework," from the Social Service Amendments of 1962 and 1967 to Title XX, reveals efforts to "manipulate" people (mostly women, particularly women of color) to teach them, train them, push them, probe them, and at times threaten them with "skills" to make them less dependent, self-supporting, and self-sufficient. It has not worked. The rates of poverty keep increasing, and only one thing is clear—women are vastly overrepresented in the ranks of the impoverished, the homeless, and the helpless.

Social workers who are concerned with social development must address these issues. It is inherent in the agenda of social development to advocate beyond an individual's concerns and examine critically the institutional biases that impede people from achieving equity in our society. Social work must address the antiwoman and anticolor biases that infuse our social welfare systems, and we must bring about the institutional changes that will correct those biases. Personal change is one strategy; an equally important strategy is institutional equity.

Carden examined from a feminist perspective two types of social goals for which feminists are striving: role equity and role change.[27] She described strategies to achieve role equity as those laws, policies, and programs that provide and ensure for women political and economic opportunities commensurate with those available to men. At one extreme, this may mean only minor modifications in current structural arrangements, such as opening job opportunities to women in areas from which they had been excluded previously or preventing overt types of discrimination against women in the work environment and as citizens. An example of this type of modification is the Equal Credit Opportunity Act, passed in 1974. Role equity implies freedom to adopt a broader variety of lifestyles but seems also to imply that women will want to assume the individualism, achievement orientation, and so-called rationality of the traditionally powerful male role in their **159**

Feminist Agenda in Social Development

attempts to gain parity with men. Perhaps it is this trait that makes this type of change easier to bring about. The male-dominated power structure seems willing to let "a few good women" in, particularly when those women emulate the existing structures to which men are so accustomed. This type of change also fits in with our "egalitarian" value statements that abhor overt discrimination and decree equal opportunities for all. The Civil Rights Act of 1964, which prohibited racial, sexual, or ethnic discrimination in employment, formed the basis for role equity, and the women's movement has been riding on the crest of that wave of reform. Both feminists and the social work profession must move on now to achieve the more crucial component of equality—that which will be brought about only through role *change.*

Role change will entail a basic alteration in the distribution of sex roles in society. It will bring about a movement away from sex-based distinctions that prescribe that women, and only women, must play the "female role," that of primary caretaker, mother, wife, housekeeper—an economically dependent status. Role change will give people, both male and female, the opportunity to become independent, self-reliant individuals, without the *expectation* that because they are of a particular gender they have or do not have *inherent* responsibilities for homemaking and child care—an expectation that all too frequently limits choices and opportunities. This type of role change will affect every individual in society. It will affect all families, social institutions, and structural foundations. This is the type of change that is required if women are to enter our society fully as equals. It is also the type of change that is necessary if all people are to become self-actualizing. Perhaps its is precisely because of the extent and breadth of these changes that the social policies, legislation, and social reforms that include role-change strategies have not yet been implemented in the United States. The Equal Rights Amendment was role-change legislation, and its passage has been stalled, perhaps indefinitely.

Social Work's Role and Obligation

Social work is in a unique position to bring about substantial and progressive changes in our society. Because we social workers work at both micro and macro levels to intervene and bring about change, we are uniquely able to bring about both role equity and role change. We are working daily to achieve both personal change and institutional equity. And we should be uniquely able to understand fully the interrelationships of such changes. Social development-oriented social workers, like feminists, are acutely aware that macro-level change will affect individuals in a variety of ways. Social workers can assist individuals to prepare and become ready for the changes that are taking place and will take place. Fear and resistance associated with role-change strategies can be easily understood by clinical social workers; support and encouragement for role-equity strategies can be easily generated by social development-oriented social workers. Feminists see the necessity for bringing about both types of change to achieve equality for women and all oppressed people. The framework for a just society has been drawn. Social work has a crucial role to play. Will it do so?

notes

1. June Axinn and Herman Levin, *Social Welfare: A History of the American Response to Need* (New York: Harper & Row, 1982).
2. Jane Addams, "Social Settlements," in *Proceedings of the National Conference of Charities and Correction,* 1897.
3. Ad Hoc Committee on Advocacy, "The Social Worker as Advocate: Champion of Social Victims," *Social Work,* 14 (April 1969), pp. 16–22; Jeffrey Galper, *The Politics of Social Services* (Englewood Cliffs, N.J.: Prentice-Hall, 1975); and Charles Grosser, *New Directions in Community Organization: From Enabling to Advocacy* (New York: Praeger, 1976).
4. Naomi Gottlieb, *Alternative Social Services for Women* (New York: Columbia University Press, 1980).
5. Phyllis Chesler, *Women and Madness* (New York: Avon Books, 1973).
6. Jessie Bernard, *The Future of Motherhood* (New York: Dial Press, 1974).
7. Steven Burghardt, *Organizing for Community Action* (Beverly Hills, Calif.: Sage Publications, 1982); Fred Cox et al., *Strategies of Community Organization* (Itasca, Ill.: F. E. Peacock, 1979); and Ann Weick and Susan T. Vandiver, eds., *Women, Power, and Change* (Washington, D.C.: National Association of Social Workers, 1981).
8. Susan Meyers Chandler, "Towards a Social Development Analysis," in Daniel Sanders, ed., *The Developmental Perspective in Social Work* (Honolulu: University of Hawaii, 1982), pp. 77–88; Frances Paiva, "A Conception of Social Development," *Social Service Review,* 51 (June 1977), pp. 327–336; and Rosa Resnick, "Women and Social Development," in Sanders, ed., pp. 63–73.

161

Feminist Agenda in Social Development

9. Dennis Falk, "Social Development Values," *Social Development Issues*, 5 (Spring 1981), pp. 67–83.

10. This concept was originally developed by Maren Lockwood Carden, *Feminism in the Mid 1970's* (New York: Ford Foundation, 1977).

11. Saul Alinsky, *Rules for Radicals* (New York: Random House, 1971).

12. Mary Bricker-Jenkins and Nancy Hooyman, "Feminist Ideology," discussion paper, Feminist Practice Project (Silver Spring, Md.: National Association of Social Workers, 1983).

13. Michael Doyle and David Straus, *How to Make Meetings Work* (New York: Jove Publications, 1983).

14. Jo Freeman, "The Tyranny of Structurelessness," *Berkeley Journal of Sociology*, 16 (1972–73), pp. 151–164.

15. Liane V. Davis, "Female and Male Voices in Social Work," *Social Work*, 30 (March–April 1985), pp. 106–113.

16. Stuart A. Kirk and Aaron Rosenblatt, "Women's Contribution's to Social Work Journals," *Social Work*, 25 (May 1980), pp. 204–209; and Kirk and Rosenblatt, "The Contribution of Women Faculty to Social Work Journals," *Social Work*, 30 (January–February 1984).

17. See Susan T. Vandiver, "A Herstory of Women in Social Work," in Elaine Norman and Arlene Mancuso, eds., *Women's Issues and Social Work Practice* (Itasca, Ill.: F. E. Peacock, 1980), pp. 21–28.

18. Cynthia J. Belon and Ketayun H. Gould, "Not Even Equals: Sex-Related Salary Inequities," *Social Work*, 22 (November 1977), pp. 466–471; and Allen Rubin, "Reexamining the Impact of Sex on Salary: The Limits of Statistical Significance," *Social Work Research and Abstracts*, 17 (Fall 1981), pp. 19–24.

19. Hide Yamatani, "Gender and Salary Inequity: Statistical Interaction Effects," *Social Work Research and Abstracts*, 18 (Winter 1982).

20. Robin Williams, Jr., *American Society: A Sociological Interpretation* (New York: Alfred A. Knopf, 1967).

21. Martha Griffith, "How Much Is a Woman Worth?" in Jane Roberts Chapman, ed., *Economic Independence for Women* (Beverly Hills, Calif.: Sage Publications, 1976).

22. Diana Pearce, "Women, Work and Welfare: The Feminization of Poverty," in Karen Wolk Feinstein, ed., *Working Women and Families* (Beverly Hills, Calif.: Sage Publications, 1979).

23. Winifred Bell, *Contemporary Social Welfare* (New York: Macmillan, 1983).

24. Richard Titmuss, *Social Policy* (New York: Random House, 1974).

25. Bricker-Jenkins and Hooyman, "Feminist Ideology."

26. Organization based in Geneva, Switzerland.

27. Carden, *Feminism in the Mid 1970's*.

162

Feminist Visions

Nancy R. Hooyman
Rosemary Cunningham

an alternative
administrative
style

this chapter grew out of the recognition that social work education and research have not addressed how women administer the feminist workplace. Instead, most social work education and research have focused on the skills and knowledge that women would need to enable themselves to advance within traditional hierarchies. The chapter begins by reviewing an individualistic, "slice-of-the-pie" approach to the role of women in administration. Next, a conceptual model of feminist administration is delineated as an alternative to this more traditional approach. Findings are then presented regarding the extent to which the components of this model of feminist administration are implemented within a national sample of women's organizations. On the basis of these findings, as well as the authors' review of the literature on feminist organizations, the organizational constraints that are faced by feminist administrators and the principles for administering feminist organizations are discussed. The chapter concludes with a consideration of the implications of a feminist administrative style for professional social work education.

163

Traditional Models of Administration

The relatively small number of women in human services administrative positions and the obstacles facing women as administrators have been extensively documented in the social work literature.[1] For the most part, men are administering and planning human services programs that have an impact mainly on women, especially low-income women. The comparatively few women in administrative positions have had primarily male models of managerial success; these models have emphasized instrumental tasks, such as the analysis of problems, negotiation and bargaining, fund raising, and decision making, which are based on male norms. As Chernesky noted, the role models for leading and for being powerful are male social models: for organizations, we have hierarchies; for power, we have oppression; and for expressing conflict, we have violence and sanctions.[2]

Women administrators have generally had to adapt to male-defined positions, rather than have the opportunity to change the positions' requirements and characteristics. Accordingly, training programs and advice-giving books have focused on how women can overcome internal and interpersonal barriers, such as passivity and lack of confidence, which supposedly constrain their movement into administration. Individuals have generally been the point of intervention, and education and skills training have been viewed as solutions. The woman manager thus is defined as a deviant, requiring special advice on how to manage her deviant identity to move up within traditional bureaucracies. In effect, the basic message to women managers is, "Think like a man, dress like a doll, work like a horse": how to dress, balance a job and family, interpret male colloquialisms, and handle premenstrual tension. Because management training programs that focus on overcoming women's socialization experiences tend to hold women responsible for their successes and failures, they do not have an impact on institutionalized sexism. Even when the importance of institutionalized barriers is recognized, most training emphasizes moving women up within existing sexist systems rather than changing institutional norms and practices that deny women access to essential resources.

A slice-of-the-pie model of leadership underlies this popular advice and training for women managers. Women are given the message that they must adopt a male model of administration and compete on male terms to get a slice of the pie. Women's weaknesses, rather than their strengths and potential, are emphasized. By focusing primarily on personal qualities, such as self-confidence and assertiveness, the slice-of-the-pie model pursues personal advancement rather than structural change. Upward mobility becomes the primary measure of liberation, which means that women with the proper credentials will succeed, and others will not. Recently, more women in social work agencies have questioned the administrative models presented to them. They are recognizing that the individualistic and self-serving aspects of assertiveness and management training oriented to individual mobility must be countered with cooperative and collective images and demands.

We must create alternatives to existing models of administration, both through developing new institutions and through changing institutional barriers in traditional organizations. A transcendence model of organizations has been proposed as one alternative to the slice-of-the-pie model. According to this model, for professional roles now requiring ambitious, competitive, and oppressive behavior to get ahead, it would be equally appropriate to change the roles themselves to accommodate alternative behaviors. Oriented toward institutional change, a transcendence model implies flexibility, plurality, personal choice, and the development of new or emergent possibilities rather than adaptation to existing male norms.[3]

Alternative Models of Administration

Since the late 1960s, there have been a number of grass-roots efforts to develop new forms of collective and democratic organizations. Although many of these "alternative" organizations remained male dominated, they represented efforts to realize different values from those undergirding bureaucracies. The strengths and limitations, potential for survival, and stages of development of consensual organizations, including communes,[4] community mental health centers,[5] and medical clinics,[6] have been described in the literature. In her study of five alternative organizations—a free medical clinic, a legal collective, a food coop, a free school, and an alternative newspaper—Rothschild-Whitt delineated eight dimensions along which collectivist organizations differed from bureaucratic organizations. These dimensions were authority, rules, social control, social relations, recruitment and advance- **165** ment, incentive structure, social stratification, and differentiation.[7]

Research specifically on women's deliberate attempts to implement feminist values in women-run organizations is more recent and limited than that on alternative organizations generally.[8] Feminist workplaces, such as rape crisis centers, centers for battered women, and women's counseling centers, evolved when traditional service systems proved inadequate for meeting women's needs,[9] yet relatively little is known about the organization and management of feminist work sites on a daily basis.

This chapter has two underlying assumptions: (1) All organizations run by and for women are not necessarily feminist, and (2) feminist administration is not necessarily limited to consensual or cooperative organizations. Regarding the first assumption, it should be noted that organizations like the YWCAs have served women well for years, but have generally not attempted to implement feminist values or modify existing male-female relationships in organizations (although this situation is changing in some urban YWCAs). This chapter focuses explicitly on how a feminist administrative style is defined and developed to affirm women's strengths, processes, and experiences.

Hartsock's definition of feminism as "a mode of analysis, a method of approaching life and politics, a way of asking questions and searching for answers"[10] underlies the model of administration delineated here. As a mode of analysis, feminism presents neither fixed political conclusions nor a right or wrong way for all women; rather, it has clear implications for action, for permitting choices, and for acting responsibly to change existing institutions. Feminism seeks to institute "female" values as legitimate, because a sexist society suffers from a surfeit of "male" values. As we reclaim our history as women, "female" values can become the basis for a positive vision of a humane, nonsexist society. In a feminist society, women (and men) act according to their wishes, inclinations, potentials, abilities, and needs rather than according to prevailing stereotypes of sex roles and sex-appropriate modes of thought and behavior.

In relation to the second basic assumption, that feminist administration is not necessarily limited to consensual or cooperative organizations, refers to the continuum of organizations, from collectives at one end to rationalistic bureaucracies at the other. Most organizations are hybrids, falling somewhere midway on this continuum. Indeed, to assume that feminist administration can be implemented only in small collectives can limit efforts to change bureaucracies that serve the majority of the consumers of human services. In addition, presumptions that collectives are the only "pure" feminist organizations can set up artificial and negative distinctions between women who are members of collectives and those who are struggling to implement their feminist values in bureaucracies. Rather, it is assumed that components of a feminist administrative style can be partially implemented in traditional bureaucracies and thereby can be a vehicle for changing hierarchical organizations.

A Feminist Administrative Style

The primary differentiating characteristics of this conceptual model of feminist administration are the valuing of women's perspectives and experiences, wholeness and the elimination of false dichotomies or artificial separations, a reconceptualization of power, the principles of democratic structuring, the valuing of process, and an orientation to fundamental structural change.[11] These constructs allow feminist organizations to be located on a continuum. Various constraints, such as the need for external funding, undoubtedly limit the extent to which an organization attains these characteristics. In addition, these dimensions are interrelated; for example, the valuing of women's perspectives and experiences is expressed in efforts to reconceptualize power, which, in turn, manifest themselves in structural modifications to enhance power sharing through democratic decision making.

Valuing of Women's Perspectives and Experiences. A feminist administrative style is based on female values. In traditional administrative models, female values have generally been defined as negative and in need of change. For example, women have been caricatured as too irrational or emotional for administrative positions. In contrast, a feminist approach affirms women's strengths, processes, and experiences. For we women to control our lives, feminism must break through male-defined stereotpyes, thereby enabling us to define our "femaleness." Women can use the male-defined stereotypes in a positive way: Women's flexibility, capacity for intuitive awareness of personal and social phenomena, empathy, multidimensional thought processes, and nurturance are examples of qualities traditionally ascribed to women and valued by feminists. In addition, women's life expe- **167** rience and perspectives are valued by feminist administrators and taken into consideration, rather than discounted, in organizational decision making.

Wholeness and Elimination of False Dichotomies.   The distinctions among managers, staff, and clients in hierarchies often translate into an expert-nonexpert dichotomy, which can become a means to keep consumers separate and powerless. This distinction has frequently been initiated and maintained during the process of deciding who defines the problems and asks the questions about who is to be served. An assumption has been that problems can be objectified into "facts." In contrast, a feminist administrator recognizes that neither the definition of facts nor the translation of facts into social problems is an objective, scientific process. Rather, the process of defining problems is always subjective—shaped by values, interests, and ideologies. There are multiple competing definitions of a problem, none of them necessarily right or wrong. Instead, there can be many truths, which, in turn, can create a need for developing a new language to convey those truths. Words can provide the means by which to define issues anew and to take action. Accordingly, more efforts are made by feminist administrators to synthesize, to see the total picture, rather than to fragment parts and set up artificial boundaries. The process of defining problems thus involves multidimensional thinking and the synthesis of many components.

Reconceptualization of Power.   The redefinition of power and its relationship to leadership is basic to a feminist administrative style. With primarily male models for power, most women have been taught to fear power, to appear helpless rather than powerful, or to use personal power as domination. As a result, women have often resorted to indirect uses of power, such as silence, passivity, and withdrawal of their time and energy.[12] But such attempts to deny the existence of leadership and power generally lead to organizational and group problems. Power and leadership can be reclaimed without negating our feminist values and ourselves. Feminist leadership is determined by the functions the leader performs and her ability to move others to action, not by her public visibility.[13]

In traditional male-based models of administration, power is viewed as finite; as property, analogous to money; and therefore as involving control and domination of subordinates to make

Feminist Visions

them do what they do not want to do. Accordingly, one person unilaterally manages the environment and determines goals; one person supervises the execution of tasks, making others dependent on her or him. Rules are created to censure behavior, information is withheld, private meetings are held, and little concern is shown for others' thoughts and feelings, except to control them so they do not intrude on the goal of "winning."[14]

In a model of feminist administration, power is viewed as infinite; as energy, strength, and effectiveness; and therefore as distributed throughout all organizational members in terms of who can deliver services or perform basic functions. Power of a position is differentiated from power as influence and responsibility that exists throughout a system and that everyone can therefore possess.[15]

An administrator who recognizes that power can be distributed throughout all members of a system empowers others. The male model, especially the male medical model, has conveyed the message, "I'll take care of you; trust me. I'll make decisions for you," and therefore has bred dependence. Although this model has increased men's absolute power, it has also given men the burden of carrying all those dependent people. Women who attempt to "take care" of their staff often find themselves cast into the "earth mother" role. In contrast, a feminist administrator encourages others to be independent, to be responsible for themselves, and thereby to develop fully their potential. Mechanisms can be created for people to work together on problems, rather than one person giving orders to another. In a feminist model, power is facilitative; empowerment to action occurs rather than domination. Personal power is then political, allowing people the ability to make decisions for themselves and to achieve self-determination and control over their lives rather than over the lives of others.

Principles of Democratic Structuring. To redefine power does not deny the reality of the power differentials that exist in most large organizations. Instead, feminist definitions of power acknowledge the differential contributions of individuals. It is a myth to believe that we are all equally powerful or that we must all be equally powerful; attempts to avoid formal decision-making structures can create informal domination if structures and tasks are not clearly delineated.[16] That one person at some point may be more knowledgeable and more influential than **169**

others cannot be structured away. But nonhierarchical structures can be created that give everyone access to the issues, resources, and information. In other words, structures can be modified to empower staff and consumers. By disclosing facts, goals, and processes through consensual decision making, administrators can create conditions under which staff and consumers are free to make choices. Structure and clarity about tasks can allow individuals to demonstrate their trustworthiness and to share in a broad set of responsibilities.[17] To give people more control over their time and activities, every job can include elements of both planning and routine execution; conception of the task can then be integrated with execution of the work. When responsibility is viewed as a source of energy shared by all members, lines of responsibility can be clear without requiring accountability to the top; members can then expand themselves by sharing in others' accomplishments through job sharing, the rotation of tasks, accountability to peers, the development of many skills, and contracts with peers. When ultimate responsibility does not rest in one person alone, administrators themselves are less likely to "burn out" from lack of support. Accordingly, when all members of the organization are involved in the decision-making process, they are more likely to feel invested in and committed to the decisions that they will be implementing.

Valuing of Process.   A feminist administrator values both process and product, with each receiving slightly more or less attention at any time; this approach allows for flexibility and the ability to respond to problems in a number of different ways.[18] For instance, at the beginning of a meeting, a feminist administrator might first be concerned with sharing people's processes, with what is going on with them, rather than with beginning on time or with going directly to the content of the meeting. Process time would be structured for critiques, for sharing opinions, for praise, and for affirmation.[19] Conflict would be dealt with as it arises, rather than be ignored until later. The importance of compromise, of avoiding polarities, also is recognized. The feminist model is developmental, concerned with long-run effectiveness and the processes necessary to attain it, rather than only with short-term efficiency. Although a feminist administrator may utilize skills that are characteristic of male-defined administrative models, she differs in her focus on the ends *in* the means. Her administration is thus value based and has a moral dimension, in contrast to

Feminist Visions

the norm-based administration characteristic of more traditional models.

Orientation to Fundamental Structural Change. Rather than focus on individual adjustment or maintenance, a feminist administrator recognizes the necessity of modifying underlying structural conditions. "The personal is political" translates into recognition of how systemic factors underlie women's personal pain. Likewise, change is to be brought about collectively, not individually, because we are responsible to one another for our actions.[20] As societal conditions are changed, we change ourselves —which, in turn, modifies the structural conditions affecting both ourselves and our clients.

Study of Women's Organizations

Given this conceptual model of feminist organizations, the following section presents empirical findings on the extent to which such feminist characteristics exist in a sample of women's organizations. As was noted, research on the administration of women's organizations, specifically on the characteristics of feminist administration, has been limited. To begin to address this gap, the authors undertook an exploratory national study of women's organizations. Because of the limited knowledge base about women's organizations, we chose not to specify hypotheses or narrow the questions asked; instead, general questions were formulated to measure the agencies' structural and organizational dimensions. Open-ended questions, which allowed respondents to describe their organizations in their own words, were included to be consistent with a feminist research perspective.[21] These open-ended variables were later analyzed.

Selection of the Sample. A national pool of women's organizations was compiled from lists of women's organizations from women's commissions and bureaus in ten federal regions and from statewide women's commissions. The primary criterion for selecting a sample of organizations from these lists was that they focus on the delivery of services to women, that is, not be a women's publishing house, bookstore, coffee house, and so on. The sample of organizations meeting these criteria was stratified to select 20 organizations from each of the ten regions. After **171** pretesting, questionnaires were mailed to 200 women's organizations. Approximately 10 percent of the questionnaires were returned as "not deliverable," often because the organization no longer existed. In such cases, the missing organization was replaced by another from a similar geographic location to ensure national representation in the responses. A follow-up card was mailed three weeks after the first mailing. Of the 200 questionnaires, 70 (35 percent) were returned.

Variables.   Given the exploratory nature of the research, the first task was to describe this particular sample of women's organizations. *Descriptive variables* included (1) the organization's age, (2) source of funding, (3) size and composition of the staff, (4) public or private status, and (5) the nature of the population served. The *administrative style* was described in terms of the organizational structure, the decision-making process, and the values that women attempt to implement through the organizations. The *organizational structure* was measured by (1) the degree of hierarchy, (2) the existence of bylaws, (3) the reliance on external funding, and (4) the clarity of lines of authority. The *decision-making process* was measured by (1) the methods used to resolve conflicts, (2) staff supervision and evaluation, and (3) the manner by which policy decisions are made. The *values* were measured by (1) the organization's political orientation, (2) attempts to share power among staff and consumers (such as the rotation of tasks), and (3) differences between their stated norms and what they actually did in decision making. In addition, we were interested in whether women-run organizations had evolved through particular stages of organizational development; how certain critical factors, such as reliance on external organizations, affected their structure; and anticipated future changes.

Analysis of the Data.   A weighted score was devised to discriminate between hierarchical and consensual organizations, which we had envisioned as falling on a continuum. Variables were classified as either consensual or hierarchical. For instance, empowerment of clients was categorized as a consensual variable, and reliance on federal funding and having policy set by a board of directors were assumed to be hierarchical variables. Organizations were given a score for each of 28 variables (consensual = 1, hierarchical = 2). The scores were added to constitute a total weighted score that ranged from 28 (consensual) to 56 (hierarchical).

Chi-square tests of independence were conducted to determine whether there were significant differences in the values, structure, and decision-making styles of consensual and hierarchical organizations. No significant differences were found between the two types of organizations; either the weighted measure was not powerful enough to detect differences among organizations or the agencies were relatively homogeneous in their orientation.

In an effort to capture the diversity of administrative styles, open-ended responses were then analyzed from a randomly selected subsample of 35 organizations. Some of the responses from this analysis are included here to illustrate the dilemmas faced by many feminist administrators and the demands and constraints created by their organizational environments.

Findings. The organizations were relatively young (a mean of 7.7 years old) and small, with a mean of 4.7 full-time staff and 3.83 part-time staff. The number of volunteer staff ranged from 14 to 250, with a mean of 32.24. The majority of the organizations attempted to serve women in general (55 percent), with 31.7 percent focusing on women only; 11.7 percent on other specific populations, such as minority women; and 1.6 percent on both men and women.

The findings are presented in terms of the six components of a feminist administrative model: an orientation to fundamental structural change; the valuing of women's perspectives and experiences; a reconceptualization of power; principles of democratic structuring; the valuing of process; and wholeness and the elimination of false dichotomies. On the basis of these findings and the authors' review of the literature on feminist administration, the authors derived some principles for administering feminist organizations and implications for social work education, which are presented after the findings.

Orientation to fundamental structural change. The organizations' statements of purpose, and, when available, brochures, bylaws, and mission statements were reviewed to determine their orientation to fundamental structural change. An underlying organizational purpose—to support women and to serve women's needs—was uniform across the organizations; the respondents saw themselves as attaining their goals for women primarily through support (45.7 percent), counseling (21.7 percent), shelter (13.0 percent), education (8.7 percent), information/referral (6.5 percent), and political action (4.3 percent). Consistent with a feminist **173** approach, several organizations were multipurpose and did not categorize or separate services. For example, a counseling center aimed to "support the development of stable, productive, and satisfying lifestyles for women through counseling, support, education, referral, and work with women in crises." A few organizations stated that they were specifically concerned with changing the larger social system to have positive impact on women. A political action agency, for example, hoped "to secure the legal economic rights of women by monitoring the enforcement of civil rights laws, conducting public education and research projects, and supporting litigation." A rural agency aimed to end " 'plantationism' in the cane field...to better the living and working conditions of women sugarcane field workers."

Although most of the organizations did not explicitly state a goal of changing current structural conditions, they nevertheless viewed themselves as alternatives to existing systems and therefore as changing the underlying conditions faced by women. For example, shelters for victims of sexual assault and battering saw themselves as meeting a gap in services in the community and providing women with a critical alternative to the criminal justice and health care systems. In fact, many organizations were founded primarily because existing institutions were not addressing women's needs. For example, one organization wrote, "After ten of us got fired for taking the 'war on poverty' seriously, we looked and listened to hear and see the poorest of the poor and discovered a whole people hidden behind a curtain of sugarcane." One organization held a conference to demonstrate the need for women's services:

> The conference exceeded the wildest expectations. Over 400 women attended, and 70 more were turned away for lack of room. The conference clearly established that there was a client group with special needs, and that those needs were not presently being met.

Respondents' political orientation also was assumed to reflect their orientation to fundamental change. Although most respondents described their organizations as "feminist" (35.2 percent), several marked more than one political description. "Liberal" was the second most common response (11.7 percent), followed by "progressive" (5.6 percent) and "other" (5.6 percent). Those who marked the "other" category defined either the political stance of their members or staff or the climate of the community or institution to which they were accountable. For example, two respondents wrote:

> We operate on a collective basis, and the tone taken by the group is liberal feminist. Many of the members are frustrated radical feminists and socialist feminists. The campus is capital 'C' conservative, and for safety's sake we keep a low profile.
>
> . . . . .
>
> Volunteers are a diverse mixture of all; the staff is progressive, feminist, liberal, and the board is more conservative.

Valuing of women's perspectives and experiences and the reconceptualization of power. These characteristics are interrelated, because efforts to empower women reflect an underlying valuing of women's strengths and skills. As can be seen from the following statements, the valuing of women's perspectives and experiences through the empowerment of staff and clients was central to the feminist philosophy of most organizations.

> That is our whole focus, to increase/improve the empowerment of women.
>
> . . . . .
>
> We promote discovery of all women's power in programs, etc. Any of our workshops "zero in" on this issue: This is also a focus of peer counseling, to locate and use strengths.
>
> . . . . .
>
> We aim to make women aware of their rights and encourage them to use power.
>
> . . . . .
>
> Empowerment is the model we subscribe to.

By their very existence, feminist organizations that provide services explicitly responsive to women's needs are making a statement about valuing women's experiences.

Accordingly, these organizations valued the skills and experiences of women staff and consumers. One respondent stated, "We are a woman-run' agency—we have each had to learn how to handle leadership, encouraging and pushing each other." In one agency, "Each staff member creates [her] own job, [so that] you can do most anything you want here." Consumers were generally encouraged to be independent, to be responsible for themselves, and to realize their full potential. For example, "A woman can try anything and if she likes it and is good at it, she **175** can create a powerful place for herself. She will get a great deal of support." In another organization, "The women make their own decisions for their own lives. We never tell women what to do." Power was thus shared by the widest possible distribution of resources and by the granting of the ability to make decisions to those persons who would be most directly affected by them. *Principles of democratic structuring.* The extent to which their structure and decision-making process were hierarchical or consensual assumed to reflect an organization's adherence to and implementation of the principles of democratic structuring. Generally, most of the organizations expressed a commitment to both a consensual organizational style and the elimination of positions of power through collective decision making. In practice, they tended to be hierarchical. In fact, almost half the organizations (46.2 percent) described themselves as hierarchical in structure, compared to 42.3 percent that indicated either a cooperative, consensual, or collective structure. In relation to indicators of hierarchy, 73.3 percent of the organizations had a formal stated purpose; 59.3 percent, a board of directors; 36.7 percent, articles of incorporation; and 28.3 percent, written charters and bylaws. The tension between their commitment to sharing power collectively and the reality of hierarchical efficiency is reflected in the following statement:

> On paper one thing, in reality another. The center is set up with a general membership which makes decisions (general goals) and a steering committee of five people to deal with day-to-day administration. Task forces are to be set up to fund raise, do the newsletter, run a 24-hour Woman's Support Line, and so forth. In reality, it took five months to get four people together for a steering committee, no one attends general membership meetings, no one is presently doing a newsletter, and we are down to half the number of women necessary to keep the crisis line working. Decisions are supposed to be by consensus in the group. But many decisions have been made by staff or one or two other people individually.

Although participatory democracy was clearly valued, respondents frequently referred to the difficulty of collaborating fully on every decision.

Organizations that are committed to a consensual structure may resort to a hierarchy when the consensual process breaks down. This statement is an example, "I'd describe us as a modi-

176

Feminist Visions

fied consensus decision-making group. We try to rely on this process, but when the situation warrants, we fall back on hierarchical decision making." Such organizations may seek to be different from traditional hierarchies but are faced with daily practical constraints.

We found that organizations that frequently interfaced with large bureaucracies, such as university-affiliated women's centers, tended to segregate their hierarchical and consensual components according to whether they were interacting with other hierarchies. For example, "Our relation to the university is hierarchical (within administration) and our paid staff structure is hierarchical. But our activities are often cooperatively structured and we're able to do what we want to do."

Another indicator of the tension between hierarchical and consensual structures faced by these organizations is their reliance on a mixture of traditional public funding and independent funding sources. Dependence on public funds was as follows: local funding, 52.5 percent; state funding, 44.1 percent; federal funding, 37.3 percent; and county funding, 33.9 percent. Such dependence generally requires compliance with guidelines that presume a hierarchical structure. Some organizations deliberately rejected outside funding for this reason: "We have not sought federal funding to stay clear of strings." "We are considering dropping United Way money because they are trying to run our agency." "We dropped CETA to be free of its restrictions." "We decided to stop seeking money that would direct what we do." One agency summed up the dilemma created by funding constraints: "There are trade-offs whenever outside funding is obtained. Funding agencies have different agendas."

The sharing of tasks was one way in which most organizations attempted to structure their activities cooperatively or consensually. Over half (54.2 percent) rotated tasks among staff members. The processes for rotating tasks included the self-assignment of tasks according to competence, the use of cofacilitators for all support groups; the occasional shifting of coordinators of special areas, the rotation of scut work, the cross-training of counselors and clerical workers, rotation within the team responsible for a project; and the inclusion in written job descriptions of the statement that all staff were to be responsible for teaching others what they wished to learn and for learning from others all that they could. One collective had an extensive job-rotation plan:

177

An Alternative Administrative Style

Eight counselors rotate every three months among three standing committees: public relations, finance and legal, and maintenance. Each moves from the top of one committee (chair) to the bottom of the next and then works her way up again. The chairs of the three committees make up the Executive Committee, which is responsible for future planning and making sure nothing is left out. The only nonrotating positions are the person who takes all the calls and makes appointments and the bookkeeper.

Another agency rotated tasks as time permitted: "As needed and as women have time, tasks are presented at meetings. Some things slide if we do not have the womanpower, e.g., grant applications and cleaning. We basically run on a survival basis." Tasks were renegotiated in another agency: "Certain people are responsible for certain areas, but may trade or renegotiate any time. Also, as things change, people are given an opportunity to move into different, new areas." One agency was developing a new method for training volunteers to rotate tasks: "In our new structure, we hope to have project coordinators rotate by training volunteers under them with the specific intent of the volunteers becoming project coordinators. This way we hope not to burn out our volunteers and yet have people who *know* what to do."

In sum, although some of the organizations occasionally resorted to hierarchy, most were oriented to principles qualitatively different from the characteristics of bureaucracies. Their very existence represented an effort to realize wholly different values; in turn, these efforts resulted in the structural dilemma of how to mesh feminist values with traditional organizational constraints.

Valuing of process. One of the ways in which these organizations valued process was through their commitment to resolving their conflicts. The majority used relatively informal consensual approaches to conflict resolution, expecting either the affected individuals or the group to resolve conflicts. For example, "We do not have an ideal conflict resolution system. It is usually worked out in the group of persons involved." Formal grievance procedures and committees were used by only 25 percent and 20 percent of the respondents, respectively. Some used a mixture of informal and formal approaches. For example, "There are written procedures, the first step is to discuss directly with the person with whom you have a grievance. If it is not

Feminist Visions

resolvable, then a third party is asked to help facilitate better communication."

Although most respondents emphasized the importance of settling conflicts, unresolved conflicts were a frequent problem. "Our biggest problem to date has been interpersonal/political conflict that the group leaves particular individuals to work out. As a result, issues don't get raised and conflicts are rarely settled." In another example, "At times women have quit. Conflict is always difficult and is usually handled between the women involved. We are not very experienced in dealing with it in other ways."

Suggestions for more effective ways to deal with conflict ranged from "less hierarchy or less management and more straightforward treatment" to "having a solid decision-making structure with clear lines of rights and responsibilities for staff and volunteers." One organization systematically trained staff in conflict resolution: "In our staff training, we teach how to confront people, how to deal with conflict. We also look at the tactics we as women use on each other to block communication so that we can get beyond them." Some respondents recommended that conflict is best handled between individuals. "Conflict should be dealt with openly; too often it is not. We should grow with conflict and respect the other's beliefs and ideology. We cannot afford to alienate any women. The problem should be dealt with as soon as it happens and in private so those involved won't be embarrassed or hurt." In contrast, other respondents felt that group meetings, sometimes with a facilitator, were the most productive means to resolve conflict. "This conflict continues to be the biggest barrier to productive work—ignoring conflict *or* hierarchical directives. Our first suggestion would be development of group decision making and regular group evaluation of project process and product."

Staff evaluation methods also reflected the organizations' valuing of process and the empowerment of staff. A combination of self-evaluation (45.8 percent) and group evaluation (62.7 percent), such as peer evaluation, staff meetings, and personnel committees, was the most frequent method.

Decision-making methods also exemplified the organizations' commitment to a democratic structure and process. Administrators (42.4 percent) or staff (45.8 percent) made almost half the agencies' policy decisions, frequently on a committee basis and then cooperatively with board approval. The following quotes reflect efforts to equalize the decision-making process: **179**

An Alternative Administrative Style

> We are a modified hierarchy with decision making
> largely accomplished through consensus and collective
> problem solving. As executive director, I do not impose
> authority, but rather act as a team leader who coordi-
> nates, moderates, enlightens.
>
> . . . . .
>
> There is a lot of team decision-making involvement at
> staff and board levels.
>
> . . . . .
>
> Policy decisions are made by group consensus after
> presentations of various proposals are made by the
> appropriate committee.

Even in hierarchical organizations, efforts were made to involve
staff in most decisions. For example, in a university-affiliated
agency,

> all decisions we can make (those not directed by the
> university) are made by staff collectively and staff
> members (collective members) make policy decisions
> that we have to run by the deans for "approval."

Wholeness and the elimination of false dichotomies. One of the most
striking findings was that most organizations did not view
themselves solely as consensual or hierarchical in structure. The
research team had implicitly assumed that most women-run
organizations would define their structure and decision-making
processes as consensual or cooperative. However, most of the
respondents indicated a diverse and flexible ability to live with
the constant tension between their feminist values and the
modified organizational structures needed to get the job done.
They pragmatically recognized that the degree of emphasis on
hierarchy or collectivity varied with either the tasks to be performed or with the organizational interface, as can be seen in
the following statements:

> We are vaguely hierarchical within consensual
> relationships between the director and the advisory
> board. We have a hierarchical relationship between the
> program and college administration and we have
> combined hierarchy/consensus of work-study students.
>
> . . . . .
>
> We've been role models in trying to establish feminist
> management. We are designing our philosophy of
> management as we go, as well as organizational
> development.

180

The respondents also adapted to the trade-offs between their feminist commitments and the need to increase in size and acquire outside funding:

> By giving up staff time to devote to the network, there was a payoff in getting state money. But a large staff meant no more consensus.
>
> . . . . .
>
> By moving from collective to hierarchy, we had more staff, clients served, diversity of programs. But we lost other things.

Being able to adapt, to change, and to develop in itself reflected an ability to see the total picture and to synthesize rather than to fragment and set up artificial boundaries. Recognition of the need to synthesize was expressed as follows:

> I would put more study/thought at the basis of our organization. We cater to feelings, identify them, and use them to become powerful women. I'd like to see thought take on an equal importance.

Most of the organizations contained internal dilemmas created by efforts to integrate the old and the new, the innovative and the traditional. These dilemmas, in turn, were expressed as the need to integrate process and product, flexibility and predictability, intuition and rationality.[22] Yet most respondents appeared to have developed the ability to understand and tolerate these dilemmas as part of a long-range process of change.

Principles for Administering Feminist Organizations

The findings of the study suggested that the challenge to these organizations' long-run survival is to maintain their commitment to principles that are qualitatively different from those of bureaucracies when faced with the daily realities of increased size, task or process constraints, and funding demands. The remainder of this chapter discusses the implications of the study findings, both for administering feminist organizations and for developing social work curricula. Although the possibility was not directly addressed by our research, these feminist administrative principles may be generalized beyond women's organizations—for example, to ethnic minority agencies.

181

An Alternative Administrative Style

As the study indicated, when women's organizations increase in size, they face a number of dilemmas. Collective decision making tends to be more time consuming; meetings grow in length as it becomes more difficult for everyone to contribute to decisions. Developing structural arrangements that save time and ensure effective collective control is a major challenge. In our sample, some organizations appeared to have achieved such arrangements by setting up small work groups or committees, open to all who wished to join and linked by two-way communication with the rest of the organization. Other organizations recognized the likelihood of dissent around decision making; instead of requiring consensus in meetings, they agreed that two or three votes against a proposal could defeat it. Negative votes, however, had to be reached by the "I can't live with it" principle.

As organizations grow and staff and consumers change, mechanisms need to be developed that allow the structure to adapt. Flexibility becomes a critical attribute. The structure evolves, rather than being fixed at the beginning. As Kanter and Zurcher noted, when process is valued, stability and permanence are seen as less important than the potential for growth and change.[23]

As organizations increase in size, the diversity of the membership undoubtedly multiplies. These individual differences, however, can result in unequal amounts of influence that are counter to collective ideals. When everyone does not devote the same amount of time and energy, people may feel imposed on, interpersonal tensions may increase, and conflicts in a large group become more difficult to resolve.

Most feminist organizations affirm the value of diversity and the resultant conflicts yet have difficulties in dealing with these conflicts. Strategies that have apparently been effective in resolving conflicts include utilizing outside facilitators and structuring specific periods to deal with conflict, such as retreats, meeting time for criticism and self-criticism, or regular group evaluations. Another effective mechanism is to construct methods of expressing conflict in ways that are not personally harmful.

The task versus process dilemma surfaced frequently for organizations that were committed to collectivity but that needed to regulate their activities more smoothly and efficiently to accomplish their service goals. Once organizations have clarified their goals, they apparently need to strive for a balance of task and process, because, over the long run, one cannot be made more important than the other. Likewise, the process issues that

Feminist Visions

impede the accomplishment of tasks need to be distinguished. Feminist organizations can set realistic benchmarks for achieving their goals while still maintaining their visions.[24]

A variety of techniques can be used to ensure that attention is given both to process in decision making and to completion of the work on schedule. These techniques include brainstorming ideas, structuring opportunities for oral and written input, small group discussions of complex issues, and rotation of the chairperson or facilitator. On the one hand, process can be scheduled as a priority. For example, regular periods can be set aside for feedback about feelings and reactions. On the other hand, structuring specific sessions to review goals, objectives, and priorities and to discuss the progress of various strategies toward objectives keeps attention focused on the task without necessarily eliminating process time.[25]

Perhaps the greatest dilemma for feminist organizations is to pursue funding without displacing goals. Among the organizations surveyed, the most widely acknowledged and desired change was to be able to increase their funding base and thereby stabilize themselves. Questions about resources basic to feminist organizations need to be raised not only in terms of how to get the money, but of how to mobilize the membership and generate the support necessary to implement the program. Resources besides money, such as personal and technical skills, contacts, and additional services, need to be identified and maximized. Staff incentives can be established, such as flexible hours, the sharing of child care, or participation in special programs or training, to compensate partially for low salaries and funding uncertainties.

Obtaining outside funding also raises the issue of boundaries with the external environment. The creation of networks among organizations with similar values appears to be one way to interface effectively with the larger environment and to work together rather than compete for resources. Feminist organizations also need to be able to present their case in a way that can be understood by outsiders without losing their integrity.

The hierarchical tendencies and dilemmas faced by organizations in the sample need not be interpreted as signs of failure. As Kanter and Zurcher indicated, the effectiveness of alternative organizations needs to be evaluated over a long time rather than labeling their difficulties as not "making it" in the short run.[26] Furthermore, the hierarchical elements incorporated by alternative organizations may not be antithetical to their deeply held **183** cooperative values. Many of these organizations may have attained consensual democracy—an organizational form that represents a stable compromise between the values and rewards of collectivity and the necessities of existing in the real world of health and social services.[27] By developing consensual forms that meet some of the needs that hierarchies fulfill (such as committees, task forces, rules, and procedures), feminist organizations may avoid moving completely to the hierarchical end of the continuum. The essential issue is whether the processes and values of the alternative organizations lead to the desired outcome, even if the ideal state is never reached.[28]

Implications for Professional Education

Content on feminist administration must be included in professional education. Courses on administration in many schools of social work present traditional, relatively hierarchical models and are technical in their problem-solving approach. Most social workers, however, interact in some capacity with women's organizations and thus can benefit from understanding alternative organizational structures and the critical issues faced by feminist administrators.

Students committed to feminist values often struggle with questions about their own administrative role and identity. Administration courses should provide opportunities for students to clarify their values and assumptions and determine their congruence with those of the organization. Some administration courses may imply that nontraditional organizations are nonprofessional and, in some way, inferior. But "nontraditional" does not equal "nonprofessional." Nontraditional organizations should be presented to students as part of an organizational continuum for service delivery from which professionals may choose, according to their values and preferences.

Administration courses also need to affirm women's strengths, processes, and experiences, as well as those of other oppressed groups who have attempted to develop more responsive programs and services. Such affirmation would counter the slice-of-the-pie model to which women and other oppressed groups are advised to adapt if they are to succeed in male-defined administrative positions. For example, feminist administrators should be invited as guest speakers and presented as role models to students.

184   Most important, students need opportunities to articulate

the issues raised throughout this chapter and to discuss them in terms of personal and institutional relationships. Through this process, changes may ultimately occur in the relationships of men and women, in the styles of administration that are exercised, and in the climate and structure of human service organizations.

notes

Cheryl Ellsworth, Ruth Ann Ruff, and Joan Tucker collected data for and helped conceptualize the study on which this chapter is based while they were graduate students, School of Social Work, University of Washington, Seattle.

1. J. S. Chafetz, "Women in Social Work," *Social Work*, 17 (September 1972), pp. 12–18; J. Szakacs, "Survey Indicates Social Work Women Losing Ground in Leadership Ranks," *NASW News*, 22 (April 1977), p. 12; and M. B. Curlee and F. B. Raymond, "The Female Administrator: Who Is She?" *Administration in Social Work*, 2 (Fall 1978), pp. 307–317.

2. R. Chernesky, "Women Administrators in Social Work," in E. Norman and A. Mancuso, *Women's Issues and Social Work Practice* (Itasca, Ill.: F. E. Peacock Publishers, 1980), pp. 241–262.

3. R. Mede, R. Hefrew, and B. Oleshansky, "A Model of Sex-Role Transcendence," *Journal of Social Issues*, 32 (1976), pp. 197–205.

4. R. M. Kanter, "Communes in Cities," in J. Case and R. C. R. Taylor, eds., *Coops, Communes and Collectives* (New York: Pantheon Books, 1979), pp. 112–136.

5. G. Hollek and W. Albion, *Alternatives to Community Mental Health* (Boston: Beacon Press, 1975).

6. Case and Taylor, eds., *Coops, Communes and Collectives*.

7. J. Rothschild-Whitt, "The Collective Organization: An Alternative to Rational-Bureaucratic Models," *American Sociological Review*, 44 (1979), pp. 509–527.

8. C. D. Mawson, "Women's Centers: A Critical Appraisal and a Case Study," *Personnel and Guidance Journal*, 58 (September 1979), pp. 61–65; M. Morgenbesser et al., "The Evolution of Three Alternative Social Service Agencies," *Catalyst*, 11 (1981), pp. 71–83; P. Parsons and C. Hodne, "A Collective Experiment in Women's Health," *Science for the People* (July–August 1982), pp. 9–13; and L. O'Sullivan, "Organizing for Impact," *Quest: A Feminist Quarterly*, 2 (Winter 1976), pp. 68–80.

9. L. Hirschhorn, "Alternative Services and the Crises of the Professions," in Case and Taylor, eds., *Coops, Communes and Collectives*.

10. N. Hartsock, "Feminist Theory and Revolutionary Strategy," in **185**

Z. Eisenstein, ed., *Capitalist Patriarchy and the Case for Socialist Feminism* (New York: Monthly Review Press, 1978), pp. 71–73.

11. J. Blanton, "Women Consulting with Women: Feminist Ideology and Organizational Structure and Process," pp. 3–19, paper presented at the Annual Convention of the American Psychological Association, Los Angeles, Calif., 1981; N. Hooyman, "Redefining Models of Power and Administration Styles," *Social Development Issues*, 2 (Winter 1978), pp. 46–54; Kanter, "Communes in Cities"; J. B. Miller, *Women and Power* (Wellesley, Mass.: Stone Center for Developmental Services and Studies, 1982); and Rothschild-Whitt, "The Collective Organization."

12. P. Johnson, "Women and Power: Towards a Theory of Effectiveness," *Journal of Social Issues*, 32 (1976), pp. 99–110.

13. C. Bunch, "Women Power: The Courage to Lead, the Strength to Follow, and the Sense to Know the Difference," *Ms.* (July 1980).

14. R. Tannenbaum and W. Schmidt, "How to Choose a Leadership Pattern," *Harvard Business Review*, 36 (1958), pp. 95–101.

15. Hooyman, "Redefining Models of Power and Administration Styles"; and J. Rothschild, "Taking Our Future Seriously," *Quest: A Feminist Quarterly*, 2 (1976), pp. 17–30.

16. J. Freeman (Joreen), "The Tyranny of Structurelessness," in A. Koedt, E. Levine, and A. Rapone, eds., *Radical Feminism* (New York: Quadrangle, 1973), pp. 285–306.

17. N. Hartsock, "Staying Alive," *Quest: A Feminist Quarterly*, 3 (1976–77), pp. 2–14.

18. G. Crow, "The Process/Product Split," *Quest: A Feminist Quarterly*, 4 (1978), pp. 15–23.

19. M. J. Lupton and A. Thompson, "Conflict on the Journal," *Women in Conflict*, 6 (1979), pp. 48–51.

20. M. McCormack, "A Feminist Perspective," *Social Policy*, 8 (November–December 1977), pp. 18–24.

21. See Joan M. Cummerton's chapter, "A Feminist Perspective on Research: What Does It Help Us to See?" in this book, pp. 80–100.

22. D. Riddle, "Integrating Process and Product," *Quest: A Feminist Quarterly*, 4 (1978), pp. 23–32.

23. R. M. Kanter and L. A. Zurcher, "Evaluating Alternatives and Alternative Valuing," *Journal of Applied Behavioral Sciences*, 9 (1973), p. 381.

24. Blanton, "Women Consulting with Women."

25. Ibid.

26. Kanter and Zurcher, "Evaluating Alternatives and Alternative Valuing."

27. Hollek and Albion, *Alternatives to Community Mental Health.*

28. Kanter and Zurcher, "Evaluating Alternatives and Alternative Valuing."

Marie Weil

women, community, and organizing

O
rganizing by women for
social justice, equality, and
human liberation is not a
new phenomenon. Women
have been powerful organizers in political and social action,
union, civil rights, human rights, and peace movements, and in
the development of social and community services, as well as in
the women's movement. This chapter focuses on feminist issues
in community organization and explores the role of women as
organizers. Furthermore, it develops a framework for analyzing
women's organizing work in general, as well as feminist community organization, articulating feminist principles for organizing.

A feminist framework for organizing integrates methods and
strategies for action with practice principles that embody feminist
values and approaches. For feminists, the framework's philo-
sophical-theoretical foundation is critical because it shapes the
questions that are posed, determines the problems that are identified as central, and sculpts the strategies for movement and
change. While political-theoretical orientations may differ among
feminists, there are strong commonalities related to the need for
altering patriarchal structures and processes. **187**

The entire history and development of feminism can be seen as a process of community organizing—from development of critical consciousness regarding the status of women and the oppression of minorities, to demystifying and reclaiming history,[1] through the development of social and political action movements, including the creation of specialized organizations and programs to serve the needs of women.

Preliminary Definitions and Orientations

Before analyzing general models of community practice and specific feminist approaches, operating definitions are needed to focus discussion on the complex issues this chapter treats.

Women are born female; we create ourselves as women through a social process of interaction of the self with family, peers, society, and culture; and we are feminists as we commit ourselves to the equality of women, to the elimination of oppression, to the empowerment of women and minorities, and to the creation of a nonsexist society.

Community can refer to any of several means of identifying connections among people. It can connote (a) the relationships among residents in a specific locale, or (b) the relationships and activities of people committed to a particular interest, concern, or problem—that is, a community of interest or a functional community. Both conceptions are grounded in the idea of community as a kind of social organism. Alternatively, it can connote (c) a particular political unit or power base.[2] Common to all three types of community is an assumption of some basis of shared concern or shared perception that can draw people together.

Organizing refers to the process of pulling together to create a functional whole.[3] It may indicate the establishment of an organization dedicated to a particular purpose or may outline and orchestrate a strategy for achieving certain goals.

Community organization was "formally recognized as a distinct field within social work in 1962"[4] and has increasingly been included in social work curricula. The mainstream community organization literature in social work has typically followed Rothman's typology of community organization.[5] Rothman identified three models: (a) locality development—incorporating goals of "self-help," community capacity and integration (process goals)"; (b) social planning—problem solving with regard to

Feminist Visions

substantive community problems (task goals)"; and (c) social action with goals related to "shifting of power relationships and resources; basic institutional change (task or process goals)."[6] As Ecklein noted, however, all social work–based community organizers are

> ...concerned with advancing the interests of disadvantaged groups, with improving social conditions, with the delivery of needed services, with redistribution of power and influence, with enhancement of the coping mechanisms of target populations, and with strengthening community participation and integration.[7]

The most recent (1985) definition of community practice, by Taylor and Roberts, is an overarching rubric encompassing practice models and theoretical orientations in the following five areas: (1) community development; (2) political action—pluralism and participation; (3) program development and coordination; (4) planning; and (5) community liaison.[8] Each of these models can, however, still embrace Rothman's earlier definition of community organization as a strategy of "purposive community change."[9] Specific goals, strategies, target systems, and action systems will change to accord with the particular model, but all are related to process of planned change.

Women and Community Organization

Many of the pioneers in social work and community organization on both local and national levels were women. Major aspects of the development of social work from the social reform movements of the late nineteenth century were led by such women as Jane Addams, Dorothea Dix, Julia Lathrop, Edith and Grace Abbott, Lillian Wald, Sophonisba Breckinridge, and Florence Kelley. Brandwein and Conway documented that women played major roles in social action, as well as managing complex programs.[10]

However, the place of women within the two major traditions of community organization in social work was markedly different. Brandwein comments that men did dominate in the conservative, social maintenance tradition of the community chests and councils, which were tied to the sanctions and models of the business community. Yet women played a larger role even in this arena than they are typically credited for.[11] In contrast to the tradition of the Charity Organization Societies and coun- **189** cils, the social reform tradition of social work, emerging from the settlement movement, "focused on social legislation, neighborhood organizing, and advocacy for the poor and other oppressed groups"; within this tradition women were very visible and maintained many leadership positions.[12]

Social work's own drive for professionalization in the 1920s related not only to clinical aspirations but to emphasis on service and cost efficiency and adoption of business management methods. This shift brought more men into leadership positions in the planning and service coordination sector, and women in this field "tended to be confined to the smaller community councils with low budgets or in planning functions closely related to clinical services."[13] Although male administrators worked with business constituencies, women continued to lead the way in "neighborhood organizing, locality development, working with volunteers, and developing services for clients."[14] This sector of community organizing has been viewed as having less status, but it is the clear descendant of the social reform movements and can be seen to have close affinities with early and current feminist orientations.

Brandwein documented the displacement of women in community organization as beginning in the late 1950s.[15] Despite women's long history in community organization and social reform, the macro-practice field within social work has come to be dominated by men in both administrative and community practice. For a period during the late 1950s and 1960s, a fairly common point of view in social work education linked the continued life of the profession and its relative professional status to its ability to attract men into its ranks.[16] Unfortunately, the effort to develop opportunity for men coincided with the advancement of macro-practice, especially administrative and planning methods, and men quickly emerged from the ranks on a fast track to leadership in community and administrative positions considered to be more compatible with societal expectations regarding male sex-role behavior.

Another factor in this change relates to some of the patterns of male dominance that developed in the civil rights and antiwar movements of the 1960s.[17] For a variety of reasons, macro-practice came to be viewed as a male preserve in social work. Kadushin even published an article that argued for the need to maintain administration and macro-practice as a male domain so that men would not feel discomforted by their entrance into a profession

190

Feminist Visions

preponderantly female and viewed as a "women's field."[18] The efforts to provide parity for men in professional social work education evolved into a pattern of male dominance in administration, community organization, and teaching. This pattern of male dominance has had a negative impact on the treatment of women's concerns and feminist issues in macro-practice curricula.

Feminist issues in community practice abound but have been largely ignored or underrepresented in the mainstream literature of community organization. Feminist thinking offers many positive parallels with basic social work theories of community organization, which emphasize values and methods grounded in democratic process, participatory democracy, civil and social rights, and social action. Many early leaders and workers in the development of community-based group practice and social and environmental action, as well as mental health and social justice, were women who in their lives and work embodied feminist principles. Those important women organizers and the movements with which they were involved include:

- The anti-slavery or abolitionist movement—Harriet Tubman, Sojourner Truth, Sarah and Angelina Grimké
- The mental health movement to provide care for the mentally ill—Dorothea Dix, Josephine Shaw Lowell
- The suffragist movement—Susan B. Anthony, Elizabeth Cady Stanton, Lucretia Mott, Lucy Stone
- The settlement movement—Jane Addams, Lillian Wald
- The labor reform movement—Florence Kelley and members of the National Women's Trade Union League
- The maternal and child health and child welfare movements—Lillian Wald, Julia Lathrop, Sophonisba Breckinridge
- The union movement and labor movement—Mary Van Kleeck, Emma Goldman, Rose Chernin, Frances Perkins
- Rights for blacks—National League for the Protection of Colored Women
- Legislative action and equal rights—Jane Addams, Florence Kelley, Alice Paul
- The civil rights movement and welfare rights movement—Fannie Lou Hamer, Angela Davis
- La Raza, United Farm Workers' Movement, and the Mexican American Legal Defense and Education Fund—Delores Huerta, Wilma Martinez, and Antonia Hernandez
- The older women's and men's movement—Maggie Kuhn, Gray Panthers, and OWL (Older Women's League)

Women, Community, and Organizing

- The women's movement—Theorists: Simone de Beauvoir, *The Second Sex;* Betty Friedan, *The Feminine Mystique;* Kate Millett, *Sexual Politics:* and Gloria Steinem, *Ms.* magazine. Groups: National Organization for Women, National Women's Political Caucus, Women's Action Alliance
- The peace movement—Jane Addams and Jeanette Rankin; Women Strike for Peace, Women's International League for Peace and Freedom, Women's Pentagon Action; Helen Caldicott, Physicians for Social Responsibility

Despite a rich and proud heritage of female organizers and movement leaders, the field of community organization, in both its teaching models and its major exponents, has been a male-dominated preserve, where, even though values are expressed in terms of participatory democracy, much of the focus within the dominant practice methods has been nonsupportive or antithetical to feminism. Strategies have largely been based on "macho-power" models, manipulativeness, and zero-sum gamesmanship.

This situation is reflected in the mainstream literature of community organization, where it is rare to find feminist case studies, a focus on organizing for and by women, or models employing feminist principles in organizing. Often this oversight extends even to the exclusion of the women's movement in discussions of social action. What is needed is attention to feminist ideology and action, as well as examination of how feminist practice is similar to and different from other forms of community organization. It is critical to develop and disseminate feminist models of community practice and organizing that focus on both women's issues and broader issues of social service and social justice. Continuous social action on behalf of the rights of women and other oppressed groups is needed, and feminist approaches have much to offer these efforts.

In order to develop feminist models for community organization, we need to focus on two subjects that have been largely ignored in the mainstream community organization literature: (a) women as organizers in general community practice and (b) women organizers and women's organizations focused on specific women's issues—women considered as a community of interest. The issues and problems encountered in these two practice sectors are different in several ways.

Women and General Community Organizing.   The first sector, women working as organizers in any general community organization, gives rise to a variety of issues that flow from the assumption

Feminist Visions

of male dominance in political, organizational, and community structure. History indicates that even when social change is stimulated by revolution, women assume large roles in development and organizing in the early stages, but are moved back into more traditional roles as postrevolutionary society stabilizes.[19] Whether in union organizing, social agency networks, academia, or community political action, a female organizer must inevitably be conscious of the social reality pointed out by Simone de Beauvoir that she is likely to be identified as the "other."[20] She is at risk of being (a) distrusted for being female, (b) disparaged for being aggressive or not "appropriately feminine" in terms of traditional gender role expectations, or (c) treated as the token or exceptional woman—usually defined as one who looks like a woman, but thinks like a man. Any one of these positions can be damaging, not only to the organizer, but to the cause to which she is committed.

Women organizers as formal or informal leaders in a group or organization must always be conscious of and examine the reactions of others within and outside their group in terms of overt or covert sexism. They must balance attention to these issues with attention to the general strategy and social change goals.

To function effectively as a woman organizer in community practice, one needs a heightened feminist consciousness, as well as the recognition that one will continually be tested as a woman and as an organizer. When feminists are involved in general community organization or social change, they must always work to include and expand feminist agendas. They must also maintain a dual focus with regard to both process and tasks, seeking to integrate feminist goals and approaches into the general problem-solving strategy. This approach requires conscious and consistent effort to shape goals, strategies, and roles so that they approach consistency with feminist values and orientations. The woman involved in general community practice as a feminist carries the risks of the boundary spanner. She will need to maintain ties in the feminist community for support and analysis, but will need to be able to function independently in the general community practice arena, which may be either tolerant of or overtly resistant to feminist ideology.

A feminist organizing model is required, in general community issues, that acknowledges and incorporates the need to deal with sexism as well as general issues of process facilitation and task accomplishment. In addition, models or a typology of models for feminist organizing around women's issues, women's organizations, and services for women are needed.

Women, Community, and Organizing

Women and Feminist Organizing.   The central issue in feminist organizing and organizations is how to embody and carry out feminist values and principles in action strategies. The values and experiences of women form the basis for all feminist orientations and approaches to social change. Accepting that premise necessitates a heterogeneous rather than a homogeneous conception of women's realities. Differences in demographics as well as political and social points of view interact with values to shape our interpretations of social reality. Understanding differences allows for building feminist coalitions grounded in common feminist commitments, such as ending sexual harassment, rape, and physical abuse; allowing for reproductive freedom; being able to choose a partner of either sex; and having the opportunity to participate fully in public life.[21]

Feminist viewpoints extend across a continuum on which one's ideological placement is a function of one's life experiences, demographics, political involvements, and education.[22] Four theoretical models for organizing women as a community of interest are the liberal, socialist, and radical models and the feminist perspective articulated by women of color.

When feminists are engaged in organizing and in developing programs and services to meet the needs of women as a community of interest, they may operate with any (or a combination) of the orienting frameworks and action approaches grounded in a particular feminist analytical framework. These frameworks indicate the specific goals, emphases, strategies, and action systems that stem from the particular ideologies and organizing perspectives of feminists who may define themselves as liberal, socialist, radical, or women of color. Table 1 (pp. 195–196) illustrates the particular emphases of the major feminist frameworks and lists the common components of feminist organizing that they all share. Because tolerance and the valuing of diversity are intrinsic feminist elements, each of the frameworks for organizing women leads to common feminist goals of equality and the empowerment of women.

Mainstream and Feminist Practice Arenas

Feminist organizers may practice in general community settings or in specifically feminist-oriented organizations and programs. For either mainstream or feminist practice arenas, the five basic community practice models detailed by Taylor and Roberts are relevant.[23] As noted in Table 2 (pp. 198–201), these include program devel-

Feminist Visions

Table 1
Women As a Community of Interest: Frameworks and Approaches

Model Components	Frameworks and Approaches			
	Liberal	Socialist	Radical	Women of Color
1. Goals and focus in organizing	Equal rights and individual liberty. Equality of opportunity, development of egalitarian gender relations. Social reform. Consciousness raising on effects of sexism.	Elimination of sexism and class oppression.	Elimination of patriarchy—meeting common human needs—creation and celebration of women's culture. Empowerment of women.	Elimination of all human oppression. Elimination of discrimination related to race, class, and gender. Solidarity within groups and among minority and other oppressed groups.
2. Assumption about causation of sexism and oppression	Sex-role socialization.	Political and economic institutions of society (capitalism and patriarchy).	Patriarchy—male power and privilege.	Racism, sexism, and class discrimination as interlocking causative factors of oppression.
3. Orientation to power structure	Gain power for women in institutions and develop institutions more responsive to feminist approaches.	Need for revolutionary social and political change.	Resist patriarchy and create a women's culture. Revolution as process.	Rejection of political and social oppression. Rejection of all biological determinism. Rejection of institutionalized racism and sexism.
4. Emphasis on strategy for change	Reeducation of public to eliminate sex-role stereotyping. Elimination of discrimination in employment. Legislative lobbying. Local political and social organizing. Local, regional, and national political action and policy action.	Analysis and action related to economic production, sexuality, reproduction, and socialization of children. Advocacy for women. Strategies to align with and advocate for other oppressed groups.	Redefinition of social relations and creation of a woman-centered culture. Emphasis on creative dimensions of women's lives. Emphasis on process and connections. Personal growth and empowerment through personal and political action.	Articulating feminist frameworks for women of color. Connecting feminism to racial and economic oppression. Building solidarity within oppressed groups. Supporting development and advancement of minority groups. Emphasis on common humanity and needs as well as recognition and support of the uniqueness of cultures and subcultures.
5. Emphasis on tactics and techniques for social change	Political and social action primarily focused within the established political and economic system.	Analysis and praxis—analysis of common grounds for oppression, and efforts to establish collective means to solve community and individual problems.	Articulating and building on women's capacities. Reclaim women's history. Analyze and validate women's experiences and perspectives.	Education, reeducation, Concentration on development of political and social positions that resist all forms of oppression.

Table 1
(Continued)

Model Components	Frameworks and Approaches			
	Liberal	Socialist	Radical	Women of Color
5. (Continued)	Development of broad-based coalitions and large membership. Development of local action networks connected to regional and national associations. Development of a national presence to articulate women's issues, and lobbying for equal rights.		Connection of the personal to the political. Empowerment of women. Emphasis on process and consciousness raising.	Building solidarity within groups. Replacing negative stereotypes of women of color and minority groups with careful analysis of capacities, strengths, and direction. Reclaiming history. Consciousness raising. Building sisterhood among women of color and other women who recognize the triple threats of racism, sexism, and poverty.
6. Major roles of change agents	Local, regional, and national level lobbying. Policy analysis and alternative policy development. Local and national political action on emerging issues. Public education and reeducation. Individual and group development through consciousness raising and mutual support.	Education, analysis, active involvement in labor activities and support of other oppressed groups. Articulation of women's issues. Development of alternative programs and services.	Analysis. Development of collectives related to services for women, support for women, women's music, arts and crafts, and literature. Definition and expansion of women's culture.	Education, analysis, consciousness raising. Redefinition of women of color. Development of political and social analysis and action frameworks. Preservation and further development of own culture. Development of groups, programs, and services to meet the needs of oppressed groups. Development of alternative programs and supports.
7. Action systems— mediums of change	Local networks to respond to emerging issues. Regional and national associations to respond to issues and to support local and national action. Mutual support and consciousness-raising groups for individual and group development.	Women's study, action, and service developing collectives. Alliances with other groups around common issues.	Collectives and small groups— emphasis on egalitarianism and shared power. Building enabling systems and mutual support. Building liberation through one's own actions.	Small groups or collectives focused on individual and political development of particular oppressed groups. Action within minority communities to build solidarity and promote social and economic development. Building coalitions and solidarity among oppressed groups.

opment and coordination; social planning; community liaison; community development; and pluralism, participation, and political empowerment. To utilize and participate effectively in these models, feminists must first analyze their practice environment and then incorporate feminist issues and roles into their own and the agency's work.

The feminist perspective articulated in Table 2 emphasizes reconceptualizing and sharing power. It furthers the democratization of macro-practice methods by emphasizing pluralism, participation, and shared decision making. In addition, the feminist perspective stresses advocacy for women and other oppressed groups and is oriented toward human liberation.

Inclusion of feminist issues and development of roles for women in these general models can assist in ensuring the following issues are addressed in community practice models: (a) empowering women and vulnerable populations; (b) demystifying the planning process; (c) diminishing power/status differentials; (d) emphasizing process; (e) clarifying the value bases of practice models and methods; (f) acting to attain the elimination of sexism, racism, and class bias; (g) questioning power structures and redefining power; and (h) establishing belief and action systems necessary for structural and institutional change.[24] A feminist perspective strengthens these models to ensure that women, minorities, and other vulnerable populations can exercise their rights as citizens and contribute to the development of society.

These generic community practice models have been adapted and implemented by feminist practitioners and organizers to develop services and programs focused on women as a specific target population and a community of interest. Feminist community practice and services may function as a specialized part of the mainstream service sector or may operate in the rapidly expanding arena of alternative services aimed specifically at women. Programs and organizations such as the Peer Consultation Project of the Southern California Rape Prevention and Study Center (SCRPSC),[25] the Family Violence Project of Jewish Family Services of Los Angeles,[26] Women Helping Women[27] in Los Angeles, the Los Angeles Commission on Assaults Against Women, the National Welfare Rights Organization, Coalition for the Medical Rights of Women, Women's Pentagon Action, National Network of Hispanic Women, and National Organization for Women all exemplify various aspects of feminist principles and commitments and community organizing. **197**

Table 2
Models of Community Organizing and Feminist Issues

Current Community Practice Models*	Incorporation of Feminist Issues and Roles into Models

Program Development and Coordination

Incorporating mediative and political processes to bring about implementation of social program and plans, and developing program coordination. Focused on a specific target population, but primary constituency is professionals and agencies. Change focus is on full range of political and organizational interests related to a particular issue. Roles in identifying needs, designing programs, consensus building, public relations for functional communities, lobbying, and education of the public on specific issues (Kurzman, 1985).

Broadening program development foci to attend to special needs of women, particularly to the needs of women who are especially vulnerable because of health, mental health or disabling conditions, or racism or poverty.

Ensuring that women's issues are considered in the development of service networks and systems for service coordination.

Giving attention to sexism as it is experienced by professional women working in the service system and to the impact of sexism, racism, and poverty on women who are service consumers or potential consumers.

Strengthening connections and collaboration between mainstream service systems and alternative feminist and minority community programs.

Assisting in development of and advocacy for community-based and culturally sensitive services for women and minorities.

Developing women's networks and support groups for women involved in service delivery with emphasis on incorporating feminist values and principles into the operation of service systems.

Social Planning

Developing plans or forecasting future conditions. Research and technological focus and skills. Use of formal structures and processes to build support for outcomes intended to be logical, rational, and beneficial. Focus on application of technical skills in planning process whether role is "neutral," "transactive," or "political" in relation to sponsors' or constituencies' expectations (Rothman and Zald, 1985).

Applying technical skills and research skills in analyzing specific service needs of women, children, vulnerable populations, and oppressed populations.

Grounding planning approaches in target populations' experiences. Validating and giving credence to women's and other client groups' appraisal of need.

Working toward democratizing planning processes.

Strengthening consideration of and integrating cultural, ethnic, and sexual preference issues in service design.

Table 2
(Continued)

Current Community Practice Models*	Incorporation of Feminist Issues and Roles into Models

Social Planning (continued)

Involving clients and staff in planning programs.

Recognizing that pure rationality is not a sufficient basis for planning, only, and incorporating cultural and value issues in planning processes.

Recognizing that planning is never "value-free" or "totally objective," and actively including women's values and perspectives in planning processes.

Intentionally using feminist ideology, values, and principles in planning.

Community Liaison

Holistic approach integrating social work roles in both environmental and interpersonal change processes. Specific community practice roles tied to goals and purpose of the agency for staff and administrators of direct service agencies. Administrative activities: interorganizational, boundary spanning, community relations, environmental reconnaissance, and support. Clinical staff activities: program development, needs identification, and client advocacy (Taylor, 1985).

Focusing on empowerment of and advocacy for oppressed groups—with particular attention to service needs of women, children, and minority populations.

Developing closer, functional ties to target populations; sharing information: reconceptualizing and sharing power.

Examining destructive and oppressive forces in the environment and personal and political lives of the target population.

Becoming actively involved to change oppressive and sexist forces affecting the target population.

Examining sexism and racism as they affect the community served and the agency and its staff.

Examining agency hierarchy and boundaries. Introducing feminist ideology, values, and principles in agency decision-making processes.

Working toward democratizing the workplace, and increasing clients' participation in decisions about service provision.

Community Development

Enabling approach—as both means to goals and a goal in itself. Dual emphasis on growth of individual and the group,

Ensuring inclusion of women's issues in social and economic development.

Table 2
(Continued)

Current Community Practice Models*	Incorporation of Feminist Issues and Roles into Models
Community Development (continued)	
neighborhood, or community. Practice roles encourage participation and social involvement for individual and group enhancement. Opportunity system for self-help. Developing local leadership and organizing structures to enable urban or rural people to improve social and economic conditions. Major strategies: building cooperation and collaboration and conflict resolution (Lappin, 1985).	Working to make women's culture and women's values and concerns an equal part of the development process.
	Developing and supporting women's full participation in decision making and social and economic development.
	Working toward empowerment of women and reconceptualization of power emphasizing inclusiveness and collective aspects.
	Working toward further development of women's culture in social and economic production and in the arts.
	Focusing specific attention on women's health needs, economic needs, educational interests, and opportunity structure.
	Developing specific women's economic and social development projects.
	Supporting self-determination of community women in developing role equity and role change.
Pluralism, Participation, and Political Empowerment	
Increasing participation and power of groups who have been excluded from decision processes in order to achieve their self-determined, desired goals. Grounded in realities of struggle, conflict, and existence of conflicting interests in any community. Roles of organizers: educator, resource developer, agitator for self-determined interests of disadvantaged groups. Individual and group growth and skill development related to central focus and goal to make democracy serve the interests of groups that have lacked power. Empowerment focus through formal citizen participation or, more important, self-generated in neighborhood and minority rights associations. Groups may develop	Maximizing the participation of women and ethnic, working class, lesbian, aged, disabled, and other relevant women's groups in social systems and institutions.
	Building process to strengthen morale and empower women in local groups and in representative groups.
	Working for inclusion of women and women's issues in social and political decision-making processes with the goal of developing collective power.
	Working for full representation of women in existing service, social, and political structures, and for development of separate women's organizations.

Table 2
(Continued)

Current Community Practice Models*	Incorporation of Feminist Issues and Roles into Models
Pluralism, Participation, and Political Empowerment (Continued)	
their own alternative services or programs (Grosser and Mondros, 1985).	Working to develop alternative women-centered programs to serve unique needs of women.
	Working to develop coalitions among women of diverse subgroups, to build, articulate, and enact common women's agenda.
	Working to increase political and service system accountability to women's concerns and the concerns of other vulnerable populations.

*Community Practice Model descriptions are drawn from specific chapters in *Theory and Practice of Community Social Work,* Samuel H. Taylor and Robert W. Roberts, eds. (New York: Columbia University Press, 1985). See Note 23 (p. 209) for full names of authors and titles of chapters.

The various roles for feminists engaged in general community practice show how women from diverse political perspectives and different ethnic and interest groups (single mothers; lesbians; older women; Asian American, black, and Hispanic women) can come together to organize around specific issues; to influence mainstream services; to develop alternative services for women; and to build unity, solidarity, and sisterhood. Unity can come from diversity when individual differences and experiences are validated and when common issues that transcend diversity can be understood in relation to shared values and articulated in unifying principles of feminist practice. The following community practice principles articulate feminist ideology and values as guides to action.

Principle One—Feminist Values. Feminist organizers will act to support female values and processes. Organizers will affirm women's strengths and capacities for nurturance and caring. The values of emphasizing process, recognizing and using multidimensional thought processes, and respecting intuitive processes will be supported.

201

Women, Community, and Organizing

Principle Two—Valuing Process.   Feminist organizers will value and act to support both process and the products that result from process. In action, organizers will support consensus development, recognizing that diversity can be supported and polar positions avoided. The valuing of process supports being nonjudgmental. The use of process to build connections can be an educative, democratizing, and empowering force.

Principle Three—Consciousness Raising and Praxis.   Feminist organizers will recognize and support the power and impact of consciousness-raising processes. Giving women the opportunity to reflect on, reexperience, identify, and analyze the social stereotypes and environmental forces that have impeded their development and liberation can serve as a bridge to reclaiming personal history, renaming, and reconceputalizing experiences, gaining self-confidence, and building individual as well as collective strength from action.

Principle Four—Wholeness and Unity.   Feminist organizers will work to build the sisterhood and solidarity of all women. Women face many societal forces that engender separation among them and prevent them from working together. Feminist organizers will act from a position of unity that also supports individual differences as well as intra- and intergroup diversity. Separations and dichotomies are often set up between various categories of women such as lesbians and straight women; women of color and white women; poor and middle-class women; single and married mothers; and young and old women. History attests to many attempts to place different ethnic, minority, and oppressed groups in opposition to one another. In social work, dichotomies are set up separating professional from paraprofessional women, and separating both of these groups from clients. Feminist organizers will affirm the variety and diversity of women's experience and will work to synthesize and build unity that transcends diversity.

Principle Five—Reconceptualization of Power and Empowerment.   Feminist organizers will work toward the reconceptualizing of power as "transactive," limitless, and collective, and as a process that "enables the accomplishment of aspirations."[28] Feminist organizers will work toward empowerment of women through the development of nonhierarchical and democratic struc-

202

Feminist Visions

tures, by the sharing power, and by supporting self-determination and egalitarianism.

Principle Six—Democratic Structuring. Feminist organizers will work to develop organizations, groups, and services that empower women—as members, staff, and consumers. Democratic decision-making processes will be developed and supported; and means to share information, resources, and power will be sought. Organizational tasks can be structured to clarify responsibilities and build autonomy.

Principle Seven—The Personal Is Political. Feminist organizers will be cognizant of the ways in which systemic factors result in problematic personal conditions for women and will work to build unity among women to achieve collective solutions to oppressive situations. The interactive factors of personal growth and political-social action will be recognized and emphasized in approaches to problems and organizing strategies.

Principle Eight—Orientation to Structural Change. Feminist organizers will recognize the need for and work toward fundamental change in organizational, institutional, and societal stuctures to eliminate sexism, racism, and other forms of oppression.

Feminist Reconceptualization of Community Practice

These principles in combination form an action framework for feminist community practice. They build on developing and converging feminist frameworks. Significantly, they also reflect basic values that are deeply rooted in American tradition, although not ascendent: "We have a long and enduring history of struggle to implement such values as egalitarianism, consensus democracy, nonexploitation, cooperation, collectivism, diversity, and nonjudgmental spirituality."[29] Feminism is clearly aligned with the two central social work value positions that support (1) the dignity and worth of each individual and (2) the responsibility of human beings for one another.[30] These two value positions undergird the feminist respect for diversity and concern for collective responsibility and action.

Feminists in community practice may be working with self-help groups, collectives, or organizations, as well as community **203** or political and social action groups. They may take on roles as organizers, community researchers, advocate-planners, administrators, clinicians, trainers, or educators to empower citizens' groups and underserved or oppressed communities. In any of these roles, the feminist principles are applicable. Given the action framework of feminism, many women who are concerned with organizing and services will concentrate on developing programs that are gender-centered or ethnic-centered. The feminist perspective leads to commitment to work with women, children, aged people, the disabled, and other vulnerable populations.

The synthesis of roles and issues that women face in community practice, central issues in feminist frameworks and models for organizing, and feminist principles for community practice lead to a feminist reconceptualization of community practice. In this conception:

A. *Goals* will always relate to the elimination of oppression, such as sexism and racism; method will be integrated with vision.

B. *Power* will be conceptualized as facilitative, enabling, and shared within and among groups. Influence will be a means of expanding feminist approaches and achieving goals. In understanding power as "energy and initiative," feminists will challenge institutions that construe power as "domination."[31]

C. *Strategies* for change will stress the necessity for congruence of means and ends and will be grounded in egalitarianism, consensus building, cooperation, collectivism, power sharing, self-help, and mutual responsibility. Strategies will be personal, interpersonal, social, and political to achieve basic social change, building toward egalitarianism in personal interactions and social structures. Coalition building will be used to expand involvement in feminist agendas—among women and other groups.

D. *Action* will be based on the eight principles for organizing that were previously enumerated.

Within this reconceptualization of community practice (1) feminist theory is incorporated into the knowledge base for community practice; (2) feminist values are made explicit, and essential components for organizing and action are derived
204 from feminist frameworks; (3) community practice models are

adapted to be congruent with feminist goals, strategies, and values; and (4) feminist principles for community practice are articulated that build toward the empowerment of women. This construct constitutes a working model for feminist community practice focusing on the goal of empowering the disadvantaged, at the same time building power and competence for both clients and professionals.

This model can be applied in all community practice relating to clients, community groups, and organizations. The settings for feminist community practice are exciting and diverse. They range on a continuum from consciousness-raising groups, through food co-ops, women's health programs, and service programs, to the movement for world peace.

The feminist agenda for organizing, service development, and community action relates to women's needs through a variety of service approaches: (1) personal and group growth through life development, crises, and transitions; (2) problems of poverty and economic stability, and needs for food, clothing, and shelter; (3) needs for employment, job training, and elimination of discrimination and sexual harassment; (4) needs for health and mental health services; (5) needs for support and services for women who are victims of violence, or who are homeless; and (6) rehabilitative services for women who have problems of substance abuse or are in the prison-probation system. The needs for service development and political action are intertwined. Collective action is necessary to deal with these issues on two fronts: (1) pressuring and challenging existing service systems to re-form their view, treatment, and interaction with women and (2) development of alternative gender-focused and ethnic-focused programs that reflect feminist principles.

Feminists need to work toward humanizing and democratizing the general service delivery system so as to increase the input received from clients as well as workers' responsiveness to client needs. In alternative structures, feminist approaches building on mutuality, self-help, and reciprocity are hallmarks of client-worker interaction.

Action to build alternative feminist and ethnic-sensitive services and action to change the existing service system and social structure are both critical areas of feminist organizing *praxis*. As we move in these areas of action, those of us who teach must also enable and empower our students to carry forward feminist agendas.

205

Implications for Professional Education

Feminist perspectives, community practice frameworks, and models need to be included in professional education. Dominant models of community organizing stress "macho" roles, tactics are often manipulative, power is construed as dominance, and democratic process and values may be sacrificed to achieve a desired end. Feminist students are bewildered at the contradiction they experience between their belief systems and action or organizing experiences; students who have no exposure to feminist approaches all too easily discount them or assume that power and dominance are the only game in town. Students interested in community and macro-practice need the opportunity to explore and engage with feminist theory and frameworks as well as to explore the differences in means and ends that feminist approaches embody.

Community and macro-practice courses need to connect students to the world of alternative services for women and minority communities and to explore ways to enlarge advocacy functions and develop positive connections between community-based, alternative services and mainstream services.[32] Students need exposure to feminist theory, frameworks, methods, and strategies. Student reports, role play, or other experiential exercises can be used to illustrate and engender reactions to different processes of decision making, different conceptions of power, and different models of group facilitation. Students need (1) cognitive exposure to feminist approaches; (2) experiential learning strategies in the classroom to examine issues of value clarification, role conflict, and leadership styles; and (3) practical exposure to community practice and social action through involvement in planning, organizing, and action tasks, such as service design, coalition development, and political action for social change through a community or political group. Participation in leading group discussions, canvassing, and lobbying are all activities that make community practice real.

Students need the opportunity to explore community practice roles, to explore feminist approaches, and to try out roles and experiment with styles. Such experiences can be designed for students specializing in macro-practice and those interested in clinical work. The community liaison role for clinicians can become the key to involving direct-service workers in community practice.[33]

206

Most important, students need an empowering model of professional education. Women students, especially those entering the macro-practice arena, need experience with a teaching-learning model that promotes feminist values and roles and that frees both women and men students from stereotypical sex-role behavior. Women students also need a learning model that is andragogical in its process. Andragogical models build on students' knowledge, values, sensitivities, and skills to promote self-directed learning.[34] Such learning models move students toward the realities, choices, values, and roles that shape professional practice and prepare them to take on responsibility. Such models are congruent with feminist approaches, can be used as a means of reconceptualizing power in the classroom as well as in the field, and can prepare students for the processes, decision making, and challenges of feminist community practice.

Conclusion

The feminist vision in community practice is one of social, personal, and political transformation. Women have always been culture bearers. As we clarify and affirm the values of female consciousness and translate them into social action, these values to preserve, support, and humanize life become principles for commitment. These feminist principles connect to community practice. Community practice is both a direct form of service to client groups and communities and an indirect form of service carried out through interagency and professional actions. Community practice moves social work firmly into the arena of social action and social justice. As feminism unites the political and the personal, community practice is the means of moving social work from case to cause and from private troubles to public concerns. The vast range of areas of commitment in feminist community practice indicates the strength and flexibility of the approach. It is increasingly important to enact the feminist agenda for social change. In neighborhood organizing, consciousness-raising groups, collectives, organizations, political action, and the peace movement—the philosophy, perspective, and direction that feminism offers are healing, holistic, and nurturing. Feminism complements humanistic approaches. We must further develop our strategies and methods; nothing less than our survival—individual, collective, community, and global—is at stake. **207**

notes

1. Mary Bricker-Jenkins, "Of, By and For the People: Feminist Perspectives on Organizations and Leadership," paper presented at the Annual Program Meeting, Council on Social Work Education, Washington, D.C., February 1985.

2. Robert Fisher, *Let the People Decide: Neighborhood Organizing in America* (Boston: Twayne, 1984).

3. *American Heritage Dictionary of the English Language: New College Edition* (Boston: Houghton Mifflin, 1980).

4. Joan Ecklein, *Community Organizers* (2nd ed.; New York: John Wiley & Sons, 1984), p. 20.

5. Jack Rothman, "Three Models of Community Organization Practice, Their Mixing and Phrasing," in F. M. Cox, J. L. Erlich, J. Rothman, and J. E. Tropman, eds., *Strategies of Community Organization* (3rd ed.; Itasca, Ill.: F. E. Peacock, 1979), pp. 25–45.

6. Ibid, p. 30.

7. Ecklein, *Community Organizers,* p. 4.

8. Samuel H. Taylor and Robert W. Roberts, "The Fluidity of Practice Theory: An Overview," in Taylor and Roberts, eds., *Theory and Practice of Community Social Work* (New York: Columbia University Press, 1985).

9. Rothman, "Three Models," p. 26.

10. Susan T. Vandiver, "A Herstory of Women in Social Work," in Elaine Norman and Arlene Mancuso, eds., *Women's Issues and Social Work Practice* (Itasca, Ill.: F. E. Peacock, 1980), pp. 21–38. See also Ruth A. Brandwein, "Toward Androgyny in Community and Organizational Practice," in Ann Weick and Susan T. Vandiver, eds., *Women, Power, and Change* (Washington, D.C.: National Association of Social Workers, 1981), pp. 158–170; and Jill Conway, "Women Reformers and American Culture, 1879–1930," *Journal of Social History,* 5 (Winter 1971–72), pp. 164–177.

11. Brandwein, "Toward Androgyny," pp. 159–160.

12. Ibid., p. 159.

13. Ibid., p. 160.

14. Ibid., p. 160.

15. Ibid., pp. 161–162.

16. Diane Kravetz, "Sexism in a Woman's Profession," *Social Work,* 21 (November 1976), pp. 421–426.

17. Susan Evans, *Personal Politics: The Roots of Women's Liberation in the Civil Rights Movement and the New Left* (New York: Alfred A. Knopf, 1979).

18. Alfred Kadushin, "Men in a Woman's Profession," *Social Work,* 21 (November 1976), p. 444.

19. Margaret L. Anderson, *Thinking About Women: Sociological and Feminist Perspectives* (New York: Macmillan, 1983).

20. Simone de Beauvoir, *The Second Sex* (New York: Alfred A. Knopf, 1952).

21. Alison M. Jaggar and Paula S. Rothenberg, *Feminist Frameworks: Alternative Theoretical Accounts of the Relations between Women and Men*, 2nd ed. (New York: McGraw-Hill, 1984), pp. xiv–xv.

22. Ibid.; and Anderson, *Thinking About Women.*

23. Taylor and Roberts, eds., *Theory and Practice of Community Social Work.* Chapters describing the five models of community practice adapted in this chapter are: Paul Kurzman, "Program Development and Service Coordination as Components of Community Practice"; Jack Rothman and Mayer N. Zald, "Planning Theory in Social Work Community Practice"; Taylor, "Community Work and Social Work: The Community Liaison Approach"; Ben Lappin, "Community Development: Beginnings in Social Work Enabling"; and Charles F. Grosser and Jacqueline Mondros, "Pluralism and Participation: The Political Action Approach."

24. Cheryl Ellsworth, Nancy Hooyman, Ruth Ann Ruff, Sue Bailey Stam, and Joan Hudyma Tucker, "Toward a Feminist Model for Planning For and With Women," in Weick and Vandiver, eds. *Women, Power, and Change,* pp. 146–157.

25. Vivian B. Brown, Barrie Levy, Marie Weil, and Linda Garnets, "Training Grass Roots Peer Consultants," *Consultation,* 1 (Summer 1982), pp. 23–29.

26. Interview with Carole Adkin, Betsy Giller, and Ellen Ledley, of the Family Violence Project, Jewish Family Service of Los Angeles, Calif., June 10, 1985.

27. Interview with Ilene Blaisch, LCSW, Director of Women Helping Women, a service sponsored by the Los Angeles, Calif., Section of the National Council of Jewish Women, July 29, 1985.

28. Mary Bricker-Jenkins and Nancy R. Hooyman, "Feminist Ideology Themes," discussion paper prepared for the Feminist Practice Project, National Association of Social Workers, National Committee on Women's Issues, presented at the Annual Program Meeting, Council on Social Work Education, Detroit, Mich., March 13, 1984, p. 7. See also Bricker-Jenkins and Hooyman, "A Feminist World View: Ideological Themes from the Feminist Movement," in Bricker-Jenkins and Hooyman, eds., *Not for Women Only: Social Work Practice for a Feminist Future* (Silver Spring, Md.: National Association of Social Workers, 1986), pp. 7–22.

29. Ibid., p. 19.

30. Paula Dromi and Marie Weil, "Social Group Work Values: Their Role in a Technological Age." Paper presented at the Sixth Annual Symposium for the Advancement of Social Work with Groups, Chicago, Ill., November 1984.

209

Women, Community, and Organizing

31. Barbara Thorne, "Review of *Building Feminist Theory: Essays for Quest,*" *Signs,* 7, No. 3 (1982), p. 711.

32. Marie Weil, "Southeast Asians and Service Delivery—Issues in Service Provision and Institutional Racism," in *Bridging Cultures: Social Work with Southeast Asian Refugees* (Los Angeles: Asian American Health Training Center and National Institute of Mental Health Asian-Pacific Social Work Curriculum Development Project, 1981), Chap. 10.

33. Marie Weil, "Community Organization Curriculum Development in Services for Families and Children: Bridging the Micro-Macro-Practice Gap," *Social Development Issues,* 6, No. 3 (December 1982), pp. 40–54.

34. Marie Weil, "Preparing Women for Administration: A Self-Directed Learning Model," *Administration in Social Work,* 7 (Fall–Winter 1983), pp. 117–131.

Mimi Abramovitz

social policy and the female pauper: the family ethic and the u.s. welfare state

the recent recognition of the feminization of poverty suggests that poverty has only recently become a women's issue.[1] But when one looks at the relationship of women and the U.S. welfare state through the lens of gender, one discovers that the impoverishment of women began a few hundred years ago.[2] However, the story of the female pauper has remained largely untold because of concerns about the provision of public aid to the able-bodied poor and the impact of relief on the work ethic, both of which focus primarily on the male pauper.

To develop a feminist vision of the U.S. welfare state, one needs, as Lerner, the well-known historian, said, "to ask questions that bring women into view."[3] In this case, one needs to ask questions about how social welfare policies, programs, and procedures affect female clientele. This article suggests that the relationship between women and the welfare state is shaped by

Reprinted with permission of the Council on Social Work Education from Mimi Abramovitz, "The Family Ethic and the Female Pauper: A New Perspective on Public Aid and Social Security Programs," *Journal of Social Work Education*, 21 (Spring–Summer 1985), pp. 15–26.

a "family ethic" that, in many ways, parallels the work ethic known to shape the relationship between the welfare state and men. The first part of this article defines the family ethic as a social norm and describes the operation of the family ethic in the welfare state. Then the role of the family ethic in public assistance programs is explored, as is its role in the social security retirement program. The article concludes with suggestions of ways in which the use of a "gender lens" helps one reconceptualize the relationship between women and the social welfare system and provides new foci for social change.

The Family Ethic as a Social Norm

The view that a woman's place is in the home informs women about their proper work and family roles. Also known as the "cult of domesticity"[4] and the "feminine mystique,"[5] this familiar social norm, referred to here as the "family ethic," says that "proper" women marry and bear and raise children while being supported by and subordinated to a male breadwinner. Since the industrial revolution, the family ethic has told women not to engage in paid labor outside the home but to work without wages, maintaining family members, managing household affairs, and providing emotional nurturance. As moral guardians of the family and the community, women must remain pure and must tame the sexuality of men. However, as the "weaker sex," women are frail and require the protection of men.

The family ethic is derived from social thought that sees gender roles as biologically determined rather than socially assigned and from standard legal doctrine that defines women's property as the property of men. It is enforced by laws and the activities of the state as well as the practices of the market. Like the work ethic, the family ethic is a method of social control. Fulfilling its terms establishes a woman's femininity, womanhood, and social respectability. Noncompliance brings penalties. The family ethic governs the traditional gender-role division of labor that assigns women to the private sphere of family, household, and community and leaves to men the more power-laden arenas of work, politics, and society.

Despite changes over time, the family ethic has persisted and has considerable influence throughout the wider social order. Not all families subscribe to this dominant norm, but few

Feminist Visions

women, regardless of race, class, or marital status, can escape its strong influence. Although it is directed primarily to white middle-class women who marry and stay home, poor, working, minority, and husbandless women experience the pressure of the family ethic, not only because they are seen as living outside its rules but because they encounter it in the welfare state to which they often must turn for support.

The social welfare system reflects and reinforces the family ethic through policies and procedures that encourage women to choose traditional family life over work, relief, or alternative family forms. The following section suggests that the system does so by rewarding women who fulfill the terms of the family ethic (such as married women) and punishing those who do not (such as single mothers). Depending on the particular program, social welfare policies deter women from seeking aid, provide incentives for women to remain at home, and penalize those who do not remain at home.

Policies that treat women differentially according to their compliance with the family ethic result in poorer services and lower benefits for many women and their families. These policies also create distinctions between women on the basis of family status, race, and class. Such distinctions can have a political role. They enable the welfare state to play an important part in mediating the economy's conflicting need for women's unpaid labor in the home and their low-paid labor in the marketplace. The following discussion indicates that welfare state policies channel poor and minority women into the paid labor force while upholding the belief that a woman's place is in the home. By dividing poor women by marital status and race, the policies also constrain women with shared economic problems from collective political action on their own behalf.

Public Assistance

It is well known that relief systems reinforce the work ethic through policies of deterrence designed to ensure that able-bodied persons choose paid labor over public assistance.[6] But this dynamic fails to account for women, who, even when they work, are told that their primary place is in the home. Public aid policies convey to women the message that, whether or not it is safe or secure, family life is more attractive than relief.

213

Just as they do for men, meager benefits and punitive procedures discourage poor women from seeking public aid and encourage them to remain married, to find a male breadwinner, or, if they fail, to accept a low standard of living. Only women without a male breadwinner can receive help, which suggests that it is the absence of a husband or the father of her child, not financial need alone, that entitles a poor woman to aid.[7]

Once eligible, relief programs punish the husbandless female pauper for stepping out of role. Ironically, the punishment consists of denying her the "rights of womanhood" under the terms of the prevailing family ethic. To receive relief, not only must a woman be husbandless, but she often is required to work[8] and may risk having her children removed from the home or her parenting strictly supervised.[9]

In contrast, the family ethic stresses marriage, motherhood, and nonpaid work in the home as the centerpiece of women's role. Because unattached women are seen as too sexually active and therefore improper guardians of family and community morality, recipients of relief face governmental regulation of their sexual and social lives—a role traditionally assigned to a woman's husband or father.[10]

Finally, relief policies treat female recipients whose life circumstances more closely approximate the terms of the family ethic better than they do those who depart from the prescribed roles of wife and mother. Although poor women generally are regarded as more worthy of assistance than employable men, relief policies distinguish between deserving and undeserving female clients based on their relationship to the family system and to a man. Married or previously married women who lack a male breadwinner through no fault of their own, such as widows or wives of sick, disabled, or temporarily unemployed men, often receive larger social benefits and more responsive services than do unwed mothers, abandoned wives, and wives of permanently unemployed men, that is, women who do not have a male breadwinner or whose male breadwinner has failed to provide steady support and who are blamed for their status.[11]

Such relief policies date back to colonial America, when from one-third to one-half the paupers were female.[12] In the labor-short agricultural economy of colonial society, in which both household and market production occurred in the home, women were expected to be economically productive. They were also

Feminist Visions

expected to marry, to bear and raise children, and to manage a household in which they were subordinate to a male breadwinner. Under the terms of this colonial family ethic, in addition to making an economic contribution, a "true woman" acquired a family and took up homemaking in her own home.[13]

Colonial poor laws supported the family ethic. They punished husbandless women who stepped out of their roles by denying them the right to receive aid in their own homes and often preventing them from raising their children. Adult paupers of both sexes faced hard labor in their own or a neighbor's home. But couples, married women, widows, and the sick were more likely to be aided in their own homes, and single mothers and "unsuitable parents" were "contracted out" or "auctioned off" to live in a neighbor's home (later the workhouse), where they exchanged labor for support.[14]

Female paupers were also vulnerable to colonial laws authorizing the removal of children from the homes of parents seen as unfit. Because poor women were more readily deemed unfit, their children frequently were apprenticed to and raised by others.[15] Women also had a difficult time proving their self-sufficiency, posting bond, or convincing town officials of their moral character, all of which were required by colonial settlement laws designed to prevent strangers without means of support from establishing a local residence.[16]

These means of punishing poor women whose life circumstances did not conform to prescribed wife and mother roles intensified with industrialization. As the industrial revolution transformed society by separating household and market production, the work ethic followed men out of the home and a revised family ethic emerged for women. Known as the "cult of domesticity," the industrial family ethic closely resembled its colonial predecessor except that it devalued women's economic role. Indeed, the new family ethic promoted the "lady of leisure" as a model for all women,[17] while expanding women's unpaid responsibilities in the home. Both helped to obscure the ways in which women's unpaid labor in the home contributed to the stability of the family and to lower production costs for industry. By fulfilling these expanded homemaking and child-rearing tasks, women nurtured, sustained, and maintained the family, whose stability was—and still is—critical for the smooth functioning of the wider social order. These same activities indirectly helped to reduce industry's costs by keeping the current adult labor force **215** fed, housed, clothed, and physically fit and by socializing a new generation of workers to assume proper adult and family roles. Moreover, the belief that women belong in the home (even when employed) rationalized low wages for women and the overall unequal treatment of women on the job.

As homemaking and motherhood became the centerpieces of nineteenth-century femininity, which also defined a woman as frail, pure, and idle, the many women who worked for wages outside the home were excluded from the only acceptable definition of respectable womanhood.[18] The claim to respectable womanhood was even less accessible to the growing number of husbandless female paupers whose low wages or unemployment caused them to turn to relief and, in some cases, to prostitution, for support.

Industrialization also brought changes in the system of relief. As poverty and the costs of relief rose, attitudes toward the poor—more and more of whom were immigrants and women—stiffened. In the early 1800s, outdoor relief came under attack and institutions became the preferred method of care. This major change in relief policy sent many women to work in the poorhouse, the workhouse, or the bottom ranks of the labor market. Others ended up in hospitals, mental asylums, or jails. Their children were placed in orphanages and reformatories, which typically restricted parental visiting rights on the grounds that the parents were unfit.[19]

In these and other ways, industrial poor law policies denied women their rights of womanhood according to the nineteenth-century family ethic that praised ladies of leisure and modernized the definition of motherhood. The laws also helped supply the labor market with low-wage, female immigrant workers, who fueled the post–Civil War industrial expansion at a time when middle-class and upper-class women engaged in no paid labor at all.[20]

In the twentieth century, changing economic and social conditions once again generated new social welfare programs. These programs continued to reflect and reinforce the family ethic but in new ways: by rewarding women who remained at home in addition to punishing those who did not.

At the turn of the century, unfounded fears surfaced that the expanding female labor force caused juvenile delinquency, took jobs away from men, and otherwise threatened the stability of the family unit; these fears began to be reflected in public

Feminist Visions

policy.[21] At the same time, rising costs and the poor performance of public institutions, liberalized attitudes toward the poor, and acceptance of an expanded role for the state revived interest in outdoor relief. Rather than place women and children in institutions, the states began to enact laws to provide financial aid to mothers in their own homes.[22] Known as Mothers' Pensions, this forerunner of Aid to Dependent Children (later Aid to Families with Dependent Children [AFDC]) substituted governmental aid for the missing breadwinner. Instead of denying husbandless women the right to maintain a home and raise children, the state now encouraged poor women to stay home and become dependent on it, although meager benefits meant that many recipients continued to work.

Moreover, distinctions between deserving and undeserving female paupers meant that only "fit" mothers and "suitable" homes qualified for aid: that is, women who were sexually inactive and from homes with a previously present male breadwinner.[23] Most fit and deserving female paupers turned out to be widowed and white, but even they received regular visits from agency workers who offered moral advice. Some lost aid or the right to keep their children on the subsequent discovery of an illegitimate child or other violations of the family ethic. Little or no help was available for families with a nonsupporting or never-present male breadwinner. As a result, poor black and immigrant women, whose numbers mounted, still worked for wages in the few jobs open to women in the paid labor force.

Mothers' Pensions became Aid to Dependent Children with the passage of the 1935 Social Security Act. The female pauper, however, continued to be punished for stepping out of role by policies that refused to give her aid. Just like Mothers' Pensions, the early Aid to Dependent Children's program provided money payments for children but not their caretakers. Not until 1950 were mothers included in the grant. Furthermore, states established AFDC more slowly than other public assistance programs and, from the outset, benefits received by poor women and children fell below those available to poor aged, blind, and disabled public assistance clients.[24]

The lack of attention to women's needs is most evident in the cessation of benefits when a woman's youngest child reaches age 18—or when her reproductive and caretaking roles are no longer needed. Few other services exist for this group of displaced homemakers.

217

AFDC continued regulating a recipient's parenting patterns and sexual activities. "Midnight raids" searching for a "man in the house," as well as "suitable-home" rules that disallowed cohabitation and even sexual relations with anyone other than a legal spouse, caused many poor women to lose their aid, as did having an illegitimate child after receiving public assistance. Mothers in such "unsuitable" homes might also be pressured to release their children "voluntarily" for placement—a pressure many women actively resisted.[25]

These means of denying poor women their rights of womanhood, under the terms of the family ethic, channeled "fit" mothers into the home and "unfit" mothers into the labor market. Prejudice and poverty meant that few immigrant and nonwhite women had the chance to stay at home. During the 1930s and 1940s, many states, especially those in the South, simply did not extend AFDC to blacks, preferring not to interfere with local demands for female field hands and domestics.[26] Meanwhile, the northern states strengthened their suitable-home requirements and added new rules to lower caseloads as more minority and single mothers applied for aid. These added requirements also sent many poor black women and single mothers into the paid labor force.

In the 1950s, AFDC programs came under sharp attack as overall public assistance costs continued to rise, when single mothers replaced senior citizens as the predominant welfare group,[27] and when nonwhite women, still a numerical minority, became overrepresented on the rolls.[28] In the 1960s, when social protests caused courts to declare midnight raids, residence requirements, and suitable-home policies unconstitutional, new ways of penalizing the female pauper were devised. In particular, coercive work requirements, introduced to reduce welfare caseloads, once again punished those women who did not properly combine the prescribed roles of wife and mother.[29] Recent changes in AFDC policy under the Reagan Administration make it more difficult for welfare mothers to receive both wages and a welfare grant.[30]

The conflicting attitudes toward keeping women in the home, the punishment of those who stepped out of the traditional female role, and the practice of deterring dependence on relief have become encoded in public aid policies that, in turn, support the family ethic and uphold the view that a woman's place is in the home. These same policies supplied an expanding econ-

218

Feminist Visions

omy with low-cost, primarily immigrant and minority female workers. The contradiction disappears if relief policies are understood as a way of mediating the conflicting demands for women's paid labor in the market and their unpaid labor in the home by making different groups of women available for each.

Social Security Retirement Program

Like public aid, the social security retirement program reflects and reinforces the family ethic. But, even more than relief, social security assumes a woman's economic dependence on a male breadwinner.

Enacted in 1935 to offset a retired worker's lost wages only, its emphasis shifted from replacing wages to replacing the breadwinner in 1939—before any payments were made. "To afford adequate protection for the family unit,"[31] Congress added dependents' benefits for a retired worker's wife, minor children, and aged parents without raising the Social Security contribution. Since then, the social security program has reflected and reinforced the family ethic through policies and procedures that encourage women to remain at home supported by a male breadwinner and that treat women who approximate the terms of the family ethic more favorably than those who depart from the prescribed roles of wife and mother.

Penalizing Working Women. Although the social security program provides benefits to women as wives, widows, or workers, its rules do not encourage or reward the employment of women. Rather, its acceptance of the economic dependence of women translates into major disincentives toward the women's market labor and conveys the message that women are better off at home.

Social security does not substantially reward working women for retiring, especially if they are single. In 1982, the average monthly benefit of retired women amounted to $362, compared to $470 for men.[32] Because many older women rely on these payments as a major or sole source of support, their poverty rate is high. In 1982, 14.6 percent of the poor were elderly. Of these elderly poor people, 71 percent were female. The poverty rate for elderly women exceeds that for the over-65 population as a whole—18.6 percent compared to 15.3 percent.[33]

The impoverishment of older women reflects the low wages of women in relation to those of men, but it also reflects the **219** social security benefit formula that penalizes women for their movement in and out of the labor force. The formula averages a worker's covered earnings over a specified number of years and then subtracts five years of low or no earnings. A number of years of low or no earnings causes benefits to fall. Women who work part time or who leave the labor force for family responsibilities receive zero credit on their earnings record for every year over five that they earn no wages.[34] This formula contrasts with other countries in which absence from the work force because of pregnancy and child care is not counted or is treated as covered employment and credited to a woman's account with some ascribed earnings.[35] In addition, the regressive social security payroll tax, which takes proportionately more from the wages of low wage earners than it does from high wage earners, hits female workers especially hard because they predominate among the lowest-paid members of the labor force.

A married woman becomes entitled to social security retirement benefits as a worker or as a spouse, whichever benefit is highest. A woman frequently receives a higher benefit as a dependent wife than as an employed worker because the wife's benefit of 50 percent of her husband's entitlement exceeds what she can claim on her own earnings record.[36] As a result, retired working women are not better off than wives who have never worked. Indeed, they are worse off, because they receive no return on the social security taxes they paid.

Likewise, one-earner couples receive higher retirement benefits than do two-earner couples with the same total family income. This disparity arises because a spouse averaging $30,000 a year realizes greater social security benefits than two lower-paid spouses earning the same amount. The inequity grows for two-earner couples who earn high and roughly equal incomes.[37]

Disabled women face even greater penalties. Regardless of sex, disabled workers become eligible for social security disability payments only if they worked five of the ten years before they were disabled. Women workers who leave the labor force to bear and raise children often cannot pass this "recency of work" test. On returning to work, they must start accumulating credits all over again.[38]

Social security provides benefits to a deceased worker's survivors as well as to a retired worker's dependents. For many years, however, employed women's survivors received no benefits or highly conditional benefits. Until 1950, social security did not cover a

Feminist Visions

working woman's survivors. That year, coverage was extended to (1) a husband over age 65 who depended on or survived an employed woman, but only if he proved he was financially dependent on his wife and (2) a female worker's surviving children under age 18, but not their father. In the mid-1970s, the Supreme Court declared these provisions unconstitutional on the grounds of sex discrimination. In 1975, the Court struck down the provision of survivors' benefits to widows but not widowers with young children. In 1977, the Court overturned the economic dependence rule for husbands because such proof was not required for wives. The Supreme Court invalidated these policies because they discriminated against women by providing working women with fewer benefits for their social security contributions than working men received.[39]

The recognition of sex discrimination in the social security program helped equalize the value of women's and men's survivor benefits. Other problems and differentials remain, however, based on women's compliance or noncompliance with the family ethic. Because these problems, to be discussed next, do not qualify as sex discrimination under the law, they will require other, even more fundamental, solutions.

Penalizing Women Who Depart from Their Proper Role. Just as social security rewards women for not working and penalizes those who do, so it supports the family ethic by treating less favorably women who depart from the prescribed roles of wife and mother than those who do not. As the following examples indicate, social security categorizes women as deserving and undeserving of benefits on the basis of their compliance with the family ethic. The program offers less coverage to dependents of single adults, neglects widows once their reproductive and home-making roles decline, and penalizes divorced women for stepping out of line.

Designed to protect the family unit, the Social Security Act provided for a worker's dependent wife over age 65, widows under age 65 with surviving minor children, and aged parents. Young widows without children, divorced women, and husbands of employed women received no benefits as spouses in their own right. Only gradually did the Social Security Act extend coverage to these groups and in some cases only conditionally. For many years, occupations employing large numbers of women, such as domestic and government work, remained exempt from the program's provisions. **221**

Social security's emphasis on the family unit means that it covers more dependents of married workers than of single workers. As a result, single workers, regardless of sex, receive less value from their social security tax payment than do married workers. Not only does a married worker receive benefits for a nonworking spouse without paying additional social security taxes, but this contribution covers children and grandchildren, who are not likely to be found among a single person's dependents. Siblings and other family members who might turn to a single worker for support are not eligible as dependents under the Social Security Act.[40] Moreover, social security taxes are not geared to family size; single and married workers with the same work history pay similar taxes but receive differential benefits. This difference is especially hard for the female single worker whose social security benefits are low.

Even the woman who complies with the family ethic loses out. Once the need for a full-time homemaker's services ceases, her social security protection ends. The program does not assume responsibility for women who lack both a male breadwinner *and* minor children, until they reach the new status of old age. Currently, a married woman who loses her husband is entitled to a mother's benefit under the Social Security Act until her youngest child reaches age 16 (lowered from age 18 in 1983). Her children might also qualify for separate dependents' benefits on their deceased father's account. However, once a married woman loses both her husband and her children, she falls into a "widow's gap"—referring to the years between the time that her youngest child turns 16 and she turns 60. During this period, widows (but also divorced women and AFDC mothers) with grown children receive no social security protection at all.[41]

Known as "displaced homemakers," these women are too young for social security and often do not qualify for other forms of aid because of their income or the composition of their family. The social security benefits they can claim at age 60 are low because of (1) their limited labor market history and (2) the 28.5 percent permanent reduction in social security benefits when claimed at age 60 instead of age 65. A full-time homemaker who becomes disabled receives no social security benefits even though the services she performs are lost to her family. Disabled widows can claim benefits at age 50, but only at 71.5 percent of the full age-65 benefit.[42]

222   Divorced women receive even harsher treatment under the

Feminist Visions

social security program. Unlike a widow who lost her breadwinner through no fault of her own, a divorced woman is treated as if she were responsible for her lack of a husband. More than others, divorced women are viewed by social security as violators of the family ethic.

The original Social Security Act made no provision for divorced women and their children. Not until 1950 did divorced women under age 65 begin to collect the mothers' benefits for their children that were previously payable only to survivors of intact families. To qualify, however, a divorced woman had to remain unmarried, caring for her ex-husband's children and dependent on him for at least one-half of her support (despite the fact that many states prohibited alimony).[43] Divorced women aged 65 or older became eligible for benefits on their former husbands' earnings records in 1965, but to obtain this benefit, they had to have been married to their former husbands for 20 years (lowered to 10 years in 1979), not remarried at the time of application, and, until 1972, able to prove economic dependence on their ex-husbands when the ex-husbands qualified for benefits. If a divorced woman met the "marriage test," she still could not collect benefits if her ex-husband chose not to retire or had not died. If she remarried, after age 60, these benefits ceased.[44]

Recent legislation has eased things for the divorced woman. It separates a divorced woman's eligibility for benefits from her ex-husband's retirement decisions and permits a divorced widow over age 60 who remarries to continue receiving benefits on the basis of her first husband's account.[45]

Summary and Discussion

Applying a gender lens to social welfare programs not only brings women into view but deepens one's understanding of the structure and functions of the welfare state. The gender lens reveals that social welfare policies and procedures contain definite assumptions about women's proper family and work roles that correspond to the terms of the prevailing family ethic.

This perspective also suggests that compliance with the family ethic rather than the work ethic determines the treatment received by women who are dependent on social welfare programs for support. Both public aid and social security distinguish between deserving and undeserving women based on a woman's **223** relationship to a male breadwinner and her role as a mother. This differentiation challenges the traditional view of social welfare programs that (1) defines the deserving and undeserving poor according to the work ethic, (2) places women, who are not expected to work, among the deserving group, and (3) sees women as receiving more benevolent treatment by the welfare state than men. It also revises the notion the social insurance programs, unlike public assistance, treat all clients the same.

This review of public aid and social security further suggests that treating women according to their compliance with the family ethic helps mediate the conflicting demands for women's paid labor in the market and their unpaid labor in the home by making different groups of women available for each type of labor. Native-born women, white women, and women who lack a breadwinner through no fault of their own tend to be channeled into the home, whereas immigrant women, minority women, and women who are held responsible for their lack of a husband end up in the labor force. By drawing on race and class distinctions, social welfare programs meet the ever-increasing demand for low-cost female labor without undermining the belief that a woman's proper place is in the home. Understanding that these distinctions are a function of social welfare programs helps explain why, in spite of claiming to strengthen family life, the programs often distort and disrupt it. Indeed, despite the predominance of women and children among public aid recipients, the policies of the programs have consistently involved some type of coerced work.

Finally, the gender lens shows that even when women adhere to the family ethic, their "place in the home" is not safe. Neither public aid nor social security provide protection for women who have no husband or children to care for. It is as if a woman's needs as a person merit no protection or recognition once the family unit ceases to need her resources and skills. Only when a woman reaches old age and is no longer expected to perform reproductive, motherhood, or homemaking roles is she reintegrated into the social welfare system.

These discoveries suggest that improved social welfare programs for women will require more than correction of the inequities between benefits for men and women. Indeed, many of the inadequacies faced by women who are dependent on social welfare benefits derive from the constraints and prejudices contained in the family ethic. Policies that do not penalize women for working, that reward women for time spent at home, and that recog-

224

nize different family structures would go a long way toward eliminating some of the problems experienced by female social welfare recipients. So would an adequate family allowance, the opening of more jobs to women, and the use of comparable worth rather than equal pay to eliminate sex-based wage differentials.

But even these reforms will only go so far unless they too are purged of the negative effects of the family ethic, the most current version of which holds women exclusively responsible for the home, even if they are not there all the time. Only by eliminating the belief in the primacy of women's responsibility for home and family life and by removing traditional assumptions about women's role, will welfare state programs properly serve all families. Only by changing this notion of women's role will women stand an equal chance throughout the wider social order.

notes

1. National Advisory Council on Equal Opportunity, "No, Poverty Has Not Disappeared," *Social Policy* (January–February 1981), pp. 25–38.

2. See M. Dinerman, "The Woman Trap: Women and Poverty," this volume, for an excellent discussion of factors contributing to the impoverishment of women today.

3. G. Lerner, "Teaching Women's History: Questions to Bring Women into View" (Washington, D.C.: American Historical Association, 1981). (Mimeographed.)

4. B. Epstein, "Industrialization and Femininity: A Case Study of Nineteenth-Century New England," *Social Problems*, 23 (April 1976), pp. 389–401; S. Eisenstein, *Give Us Bread But Give Us Roses* (London, England: Routledge & Kegan Paul, 1983); M. Ryan, *Womanhood in America* (New York: New Viewpoints, 1975); and B. Welter, "The Cult of True Womanhood," *American Quarterly*, 18 (1966), pp. 151–174.

5. B. Friedan, *The Feminine Mystique* (New York: Dell Publishing Co., 1963).

6. See, for example, J. Axinn and H. Levin, *Social Welfare: A History of the American Response to Need* (New York: Harper & Row, 1975); K. DeSchweinitz, *England's Road to Social Security* (Philadelphia: University of Pennsylvania Press, 1943); J. Leiby, *A History of Social Welfare and Social Work in the United States* (New York: Columbia University Press, 1978); S. Mencher, *Poor Law to Poverty Program* (Pittsburgh: University of Pittsburgh Press, 1967); and F. F. Piven and R. A. Cloward, *Regulating the Poor* (New York: Pantheon, 1971). **225**

7. W. Bell, *Aid to Dependent Children* (New York: Columbia University Press, 1965); B. Coll, *Perspective in Public Welfare* (Washington, D.C.: U.S. Department of Health, Education & Welfare, 1969).

8. M. Dinerman, "Catch 23: Women, Work, and Welfare," *Social Work*, 22 (November 1977), pp. 472–478; P. Day, "Sex-Role Stereotypes and Public Assistance," *Social Service Review*, 53 (March 1979), pp. 106–115; Barbara Joe, "What's Wrong with Workfare And Why Did It Fail in California?" *NASW News*, 26 (September 1981), pp. 8–10; B. Bernstein, "The Case for Work Requirements," *Public Welfare*, 36 (Spring 1978), pp. 36–39; M. Rein, "Work in Welfare: Past Failures and Future Strategies," *Social Service Review*, 5 (June 1982), pp. 211–229; Rein, *Work or Welfare* (New York: Praeger Publishers, 1974); S. M. Chambré, "Welfare, Work, and Family Structure," *Social Work*, 22 (March 1977), pp. 103–108; and K. S. Hill, "Work Requirements for AFDC Mothers," in A. Weick and S. Vandiver, eds., *Women, Power, and Change* (Washington, D.C.: National Association of Social Workers, 1981), pp. 137–145.

9. E. Abbott, *Women in Industry* (New York: D. Appleton & Co., 1910); Axinn and Levin, *Social Welfare*, pp. 9–25; and D. Rothman, *The Discovery of Asylum: Social Disorder in the New Republic* (Boston: Little, Brown & Co., 1971), pp. 206–237.

10. J. Handler, *Reforming the Poor: Welfare Policy, Federalism and Morality* (New York: Basic Books, 1972); and Bell, *Aid to Dependent Children.*

11. Handler, *Reforming the Poor*, pp. 11–13.

12. A. Kessler-Harris, *Out to Work: A History of Wage-Earning Women in the United States* (New York: Oxford University Press, 1982), pp. 16–19; J. Matthaei, *An Economic History of Women in America* (New York: Schocken Books, 1982), pp. 51–53; Rothman, *The Discovery of Asylum*, pp 33–34; and Ryan, *Womanhood in America*, pp. 100–101.

13. Matthaei, *An Economic History*, Chaps. 1–3; and Ryan, *Womanhood in America*, pp. 9–82.

14. Matthaei, *An Economic History*, Chap. 3; Rothman, *The Discovery of Asylum*, Chaps. 1–2; and Ryan, *Womanhood in America*, pp. 19–82.

15. See Abbott, *Women in Industry;* Axinn and Levin, *Social Welfare;* and Rothman, *The Discovery of Asylum.*

16. Ryan, *Womanhood in America*, p. 67.

17. See Lerner, "Teaching Women's History"; and Lerner, "The Lady and the Mill Girl: Changes in the Status of Women in the Age of Jackson," in J. Friedman and W. Shade, eds., *Our American Sisters: Women in American Life and Thought* (Lexington, Mass.: D. C. Heath & Co., 1982), pp. 183–195.

18. Eisenstein, *Give Us Bread.*

19. Axinn and Levin, *Social Welfare*, pp. 115–150.

20. For a more detailed discussion of the history of the family ethic, see M. Abramovitz, "The Family Ethic: The Female Pauper and

226

Feminist Visions

Public Aid, Pre-1900," *Social Service Review,* 59 (March 1985), pp. 121–135.

21. Axinn and Levin, *Social Welfare,* Chap. 5, pp. 115–150.

22. Bell, *Aid to Dependent Children;* R. H. Bremner, *From the Depths* (New York: New York University Press, 1964); W. Trattner, *From Poor Law to Welfare State* (New York: Free Press, 1974); and K. Woodruffe, *From Charity to Social Work* (London, England: Routledge & Kegan Paul, 1962).

23. Bell, *Aid to Dependent Children.*

24. Axinn and Levin, *Social Welfare,* p. 187; and Bell, *Aid to Dependent Children.*

25. Bell, *Aid to Dependent Children.*

26. Ibid., p. 35.

27. Axinn and Levin, *Social Welfare,* p. 235.

28. Bell, *Aid to Dependent Children.*

29. Handler, *Reforming the Poor,* pp. 9–46.

30. M. Abramovitz, "The Conservative Program Is a Women's Issue," *Journal of Sociology and Social Welfare,* 9 (September 1982), pp. 389–424.

31. B. A. Mikulski and E. L. Brown, "Case Studies in the Treatment of Women under Social Security Law: The Need for Reform," *Harvard Women's Law Journal,* 6 (1983), p. 34.

32. U.S. Department of Health and Human Services, Social Security Administration, *Social Security Bulletin, Annual Statistical Supplement, 1982* (Washington, D.C.: U.S. Government Printing Office, 1982), Table 80, p. 150.

33. U.S. Bureau of the Census, Current Population Reports, Series P-60, No. 140, *Money, Income and Poverty Status of Families and Persons in the United States, 1982* (advance data from March 1983 *Current Population Survey*) (Washington, D.C.: U.S. Government Printing Office, 1983), Table 15, p. 21.

34. *Report of the HEW Task Force on the Treatment of Women under Social Security* (Washington, D.C.: U.S. Government Printing Office, February 1978), pp. 11, 16.

35. Ibid., pp. 129–130.

36. Ibid., p. 6.

37. Ibid., pp. 16–17. See also B. A. Lingg, "Social Security Benefits of Female Retired Workers and Two-Worker Couples," *Social Security Bulletin,* 45 (February 1982), pp. 3–24, for a report on research suggesting that two-earner couples do better than couples in which the wife receives only a spouse's benefit.

38. *Report of the HEW Task Force,* pp. 18–19.

39. Ibid., p. 13; Mikulski and Brown, "Case Studies," pp. 32–37.

40. Mikulski and Brown, "Case Studies," p. 40.

41. M. Forman, "Social Security Is a Women's Issue," *Social Policy,* 14 (Summer 1983), pp. 35–38; and C. Muller, "Income Supports for Older Women," *Social Policy,* 14 (Fall 1983), pp. 23–31.

42. Forman, "Social Security Is a Women's Issue," p. 38.

43. *Report of the HEW Task Force,* p. 108; and S. Chambre, "Women and Income Maintenance Programs," in E. Norman and A. Mancuso, eds., *Women's Issues and Social Work Practice* (Itasca, Ill.: F. E. Peacock, 1980), pp. 219–239.

44. Forman, "Social Security Is a Women's Issue," p. 37.

45. Ibid.

Feminist Visions

Miriam Dinerman

the woman trap: women and poverty

the "feminization of poverty" is a complex phenomenon with a number of forces and factors that push women—especially women who head families—into poverty or inhibit their escape from it. It is a rapidly growing phenomenon, peculiar for a society that claims to care for children and women. This article examines the efficacy or failings of systems supposed to take care of women who head households with children, as well as barriers that prevent their escape from poverty. Strategies to improve the situation are examined. Comparisons with other industrialized nations provide a yardstick by which to measure how this society lives up to its statements of concern. An analysis of the feminization of poverty is offered from a feminist point of view.

Historical Perspectives on Poverty

The United States periodically rediscovers poverty as an issue of widespread concern. It did so in the 1830s, the 1890s, the 1930s, and, again, in the 1960s. Some of these rediscoveries coincided **229** with a great upsurge in the number of poor people and in the direness of their plight—for example, the period of the Great Depression in the 1930s. Other periods of poverty have not elicited much concern, and at least once, in the 1960s, the concern grew at a time of considerable affluence. Clearly public attention to a social problem is not caused solely by a change in its prevalence, nor by data on the condition of its victims. Rather, there seems to be a process shaped by economic, political, social, and moral attitudes that are, in turn, affected by contending and shifting power groups in society.[1]

As Abramovitz explains earlier in this book, only certain categories of women—for example, widows or wives of disabled men—used to be considered deserving of aid. The Mothers' Pensions program, created at the turn of the century, and Aid to Dependent Children, established in 1935, gave minimal assistance to women, provided that they had children.

In response to a rising concern about the standard of living and the number of poor people in the United States, the Social Security Administration developed the basis for an official poverty line starting in the early 1960s. The poverty line has been adjusted annually for inflation but not for the rising affluence and changing standards of living of the rest of American society. Some of the assumptions inherent in the poverty line standard are that there will be no dental or medical costs (these are assumed to be postponable), only public transportation will be used (this is assumed to be available), and only free forms of recreation will be used (not even television, unless the set is a gift and needs no repair). The poverty line assumed $1.52 per person per day for food in 1980.[2] In 1982, the official poverty line for a family of four was $9,862; the U.S. median family income was $23,433.[3]

Despite its limitations, the poverty line is the only measure we social workers have to examine the differential risks of poverty and to determine how effectively social welfare programs have been able to help some people escape above this rigorous standard. When first developed, the poverty line showed that the aged, nonwhites, and female-headed households all had many times the rate of poverty of white male-headed families. These patterns have persisted through good times and bad, with only one exception; there has been a decline in the proportion of poor among the aged.[4]

The data suggest that families with earners—and especially two earners—can escape poverty better than families with no

Feminist Visions

earners or only one earner. High employment helps some more than others. Even so, families headed by a full-time, yearlong employed person still represented 27 percent of all poor families in 1981.[5] Table 1 shows that the risk of being poor is nearly triple for black households compared to white ones, with a 36 percent rate for blacks. The comparable rate for whites is 12 percent.[6] Regardless of race, two-parent families are at less risk than one-parent families. Over 95 percent of all one-parent families are headed by women, and almost half of these fall below the poverty line. That rate increases to 70 percent for comparable black families. Although households with heads over age 65 ran about the same risk of poverty in 1965 as female-headed households, the rate for the former has been consistently reduced over the years. At present, after counting cash-benefit program receipts, one can see that the aged are no more at risk than the U.S. average. Clearly, because the aged are not greatly affected by changes in the job market, improvement can only be attributed to the effectiveness of the income transfer programs. In addition, because American patterns of savings showed a steady decline in this period, self-help cannot be considered as an explanation.

The major income support program for the elderly is social security, but Supplementary Security Income (SSI) and food stamps also are to be considered. Women are overrepresented among the very old, and are among those beneficiaries of social security with the lowest levels of benefits.

Precipitants of Poverty

It has clearly been shown that women, especially women heading families with children, are disproportionately the victims of poverty whether one compares white women with white men, black women with black men, or old women with old men. What are the systems that are supposed to protect women and children from poverty? The most traditional means for providing for women, with or without children, of course, has been the conventional family pattern in which the father earns the family income in a job outside the home while the mother manages the care of the house and children. That this pattern now holds true only for a distinct minority of American families has not caught up with beliefs, policies, or programs.

In 1983, fewer than half the children living in married- **231**

Table 1
**Incidence of Poverty after Transfers in Different Types of Families,
1965–82 (percentage)**

Type of Family	1965	1972	1978	1982
All persons in the United States	17.2	11.9	11.4	15.0
Two-parent families	9.7	7.4	6.9	13.6
White female-headed families with children	52.9	41.1	39.9	46.5
Black households	40.9	33.3	29.5	36.0
Black female-headed families with children	81.6	69.5	66.4	70.7
Households with a head over age 65	32.3	18.6	14.0	14.6

SOURCES: U.S. Bureau of the Census, "Characteristics of the Population Below the Poverty Level, 1982," *Current Population Reports,* Series P-60, No. 144 (Washington, D.C.: U.S. Department of Commerce, 1984); and *New York Times,* August 7, 1983, p. 4E, and August 4, 1983, p. A1ff.

couple families had only one working parent, the father. Half had two working parents.[7] Furthermore, not only are women entering and remaining in the labor force in great numbers, but they are doing so at ever-younger ages of their youngest child. The myth of the father-as-sole-breadwinner is less and less true. Further deviation from the traditional pattern is to be found in the large and increasing numbers of broken or never-married families with children. In the 1970s, the number of households headed by women, with children under age 18, rose from 2.9 million to 8.5 million; by 1983, the number was up to 9.8 million, representing 16 percent of all families.[8] And virtually all one-parent families are headed by women.

Financial support from the absent father becomes the next traditional line of defense against poverty for this group, however, in the vast majority of female-headed families, the absent father's contribution is lacking or inadequate, even though the father is legally bound to contribute. Of the 7 million women heading families with minor children in 1978, just over 4 million, or 59 percent were awarded child support payments by the courts. Almost 3 million more were denied such support. The amount of the award varied from place to place; it depended on such factors as the presence or skill of a lawyer, the attitude of the judge, the tax consequences, and, seemingly last, if not least, the

232

Feminist Visions

needs of the children and the ability of the father to pay. Nevertheless, only 49 percent of the women who were awarded child support actually received the full amount, and 28 percent received nothing at all.[9] For another 14 million divorced women who sought alimony, the odds were even worse. Only 14 percent were awarded alimony and, of these, 41 percent received the full amount; almost one-third received nothing. Lest one imagine wealthy women who did not need support, it should be noted that the mean income for child support families, if the support due them had been received, was only $8,172 a year in 1978, and the average child support award was $2,003 per year. The picture with voluntary written agreements, as opposed to legally derived plans, was no better. Twenty-eight percent of all households that were due support from an absent father fell below the poverty line.[10] Many more fell into the near–poor category. The legal and criminal justice systems that are supposed to oversee child support and alimony for the protection of the vulnerable have not done so.

Systems to Aid Poor Women

When the traditional systems, based on the male breadwinner, do not provide for the needs of women heading families, there are two remaining alternatives, either or both of which may be used. One is publicly provided financial assistance or welfare. The second is a well-paying job.

The public assistance designed to take care of one-parent families with children is Aid to Families with Dependent Children (AFDC), a highly stigmatizing program. The negative image of its recipients has been fostered by politicians and the media. In actuality, there are far more white than nonwhite recipients, although the *rate* of receipt among nonwhites is higher. Moreover, the average number of children in AFDC families is the same as the average number of children in non-AFDC families with children. In spite of welfare policies that deter working and the limited amount of child care available, 25 to 30 percent of AFDC mothers have worked part time or full time during any given year. Half the AFDC recipients received aid for no more than two years in the decade 1969–1978, despite fluctuations in the economy. Only 2 percent of the University of Michigan's longitudinal study of 5,000 families received welfare for seven years **233** or longer. One-third of these long-term recipients were old or lived in families headed by an aged person. The remaining two-thirds were members of female-headed households or were black—not surprising in that "both women and blacks are affected by restricted labor market opportunities."[11] Although these general facts are known, they seem to make no dent in the continuing beliefs that AFDC women are lazy and shiftless, are cheaters and promiscuous breeders, and are all minority members. When belief is resistant to data, one must ask why.

The AFDC program is inequitable in its treatment of recipients and is a maintainer of poverty because the benefits paid are usually well below the poverty line even if the value of food stamps is added in. The maximum benefit to a three-person family in 1983 was $96 a month in Mississippi and $530 a month in Vermont. Few states have corrected even partially for the impact of inflation on purchasing power in a highly inflationary decade—a policy that is in sharp contrast to that for social security and SSI, both of which are indexed to rise as the cost of living rises. SSI paid $238 per person per month in 1980, and some states added a supplement to that. This is nearly twice the per-person payment in the highest-paying AFDC state. Thus, AFDC recipients are now living at a lower standard, compared to the rest of the people in this country, in relation to both their earlier purchasing power and to the old and disabled who receive public aid. To bring all AFDC recipients up to the poverty line—not a generous standard—expenditures on food stamps and AFDC would have to rise by another $2.3 to $3 billion.[12]

In the last few years, inflation has pushed a large number of the working poor into tax brackets in which they owe taxes, rather than receive credits. A family of four at the poverty line now will pay 10 percent (or about $1,000) in federal income taxes, and this rate is expected to increase. We also know that state and local taxes tend to be regressive; that is, together they exact a larger proportion of income from the poor and they gradually reduce that proportion as income goes up.

The poor have also lost the services and benefits of many federal programs designed to aid them. Forty percent of the cutbacks in federal programs in the budgets for fiscal years 1981, 1982, and 1983 affected families with incomes below $10,000, although such families are only 23 percent of the population.[13] A study by the Congressional Research Service reported that over

2 million people who would otherwise have escaped poverty have

been pushed below the poverty line since 1981 by the combination of the recession (1.6 million persons affected) and the budget cuts in a variety of social programs (557,000 persons affected).[14] Because women heads of households have been major recipients of the social programs and have been particularly affected by the reduction in low-earning supplementation in AFDC, one must assume that women are overrepresented in this newly poor group. This assumption is substantiated by the estimate of 331,000 more children in poverty, over half of whom can be attributed to cutbacks in social programs.[15]

Another comparison between AFDC and programs aiding the elderly showed that 37 percent of the families headed by a non-aged woman received cash aid in 1965, while 88 percent of families with an aged head received such help. By 1978, there was no change in the proportion of female-headed families being aided, but 96 percent, or virtually all, of the aged families received cash transfers. Even after receipt of cash transfers, roughly a third of the female-headed households were still below the poverty line—both in 1965 and in 1978. The poor households headed by an aged person declined from 32 percent to 17 percent in that same period.[16]

Why Poverty Persists

At this point, it may be useful to ask a few questions. Why are mothers with young children treated less generously than the old or disabled in financial aid? Why are child support payments neither adequate nor enforced? Why does racism contaminate popular judgments of female-headed families? Why do these conditions persist when more and more women with young children are becoming economically vulnerable as the rate of family breakup escalates? And why do myths about the prevalence of the patriarchal family pattern persist in the face of data showing its decline? Most of all, why does all this continue in a nation that enshrines motherhood in all its Fourth of July speeches?

The picture drawn thus far suggests that there must be strong covert reasons for the persistence of this situation. Let us look at it from a feminist perspective to find some answers. One fact immediately leaps forward. That is the total lack of value this society attaches to the tasks of home care and child care. Were these tasks valued, those who perform them would be **235** valued as well, and their work would be considered as worthy as any other (paid) work. This society seems to see the nurturing functions on which feminists place high value as necessary but only of use when carried out in a patriarchal family structure.

Second, the nasty and stigmatizing attitudes toward welfare recipients apply only to mothers with children (and childless adults who are not aged). The categories of "worthy" and "unworthy" poor may be politically useful because they create divisions where in reality none exist. Racism also serves to divide one needy group from another. Feminists oppose such dichotomies and see the common conditions of poverty and need as overriding.

Some legislators and others have voiced concern that the AFDC program, by its eligibility requirements, causes fathers to leave their families, actually or seemingly, thus promoting the breakup of families. A feminist view of AFDC turns this notion on it head—AFDC may actually keep unhappy or abusive marriages together because welfare is so harshly punitive. As one battered woman said, to explain why she had returned yet again to her abusive husband: "When my husband beats me up, I know in his perverted way he loves me. When the Welfare Department beats me up, I know they despise me. Which would you choose?"

Third, it is the largely male world of the legal and criminal justice systems that determines and enforces child support and alimony payments. That must help to account for such a uniform pattern of inadequate and unenforced payments across thousands of courts and police departments. The sum of these actions is more concern for the finances of the absent fathers than for the well-being of their children. Again, these inadequacies protect and maintain the patriarchal family pattern because the alternative sources of support are so meager. It seems no accident that all welfare mothers are thought to be nonwhite, while the elderly recipients of aid are thought to be only white, against all evidence. The perpetuation of these erroneous ideas must occur because of covert needs: aid to the old poses no threat to the traditional family, but aid to mothers with children does.

What about employment—the all-American solution for poverty—as a means of rescuing women and children from poverty? To understand the potential of this solution, two questions must be addressed: How do women fare in the labor market, and who takes care of the children when women work? Women's

236

educational levels, job opportunities, and pay levels—in other words, women's marketability—must be looked at; it is important also to look at the availability, kinds, and costs of child care.

Women in the Work Force

There is widespread awareness of the rapid increase in the number of women who are working full time and all year long, whether they are married or have children and whether the children are young or considered old enough to care for themselves. One could speculate that the recent severe economic depression may have enhanced this movement of women into the labor force because the second earner's wages became a kind of added insurance for the family against the rigors of unemployment. In 1983, for the first time, more than half the mothers of children under age 6 were in the work force. Women maintaining families constituted 60 percent of the labor force; three-fourths of these working women had children aged 6–17, and 55 percent had children under 6. For most of these women, work was an economic necessity. Only 9 percent of the mothers heading single-parent households who were unemployed had any family member in the household with a full-time job, unlike two-parent families where the likelihood of a spouse being employed was high.[17] Over four-fifths of all working women worked full time.

"Most employed women maintaining families have tended to remain in the generally lower paying or lesser skilled jobs within a broad occupational group. . . ."[18] A closer look at patterns of the labor market will clarify why these outcomes happen. Most people can easily name occupations that are heavily staffed by women, such as secretary, nurse, or social worker, and others that are equally heavily male dominated. This labor market segregation is associated with pay scales that are different and with unionization patterns. Those industries that are the highest-paying had no more than 23 percent women among their work force, and one-third to two-thirds of their workers were represented by unions in 1981. For these workers, the median weekly wage was $400 in 1981. In contrast, in the lowest-paying industries as a group (excepting agriculture), between 66 percent and 90 percent of the work force was female, less than a quarter of the workers were represented by a union, and the median wage ranged from $114 to $188 per week. (At that time, the minimum **237** wage of $3.35 per hour for a 35-hour week would equal $117.25). "Earnings below $150 a week were most common among youth, women and minority employees."[19]

The National Organization for Women (NOW) has publicized the "59-cents" slogan—that women earn 59 cents to every dollar earned by comparable men—and that this differential has persisted for several decades. As Table 2 shows, a significant differential is found at every level of educational attainment. The data indicate a hierarchy of earnings levels, with white men at the top, black men next, followed by white women, and, last, by black women (except that the last two have recently become reversed for women holding graduate degrees). Black women earn between 70 and 81 percent of what black men earn, but both earn less than whites. Black women who are high school graduates earn 56 percent of what white male high school graduates earn. Because the data in Table 2 cover only full-time workers, the differences cannot be explained by part-time status of women or blacks. Furthermore, this difference in wages of men and women has persisted for the past 40 years in spite of two decades of national legislation that was supposed to correct it.

Another consequence of a segregated labor market is the distribution of fringe benefits. These benefits not only provide protection against the economic consequence of illness and retirement, for instance, but, in effect, increase the disposable income of persons who have them. Without such coverage, individuals and families would have to spend some of their income to purchase medical care or annuities. As has been shown, most women workers are in nonunionized industries. Unionization dramatically increases the likelihood of job tenure, health insurance, pensions, and other protections.[20]

Although a woman has been appointed to the Supreme Court and another was chosen as a candidate for vice president of the United States, these women are still rare exceptions. Eighteen percent of all working men were classified as professional in 1981, compared to 8 percent of all working women; 41 percent of working women were in sales, compared to 5 percent of working men. Similarly, 10 percent of men, but 22 percent of women, worked in service jobs, and 28 percent of all women workers were in clerical positions, compared with 19 percent of all men. Thus, occupational distribution is skewed and depends on the sex of the workers. Sales, service, and clerical jobs, it need

238 hardly be said, are among the lowest paid of all jobs.[21]

Feminist Visions

Table 2
Median Weekly Earnings of Full-Time Workers in 1981,
by Educational Level, Sex, and Race (in dollars)

Educational Level	All Men	White Men	Black Men	All Women	White Women	Black Women	Ratio of White Women to White Men
Less than a high school degree	290	301	241	180	182	172	.60
High school graduate	363	372	294	222	224	209	.60
College graduate	459	471	354	299	301	296	.64
Graduate degree holder	507	510	449	362	359	384	.70

Source: Earl Mellor and George Stamas, "Usual Weekly Earnings: Another Look at Intergroup Differences and Basic Trends," *Monthly Labor Review*, 105 (April 1982), pp. 15–24.

Increased attention has been paid lately to the practice of giving similar jobs different titles and different pay, the higher titles and pay to those filled by men and the lower to those filled by women. Another issue, now being tested in the courts, is comparable worth. This issue involves jobs with comparable degrees of responsibility or usefulness that have different levels of pay if they are usually filled by men or by women. Whether the secretary is more useful to the continued functioning of the university, for example, than the groundskeeper, *she* earns far less than *he* does (the gender terms used here are deliberate and are not inappropriate or irrelevant to understanding the issue). If her salary is one-third lower than his, yet both are required to have at least a high school diploma and some additional skills, is not their worth comparable and should not their salaries also be?

The data show that women earn less than their male counterparts and tend to work in a limited range of female-intensive occupations that offer not only lower wages but fewer fringe benefits. As with other victims of bias and oppression, they are often blamed for their own plight, faulted that they lack skills to compete according to male values. The economic consequences of such biases are severe for women and the children dependent on them. Some years ago, a study estimated that if women recipients of AFDC who were working were paid at the rate of men in similar jobs, 40 percent would earn enough to leave the welfare rolls without any added work effort.[22] More important, they could substantially improve their living standards and those of their children. **239**

Child Care and Employment of Women

Working women with children, whether they are single parents or married, face another set of concerns: care for their children while they are at work. Some two-parent families can stagger working hours, but flextime is not yet a widespread policy. Women still carry the major responsibility for child care: It is the woman who leaves work when a child is sick and who assumes the larger share of child and home care after work. It is interesting to note that this seems to be an international pattern.[23]

Unlike many European nations, this country has eschewed public provision of child care. A study of child care in Western industrialized nations found that "the United States is the only nation to construct its child care program with such a heavy emphasis on problems....The result...is that child care programs are imbued with strong negative overtones....[They] segregate a community by grouping together the poor, the abused and those with other problems."[24]

One estimate, in 1982, reported about 15 million children 13 years or under living in households where all resident parents worked full time. "There are less than one million slots in child care centers; family day care and in-home care by relatives or non-relatives serves another 6.8 million children." That leaves nearly half these children under 13 years as latch-key children who "probably take care of themselves when they are not in school."[25]

Probably most child care is provided by informal systems—babysitters, housekeepers, and family day care providers who are unregulated, unsupervised, and unreported. Even in states that try to license family day care—and some 30 do so—there is general agreement that a large but unknown number of day care providers, especially small providers, slip through these regulatory efforts. Standards of safety, staffing, training of staff, quality of programming, and so on vary greatly; they are probably low, but, in any case, they are unknown.

Although these kinds of private arrangements are the most widely used, it is not known whether they are used because parents prefer them or because there is a shortage of desirable alternatives. Several surveys have reflected parents' dissatisfaction with the child care choices available to them and a "preference for well-staffed day care centers to family-based day care."[26] All the evidence suggests an absolute shortage of child care relative to the need, aggravated by geographic patterns in the distribution

240

Feminist Visions

of services and by a serious shortage in the *kinds* and *quality* of child care that parents would prefer.

In 1978, the average cost per child in a private day care center was $1,300 per year; it was $2,500 in a public day care center.[27] This cost was subsidized for the very poor—if they were eligible. When such costs for one or two children are placed against the earnings, particularly of one-parent families and, most particularly, the earnings of women, who represent over 95 percent of the heads of such families, it can be seen that this sum represents a huge proportion of their earnings. To illustrate, the median weekly wage of women over age 16 and working full time was $224 in 1981.[28] If such a woman were a single parent and had two children in need of child care, the cost of that care would absorb about one-quarter of her total gross earnings. Her remaining income would put her below the poverty line. However, her gross earnings level would probably place her above the cutoff for subsidized day care in many states.

In spite of such disincentives, the policy for recipients of public assistance is to require participation in job training or work, provided there is no child under age 6 in the home. It is likely that most welfare recipients would earn less than the median wage because of discrimination and their lower-than-average levels of education. In effect, many mothers on welfare are faced with a draconian choice similar to that facing women in the nineteenth century before Mothers' Pensions: to feed and clothe one's children, one must place them in child care arrangements that are well below what one would choose. It seems that most working mothers with young children face a situation of "damned if you do, damned if you don't." Although many European nations, as will be shown later, view children as a major national resource for whom the state shares the responsibility with parents for both costs and care, this country clearly has taken a different tack.

Work Incentives and Women's Poverty

In this book, Abramovitz discusses how women and children are punished for deviating from traditional family patterns. Unlike the elderly and the disabled, women who head families are considered able-bodied and therefore able to work for pay with little regard for the availability of resources for the care of children.   **241**

In the 1970s, economists discovered the issue of work incentives. They pointed out that welfare recipients were, in effect, taxed 100 percent if they were able to work and earn while on the welfare rolls. By reducing the welfare grant $1.00 for each $1.00 earned, they observed, work—even part-time or part-year work—was discouraged. The only job worth taking under such conditions would be a job that offered a wage sufficient to bring the family well above the welfare eligibility level and that promised long tenure. (Needless to say, such jobs are scarce.)

Therefore, AFDC policies were changed so that working recipients were given a flat sum to cover the extra costs of working (usually about $1.00 a day), and the so-called tax rate was reduced from 100 percent to 70 percent. Generously, women were allowed to keep 30 percent of their earnings up to a certain amount. The costs of welfare were supposed to go down when welfare recipients went to work.

These policies were enacted at a time when more women were entering the labor market and employment levels were relatively high. They have been revoked under the Reagan Administration during a time of high unemployment. Because they were never tried under poor economic conditions, it is not clear that work incentives were necessary or that they attained the goal of a greater work effort by welfare recipients. One might also ask how fair this now-revoked policy could have been since it taxed these poor women more highly on their earnings than taxpayers in any other tax bracket were taxed.

The systems that are supposed to guarantee equal pay and equal working conditions to men and women and to whites and nonwhites have been in place for over 20 years. The Equal Pay Act of 1963 forbids wage discrimination on the basis of sex or race. The Civil Right Acts of 1964, with later amendments, prohibits discrimination in hiring, promotion, conditions of employment, and classification of employment. Executive Order 11375, of 1968, prohibits discrimination by anyone doing business with the federal government and requires such employers to develop affirmative action plans and goals. Title IX of the Educational Amendments of 1972 forbids such discriminatory patterns in educational programs or the institutions that provide them as differences in access, in requirements, in spending. All these pieces of legislation rely on the individual's filing a complaint— the weakest form of enforcement. The complaint is filed with the

242 Equal Employment Opportunity Commission, which has long been underfunded and understaffed. The time between filing and processing a complaint can be as long as three years. Final recourse lies in the courts. Most of these processes presume that the person filing the complaint is able to withstand pressure on the job, the loss of the job, and sufficient income to hire a lawyer. Class-action suits, although dramatic, are rare and not permitted in all categories. The courts have held to a more stringent standard of proof in sex discrimination cases than in racial ones, which has made progress on this front even slower. Furthermore, the federal government is itself one of the worst offenders. For example, the U.S. Government Printing Office hired women as "sewing clerks" and men as "bookbinders," even though both operated the same machines and did the same work; the only difference was in the rate of pay. The Reagan Administration has opposed quotas in hiring and attacked still further an already weak affirmative action effort. The gender gap in earnings continues unchanged. The job market strategy, which also ignores child care, seems to be of only limited value in defeminizing poverty.

International Comparisons

All industrialized nations are seeing the same broad trends of an ever-increasing number of women, including mothers, entering and remaining in the labor force; of more children living in one-parent families; and of an ever-increasing number of women maintaining families. Other nations, however, have defined the problems differently than has the United States, and they have developed a number of strategies that have sharply reduced the incidence of poverty among such families.

Two broad areas of belief seem to undergird the actions of these nations. One is that children are a resource of the nation; thus, the society has a stake in their healthy development. An outgrowth of this view is a sense of responsibility for sharing in the costs of childbearing and childrearing, in recognition that the wage system is based on the productivity of a worker—not on the number of mouths to be fed by the wage the worker earns. A second area of belief is of a national community, which promotes the idea of a national minimum below which no member of the community should fall, as well as a strong sense that every citizen is entitled to at least that standard. A feminist view supports the right of all human beings to live in decency and the **243** right of all children to receive the care they need to grow and develop to their fullest capacity.

All industrialized nations, except the United States, have enacted a children's allowance.[29] The children's allowance is an automatic monthly cash grant to every family, regardless of income, that begins at the birth of each child (in some cases only after the birth of the second child) and continues to a certain point, usually to the end of schooling. Although not sufficient alone for an adequate standard of living, the children's allowance raises the family's income. The effect has been a significant reduction in the number of families and children in poverty.

The rise in the number of families in which all resident parents are working outside the home in recent years has caused most industrialized nations to identify four concerns and to develop policies to deal with them that are fully consistent with feminist perspectives. These concerns are (1) the need for financial help with the costs of childrearing for most or all families, (2) the need for child care while parents are at work, (3) the need to permit changes in the way work, home, and child-tending tasks are shared by men and women, and (4) the need to encourage a better balance between the demands of work and home so that parenting can be carried out without a labor-market (and thus income) penalty for mothers or fathers. Many countries provide tax credit to families with children and refund it as a cash benefit to those whose income is too low to receive full advantage of the credit. In the United States, the tax exemption benefits only those whose incomes—and tax bills—are high enough to derive advantage from it; and, because of the progressivity of the tax structure, the higher the income bracket, the more the exemption is worth.[30]

Most European nations, unlike the United States, also have maternity policies that provide an income-replacement benefit during the leave period (which averages six months to a year) and guarantee the protection of the leave taker's job, seniority, and fringe benefits, including health benefits. Hungary extends this protection through a cash benefit equal to about 40 percent of the average female wage until the child reaches age 3. This policy surely is a more humane way to maintain the traditional roles of the father as breadwinner and the mother as child rearer than is the U.S. AFDC program.

All the benefits discussed so far go automatically to families with children, regardless of income, without stigma. France, in

Feminist Visions

addition, gives an income-tested benefit to low- or middle-income families with preschoolers or to families with three or more children. This policy is based on the assumption that the presence of many or of young children hinders the financial well-being of the family. A number of countries also give rent subsidies on an income-tested basis to one-parent families or to large families.

All European countries provide for the health care of pregnant women and of all children through a health service or a health insurance scheme. They provide child care services as well. In France, Belgium, West Germany, and almost all the countries in Eastern Europe, the public school systems include preschools, some include children as young as 2 years. Child care is provided, at no cost to parents, to more than three-quarters of all children aged 3–6. There is a widespread belief that such preschool programs are beneficial and educational for children. Only secondarily are they seen as a way of providing child care while parents are at work.

In contrast, care for children under 3 is considered day care and is most often administered as a social welfare program. It is usually family day care, but there is a clear trend toward increasing the availability of group care for ever-younger children. Countries differ on the public-private mix and on the degree of subsidization for low-income families for this latter form of day care. The need for after-school programs for primary school children of working parents also is widely recognized, but, thus far, the need has far outstripped the supply.[31]

European employers are experimenting with a variety of ways to ease the strains of carrying the dual tasks of work and home. In addition to flextime, job sharing, and shorter workdays for the caretaking parent of young children, there are a variety of fringe benefits, such as providing or paying for day care. The net effect of these various policies may best be illustrated by contrasting Sweden and the United States. Table 3 shows that relatively few of the one-parent families in Sweden receive public assistance, although there are more of such families there than in the United States. The explanation lies largely in the public programs provided to *all* families with children in Sweden, which help to raise their standards of living, and in the widespread availability of child care programs that are subsidized for low-income families. These child care programs permit a much higher rate of participation in the labor force of Swedish mothers of preschoolers than exists in the United States. Work, therefore, **245**

Table 3
Treatment of One-Parent Families with Children: United States (1975) vs. Sweden (1976)

Type of	United States	Sweden
1. One-parent families as percentage of all families with children	16 percent	23 percent
2. One-parent families as percentage of all public assistance recipients	86 percent	17 percent
3. One-parent family, two children, no earnings or resources; all benefits; monthly income in U.S. dollars, 1976	$311.00	$586.00
4. Monthly income of two-parent family, two children, only the father working, at median male wage, plus benefits	$937.90	$911.90
5. Net income of No. 3 as a percentage of No. 4	33 percent	64 percent

SOURCE: Derived from C. T. Adams and K. T. Winston, *Mothers at Work: Public Policies in the U.S., Sweden and China* (New York: Longman, 1980), copyright © 1980 by Longman Inc. Tables 2–11 and 2–12, pp. 89 and 91.

becomes a real option because child care is available at low cost.

Table 3 also permits a comparison between the one-parent, no-earner, no-resources family with two children (Item 3) and the two-parent, one-male-earner family at the median male wage (Item 4) in each country. Included in both family incomes are all the public benefits for which they are eligible. For the American family in Item 3, for example, those benefits are public assistance and food stamps. It is evident that the net monthly incomes of the two-parent families in the two nations are similar in U.S. dollars. Net incomes of the one-parent families, however, are disparate. The public assistance grant in the two countries for this type of family is similar, but the difference is accounted for by the Swedish family's receipt of a family allowance ($78.00), a child-maintenance grant ($164.00), and a housing allowance ($119.00). Although these data are for 1976, there have been no significant changes since that time.[32]

Conclusion

The woman trap need not continue if feminist visions are applied to policies designed to eliminate poverty. For example, a feminist

246 approach eliminates false dichotomies and categories. It is not concerned with separating the worthy from the unworthy; instead, it places major importance on the provision of adequate income and care—certainly for children, but also for all people. Guided by such values, it is possible to design programs to keep women who head families with children from poverty. Feminist values would demand that parents share equally the costs and the care involved in raising children, which would require reorienting many families and many services, as well as enforcing child support laws.

Feminist values would require that all bias and discrimination in the labor market be ended—again, an approach that would require the enforcement of existing laws and probably the creation of some new ones. Even these small steps would go far toward allowing women heading families to escape from the poverty trap. Bringing the level of the AFDC benefits up to the level of welfare for the aged would improve the condition of recipient families. A feminist approach would be to set one benefit level for all the poor, regardless of why they are poor and regardless of their age or status. When SSI was passed, it combined the previously separate categories of Old Age Assistance, Aid to the Blind, and Aid to the Disabled. Why not fold all the poor into SSI? If a children's allowance were enacted in this country, as it has been in all the other industrialized nations, the level of living of *all* families with children would be raised.

Although some of these proposals would require large new expenditures, others would require merely the enforcement of laws already on the books. There would be offsetting savings in that many women heading families would be earning more for the same amount of work effort and would not need public aid to support themselves and their children. Clearly, a child care system would also need to be developed—in many forms, in larger quantity, and with better quality—so that children would not be left untended while mothers work. Were all these options to be implemented, still another feminist value would be enhanced: that people should have choices. One has to ask why it is that these failures persist in the face of rhetoric and legislation that seems to be aimed at correcting them. Is the underlying reason for these identified failures the covert purpose of maintaining the patriarchal family and its traditional division of labor as well as power?

The Woman Trap

notes

1. For a discussion of the social processes by which social problems become such, see Herbert Blumer, "Social Problems as Collective Behavior," *Social Problems,* 18 (Winter 1971), pp. 298–306.

2. A description of such assumptions can be found in Clair Wilcox, *Toward Social Welfare* (Homewood, Ill.: Dorsey Press, 1969), p. 27; and Betty Peterkin, *The Measure of Poverty* (Washington, D.C.: U.S. Department of Health, Education & Welfare, 1976). See also Andrew Levison, "The Working Class," *The New Yorker,* September 2, 1974, p. 38ff. *Monthly Labor Review* publishes annually the updated monetary components of the standards.

3. U.S. Bureau of the Census, "Characteristics of the Population Below the Poverty Level, 1982," *Current Population Reports,* Series P-60, No. 144 (Washington, D.C.: U.S. Department of Commerce, 1984).

4. Ibid.

5. U.S. Bureau of the Census, *Current Population Reports,* Series P-60, No. 138 (Washington, D.C.: U.S. Department of Commerce, 1983), p. 25.

6. See *IRP Focus,* 8 (Summer 1985), p. 2.

7. Howard Hayghe, "Married Couples: Work and Income Patterns," *Monthly Labor Review,* 106 (December 1983), pp. 26–29.

8. U.S. Bureau of the Census, *Current Population Reports,* Series 107 (Washington, D.C.: U.S. Department of Commerce, 1980); and Beverly Johnson and Elizabeth Waldman, "Most Women Who Maintain Families Receive Poor Labor Market Returns," *Monthly Labor Review,* 106 (December 1983), pp. 30–34.

9. U.S. Bureau of the Census, *Current Population Reports,* Series P-23, No. 106 (Washington, D.C.: U.S. Department of Commerce, 1980).

10. U.S. Bureau of the Census, *Current Population Reports,* Series P-60, No. 138 (1983).

11. Greg Duncan, *Years of Poverty, Years of Plenty* (Ann Arbor: Institute for Social Research, University of Michigan, 1984), p. 167.

12. "Poverty in the United States: Where Do We Stand Now?" *IRP Focus,* 7 (Winter 1984), pp. 1–4.

13. *New York Times,* October 23, 1983, p. A29, and August 26, 1983, p. A24.

14. "Poverty in the United States."

15. Ibid.

16. Ibid.

17. Elizabeth Waldman, "Labor Force Statistics from a Family Perspective," *Monthly Labor Review,* 106 (December 1983), pp. 16–20.

Feminist Visions

18. Johnson and Waldman, "Most Women Who Maintain Families Receive Poor Labor Market Returns," p. 31.

19. Earl Mellor and George Stamas, "Usual Weekly Earnings: Another Look at Intergroup Differences and Basic Trends," *Monthly Labor Review*, 105 (April 1982), p. 19.

20. Ibid., pp. 15–24.

21. Ibid. See also Johnson and Waldman, "Most Women Who Maintain Families Receive Poor Labor Market Returns."

22. Richard Wertheimer, "Earnings of Women: Implications of Equality in the Labor Market," Working Paper No. 980-1 (Washington, D.C.: The Urban Institute, 1974).

23. Alice H. Cook, "Working Women: European Experience and American Need," in *American Women Workers in a Full Employment Economy*, Joint Economic Committee, 95th Cong., 1st sess., 15 September 1977 (Washington, D.C.: U.S. Government Printing Office, 1977).

24. Ellen Galinsky and William Hooks, *The New Extended Family: Day Care That Works* (Boston: Houghton Mifflin Co., 1977).

25. *Employed Parents and Their Children: A Data Book* (Washington, D.C.: Children's Defense Fund, 1982).

26. Ellie Aronowitz, "Day Care: A Challenge for Policy Makers." Unpublished manuscript, Rutgers-The State University of New Jersey, New Brunswick, 1984. (Mimeographed.)

27. Bryna Siegel-Gorelick, *The Working Parents' Guide to Child Care* (Boston: Little, Brown & Co., 1983).

28. Mellor and Stamas, "Usual Weekly Earnings."

29. Sheila Kamerman, "Child Care and Family Benefits: Policies of Six Industrialized Countries," *Monthly Labor Review*, 103 (November 1980), pp. 23–28.

30. Ibid., pp. 24–25.

31. Ibid., p. 27.

32. C. T. Adams and K. T. Winston, *Mothers at Work: Public Policies in the U.S., Sweden and China* (New York: Longman, 1980).

Ruth A. Brandwein

a feminist approach to social policy

how is it that this world has always belonged to men? — Simone de Beauvoir, *The Ethics of Ambiguity*, 1948.

What is feminist social policy? What does it look like? Is policy not just policy? Does feminist social policy mean policy pertaining to women? Before I address these questions and attempt to suggest a feminist vision of social policy, it would be well to answer a prior question—"What is social policy?"

Social policy, according to the *Encyclopedia of Social Work,*

> may be regarded as the principles and procedures guiding any measure or course of action dealing with individual and aggregate relationships in society. . . . Established social policy represents a settled course of action with respect to selected social phenomena, governing social relationships and the distribution of resources within a society. . . . It concerns the myriad relationships between individuals, groups, and the larger society; it defines social status and roles and governs the distribution of economic resources among the mem-

250

bers of society. . . .Social policies. . .regulate the development, allocation, and distribution of statuses and roles and their accompanying constraints, rewards, and entitlements among individuals and social units within a society.[1]

Briefly, then, social policy concerns a set of procedures and principles, whether formalized or not, that deal with, regulate, or govern relationships between people, as individuals or as part of groups, and with the larger society. It is concerned with the distribution of resources, whether material or in the form of roles and statuses, and of sanctions. Included among the resources that may emerge from social policies are social programs that benefit certain portions of the population.

In social policy, economic, political, and social issues, values, and beliefs converge to affect who will benefit or suffer and in what way. Public policy defines how the government encourages or discourages courses of action and distributes rewards and punishments. In addition, other formal institutions such as the corporate sector and the church also have policies that, although not developed through a public process, have a profound impact on the public. In short, social policy is the arena in which impersonal societal forces affect people's lives.

What is a feminist approach to policy? In the introduction to this book, feminism was defined as "a transformational politics, a political perspective concerned with changing extant economic, social, and political structures," which can be put into operation by the elimination of false dichotomies, the reconceptualization of power, valuing process equally with product, renaming or redefining reality consistent with women's reality, and acknowledging that the personal is political.[2] Other writers have offered similar definitions, adding such concepts as holism, nonhierarchical relationships, an acceptance of the spiritual dimension, acceptance of uniqueness including the valuing of diversity, and the importance of connections or webs of relations.[3]

Some of these values, such as egalitarianism, valuing process as well as product, integrating personal and political spheres, and acknowledging the intuitive or spiritual, are shared by many value systems, including those of some American Indian and non-Western cultures, humanists, and, to some extent, the profession of social work. What makes an approach to policy uniquely feminist is that it incorporates these values but in addition is centrally concerned about the oppression of women, which it connects with that of other historically oppressed groups. Such an   **251** approach seeks to develop policy solutions to reduce that oppression and to empower women.

There are three levels on which to approach feminist social policy. The first and most obvious level is to examine those policies dealing with what are inherently "women's issues." The second level is to analyze all policy issues from a feminist perspective, and the third is to examine how a feminist approach affects not only policy outcomes but also the process of policy-making itself.

This article systematically addresses each of these levels, using particular policies as illustrations rather than dealing with them exhaustively. The article concludes with suggestions on how social policy can be taught from a feminist perspective in the social work curriculum.

Women's Issues in Social Policy

Just as all women politicians do not define themselves and their beliefs as feminist and women's studies are not necessarily feminist studies, policy issues that affect women do not necessarily constitute feminist social policy. Indeed, the history of social policy is replete with issues that have affected women. For example, public welfare policies and concomitant financial programs such as Aid to Families with Dependent Children are primarily, and in many states exclusively, programs for women and their children. Because women have been, and overwhelmingly still are, the primary child rearers, child welfare is also a "women's issue."

In the past 15 years, other issues that exclusively or primarily affect women have come to the fore in policy debates: violence against women (rape, domestic violence, sexual abuse); reproductive rights (family planning, sterilization, abortion); discrimination (equal pay, sexual harassment, affirmative action); child care, divorce, and custody (displaced homemakers, joint custody, enforceable child support); and, most recently, the feminization of poverty. Although it is true that all these issues could affect men—even men can be raped by other men—these policy issues have been seen as women's issues because of women's particular biology or social roles.

Child welfare policy is a key example of how a subject that primarily affects women (as mothers) has not traditionally been addressed from a feminist perspective. Early child welfare advo-

252

cates were frequently critical of the natural parents, especially mothers, who were seen as neglectful, irresponsible, slovenly, and too fertile. There was often an underlying but unacknowledged cultural and class bias in the middle-class, Protestant, native-born American, frequently unmarried child welfare workers who made judgments about poor, immigrant mothers. The legitimate concerns of child welfare advocates about the "best interests of the child" have often been translated in practice into an adversary relationship between children and parents.[4]

An alternative, feminist approach would recognize the oppressive forces in society that prevent mothers from adequately caring for their children and attempt to develop policies and programs to rectify the situation. An excellent example of such an analysis was the Carnegie Council's report, *All Our Children,* which identified economic factors as a key determinant to good parenting:

> In keeping with our view that a family's economic position is still the single most powerful determinant of the opportunities open to families and to children, we support above all national policies to equalize the impact of economic forces on our entire citizenry. This will take a commitment to creating jobs and achieving full employment so that no American child will suffer because a parent cannot find work or earn enough to provide a decent living.[5]

Such preventive programs as family life education developed by the Family Service Association of America (now Family Service America) are examples of efforts to empower women (and men) to be better parents.

A second policy area, which has recently been redefined from a general policy issue to one that is centrally of concern to women, is that of poverty. Poverty has been on the front burner of American social policy since the early 1960s. Reframing the issue as the feminization of poverty is an example of a redefinition or renaming of reality that is consistent with women's reality and constitutes a feminist approach. The feminization of poverty focuses on the fact that most of the poor people in this country are now women and their children. Among the reasons for this phenomenon are the increase of single-parent families, the inequitable salary distribution between women and men, inadequate child support enforcement mechanisms, and the demography of the elderly: The majority of the elderly **253** are women; they are less likely than men to have private pensions and thus are more likely to fall below the poverty line. Indeed, the National Advisory Council on Economic Opportunity has predicted that if current trends are projected to the year 2000, all the poor people in this country will be women and their children.[6]

Obviously, redefining and reanalyzing the problem in this way is feminist in that it exposes the oppression of women in the society. The policies and programs proposed to overcome the problem may or may not be feminist. On the one hand, policy initiatives that promote equal pay for comparable work promote justice and equality for women. On the other hand, a policy that discourages divorce to "keep families together" to "solve" the problem of underpaid female single parents who are heads of families would be more oppressive to women.

Abortion is a classic example of a women's issue that may or may not be approached from a feminist perspective. Abortion is of primary concern to women because it affects their bodies. Those who advocate "anti-choice" policies are, in effect, choosing between a woman's right to control her body and certain norms and moral codes. Feminists would argue that such a position reduces a woman's body to an incubation machine for the unborn child. Although anti-choice (or "pro-life") advocates define their adversaries as "anti-life," most women do not see themselves as pro-abortion so much as they see themselves as pro-choice (another example of redefining women's reality). They favor reproductive rights for women, which include not only the choice about whether to bring a pregnancy to term but the choice of whether to be sterilized. This choice, in the past, was denied to many women who were poor, black, on welfare, or in institutions for the retarded or mentally ill where they were forcibly sterilized.

Unlike the issues of child welfare or abortion, it would seem that the issues of rape, battered women, and sexual harassment are inherently feminist because the problems addressed are specifically ones in which the oppression of women is the defining factor. Yet even in such de facto feminist policy issues, the proposed solutions can be more or less feminist. Shelters for women, for example, can focus primarily on women's empowerment or can merely provide clinical services to help them cope. Valentich and Gripton's article developed a model for such an analysis.[7]

254 Feminist Visions

General Policy Issues

Identifying certain issues as "women's issues" and limiting feminist concerns to these alone is indicative of a patriarchal society in which women are the "second sex."[8] In distinguishing those policies that are clearly and undeniably of concern to women, one assumes that other policies are not. Moreover, the policies that concern women (like those professions in which women predominate) are usually accorded inferior status. As in other spheres, what is human is considered male, and what is female is "other."

In mental health policy and programs, for example, mental health was defined from a male perspective, as the work of Broverman et al. documented.[9] In a classic study, they found that mental health professionals equated attributes of a healthy adult with those of a healthy male and contrasted them with those of a healthy female. Chesler found that women and men were diagnosed differentially and channeled into different types of treatment settings.[10]

In health policy, traditional medical policies and practices have been altered only since the new wave of the women's movement. Patients' rights and informed consent are long-term empowerments for all people that emanated from women's health collectives and their insistence on these rights for women. Similarly, the discovery that a radical mastectomy was not any more effective in most cases than a modified mastectomy or lumpectomy has led to a change in policy that has affected millions of women and that came about when women were empowered to question their physicians and to seek information from other sources.

What about policy issues related to housing, physical planning, and economic development—areas in which special efforts must be made to redefine or transform the issues to address women's concerns? Suburbanization, it is now acknowledged, created a major social change in the lives of women, their roles, and their relationships to their families. Women were moved out of close, supportive neighborhoods—in which webs of relationships existed—into isolated nuclear-family homes in which women's roles as wives, mothers, and consumers were paramount. The impact of a policy on women is rarely considered; when it is, it is often considered in the light of patriarchal values.

I have firsthand knowledge of one example in which a Washington policymaker denied a request by a social service agency to fund a housing development for female-headed house- **255** holds. Besides apartments, the development would have provided laundry rooms, a day-care center, and other supportive facilities. His explanation was, "Of course we turned it down; it would just discourage them from ever getting remarried."

Until recently, economic development and job training have focused almost solely on men. Despite the increased number of female-headed families, especially among minorities, most job-training programs choose men preferentially over women, especially for training that may lead to higher-paid jobs. Only since the women's movement has there been pressure for women to be trained for "nontraditional" jobs, such as the skilled crafts, which pay higher wages than the traditional low-paid women's occupations, such as secretary or nurse's aide. As Pearce and McAdoo observed, jobs have been a strategy for leading men out of poverty—but not women.[11] The policy of equal pay for comparable worth, mentioned earlier, which was won recently in the Washington State courts but was lost on appeal to the federal court and is now under study in New York State, is a strategy for providing compensation to those in traditional "women's" jobs that is equal to the compensation paid to those in traditional "men's" jobs when the level of training and responsibility are comparable.

A final example of general policies that need to be transformed and redefined to consider women's oppression and empowerment is in the area of peace and war. Historically, peace has been a women's issue worldwide because of women's roles as child bearers and nurturers. Women have been in the forefront of the antinuclear and nuclear freeze movements. Traditionally, women have been the "peacemakers" in the family. Because of their lesser physical strength, they have tended to develop strategies of negotiation, persuasion, and bargaining instead of the use of brute force to solve disagreements. Moreover, peace is a women's issue because it is everyone's issue. Nuclear armageddon would threaten the survival of the world's population, of which women are one-half.

The Policymaking Process

A feminist approach to policymaking must first address how social problems, policies, and programs differentially affect women and men

and must be sensitive to the problems of oppression and to solu-

Feminist Visions

tions that promote empowerment. Although such a step is necessary, it is not sufficient.

A feminist approach to social policy is inherently different in a number of other ways. Operationalizing the value of process and of product, the feminist policymaker is concerned with means as well as ends. It is not enough to believe that a policy is right and, therefore, that any means to achieve it is justified. For example, the War on Poverty introduced the concept of "maximum participation of the poor" into the design of policies and programs geared toward the poor. True participation means that the policymaker, the agency director, or whoever else is the key professional "decision maker" must enter a partnership with the targets of policies or recipients of service. One can guide, persuade, and try to influence decisions, but one must be more wedded to a belief in the process than to one's particularly favored outcome. If the latter prevails, then coercion or manipulation will be the result.

If one truly believes that a particular outcome is essential, then, to be authentic, one must state one's belief explicitly; then others have the option of evaluating the correctness of such a judgment. In fact, there are so few absolutes in working with people that it is rare that one or another policy or program is objectively the "best." Rather, it is often the one that people believe in and invest in that will yield the best results.

A second principle the feminist policymaker must implement is that "the personal is political." Often policymakers operate so high in the macrosphere that they have little to do with the actual implementation of policy, which is left to the administrators or deliverers of service. Such policymakers seem to be taking onto themselves a certain arrogance of godlikeness—being above mere mortals, treating people as objects or as things, entering into an I-It rather than an I-Thou relationship with those who will be affected by their policies.[12]

Although it may be true that in a complex society not everyone can do everything all the time and do it well, it is essential that policymakers know what a real client looks like and be aware of the bureaucratic obstacles in the organizations that are to implement policy. Too often, it is not that a policy is "bad" or "wrong" but that there is a "slip between the cup and the lip." It is incumbent on the policymaker to take some responsibility for the realistic implementation of policy. Moreover, unless the policymaker has some firsthand understanding of the objective **257** reality of those who are most directly affected by the policy—client and worker alike—she or he cannot know whether the policy is appropriate or implementable.

In putting into practice the concepts of process as well as product and the personal is political, we feminists are, in effect, introducing a more egalitarian model of policymaking and redefining power. If those who are the recipients (or, in systems terms, the output constituency) of policies are to be authentically involved in making those policies (the input constituency), then power is shared; power is transformed to influence rather than to coerce or force.

This sharing of power means adopting a "win-win" rather than a "win-lose" approach to power. If we are so invested in our own policy preference, then if it is not adopted we define that as a loss. But if instead we believe that through an authentic process of involvement a synthesis will emerge that will be better than any individual's favorite solution, then everyone has won—there need not be any losers. This process also illustrates the value of the collective over the individual and the value of diversity. Solving a problem using knowledge and understanding from multiple viewpoints will create a final product—in this case, a policy —that will be superior to what any one individual could develop.

The feminist policymaker must also approach problems and issues holistically. That is to say, as we examine an issue, we must look at the connections, the web of relationship that are affected. For example, in promulgating a policy to establish filial responsibility for elderly parents, it is not enough to look merely at the economic implications for the government and the family. One must ask, Who will be the caregiver?[13] All too often, it is the woman in the family. How does this answer fit in with the phenomenon that over 50 percent of the work force is now female? That most women work because of economic responsibility? That increased housing costs may mean that there is less physical space to house the elderly? What are the psychological implications of intergenerational families? Of role reversal in authority? These are just a few examples of a holistic rather than a linear analysis. Mayer described this approach in greater detail as being inherent in the developmental approach to policymaking that emerged from the "City Beautiful" movement in which physical planning was undertaken organically.[14]

Finally, although not all women are feminists and not all **258** feminists are women, it is essential that more women be involved

Feminist Visions

in the policymaking process. Why? Simply because women constitute at least 50 percent of the population and they have had different experiences and perceptions that can enrich the diversity of input into policymaking.

As Eleanor Roosevelt observed,

> Too often the great decisions are originated and given form in bodies made up wholly of men or so completely dominated by them that whatever of special value women have to offer is shunted aside without expression.[15]

For example, no man has experienced an abortion or a pelvic examination. Few have been single parents or have done the weekly shopping or have had to adjust family schedules to the exigencies of a mate's employer. Although we do not advocate that only those who have directly experienced something should be involved in policy deliberations about that subject, involving those who have the experience brings a reality base to such deliberations. Moreover, because of women's differential socialization and roles, they more often have learned to approach decision making from a consensus rather than a conflict orientation. Women are, in general, more skilled at seeking various viewpoints and inputs, less likely to have ego needs in having their particular solution adopted, and more likely to be sensitive to issues of oppression. The more we move to an androgynous society with shared roles and the elimination of oppression, the less this will hold true. It is to be hoped that, as we move in that direction, more men will gain these feminist qualities rather than women losing them.

Implications for Social Work Education

The Council on Social Work Education's accreditation standards require some curricular content on women in foundation courses.[16] In social policy courses, policy analysis should include not only those policy areas defined as women's issues, but an exploration of how all issues, programs, and policies differentially affect men and women, as well as different groups of women. Topics for consideration can include the elderly, criminal justice, health, and all specific social welfare policies, such as social security. Also, issues of women of color should be explicitly addressed. Too often women's issues are confined to those that affect only white middle-class women. The double jeopardy of race and gender is a primary concern for social work practitioners.   259

Moreover, social work students should be introduced to the important women role models who were key policymakers. A course, or section of a social policy course, on our "founding mothers" could include not only those best-known social workers, such as Jane Addams, Dorothea Dix, and Lillian Wald, but Florence Kelley, who researched and developed legislation on women and child labor and introduced minimum wage legislation in nine states; Grace Abbott, who organized the first White House Conference on Children and, as head of the U.S. Children's Bureau, established 3,000 child health and prenatal centers throughout the country; Josephine Goldmark, who researched working conditions of women for Justice Brandeis's Supreme Court case and drafted legislation for working women's protection introduced by Senator LaFollette; and others.

Finally, and most difficult, a feminist approach to policymaking should be introduced not only in foundation policy courses, but in practice courses. This would be consistent with the concepts of holism, of process and product, of personal and political. It is incumbent on social work educators to bridge the gap between the thinking and the doing, the macro and the micro, the theory and the practice.

A feminist approach to social policy will not be achieved overnight, but the seeds of the approach are already there. Social work, because of its origins and values, is compatible with such a model. We have a history, too often hidden, of women and feminists who have been involved in policymaking. A feminist approach to social policy is both new and old, radical and traditional. A feminist vision is authentic social work. Only by educating both men and women in this vision will we achieve a feminist approach to social policy.

notes

1. A. L. Schorr and E. C. Baumheier, "Social Policy," *Encyclopedia of Social Work,* Vol. 2 (16th ed.; New York: National Association of Social Workers, 1971), pp. 1361–1362.

2. See Introduction, p. 1.

3. R. Brandwein, "Feminist Thought Structure: An Alternative Paradigm of Social Change for Social Justice," in D. Gil and E. Gil, eds., *Toward Social and Economic Justice* (Cambridge, Mass.: Schenkman Publishing Co., 1985); N. Hooyman, "Toward a Fem-

Feminist Visions

inist Administrative Style," paper presented at the National Association of Social Workers' Conference on Women in Social Work, Washington, D.C., 1980; C. Gilligan, *In a Different Voice* (Cambridge, Mass.: Harvard University Press, 1982); and J. Wood Wetzel and the Feminist World View Educators, "A Feminist World View Conceptual Framework," paper presented at the Annual Program Meeting, Council on Social Work Education, Ft. Worth, Tex., 1983.

4. R. Brandwein, "Children, Parents and Society: Partners or Adversaries," *Social Development Issues,* 5 (Spring 1981), pp. 27–32.

5. K. Kenniston and the Carnegie Council on Children, *All Our Children: The American Family Under Pressure* (New York: Carnegie Corp., 1977), p. 79.

6. National Advisory Council on Economic Opportunity, *Critical Choices for the 1980s* (Washington, D.C.: August 1980).

7. M. Valentich and J. Gripton, "Ideological Perspectives on the Sexual Assault of Women," *Social Service Review,* 53 (September 1984), pp. 448–461.

8. S. de Beauvoir, *The Second Sex,* H. M. Parshley, trans. and ed. (New York: Modern Library, 1949).

9. I. K. Broverman et al., "Sex Role Stereotypes: A Current Appraisal," *Journal of Social Issues,* 28, No. 2 (1972), pp. 59–78.

10. P. Chesler, *Women and Madness* (Garden City, N.Y.: Doubleday & Co., 1972).

11. D. Pearce and H. McAdoo, *Women and Children: Alone and in Poverty* (Washington, D.C.: National Advisory Council on Economic Opportunity, 1981).

12. M. Buber, *I and Thou,* W. Kaufman, trans. (New York: Charles Scribner's Sons, 1970).

13. E. Polansky, "Caregiving of the Chronically Ill at Home: The Social, Physical and Financial Impact on the Family Caregiver." Unpublished doctoral dissertation, Columbia University, 1982.

14. R. Mayer, *Policy and Program Planning: A Developmental Perspective* (Englewood Cliffs, N.J.: Prentice-Hall, 1985).

15. E. Roosevelt, speech to the United Nations, December 1952, quoted in E. Partnow, ed., *The Quotable Woman* (New York: Anchor Books, 1978), p. 528.

16. Commission on Accreditation, *Handbook of Accreditation Standards and Procedures* (New York: Council on Social Work Education, July 1984).

261

Feminist Approach to Social Policy

Patty Gibbs
Becky Fowler
Hilda R. Heady

feminism and rural america: vision or hallucination?

feminism has been a major social current for nearly two decades but has made little appreciable impact on the character of rural people. This statement alone, however, creates another in a series of misconceptions about rural America—misconceptions that leave change agents with a distorted and one-sided view of rural American life.

Although feminist theory has come of age in contemporary America, a feminist analysis of rural American dynamics has been given limited thought and little press—and probably for good reason. The character of rural America makes its compatibility with feminist ideology seem less of a vision and more of a hallucination. That is, the stereotypes connected with both feminism and rural dynamics suggest a possible conflictual relationship between the two. A careful feminist analysis of rural America and the strengths of its people, however, refutes the notion of an inevitably conflictual relationship.

To contrast the stereotypic view of rural America with an alternative view, the authors divided this chapter into two major parts. The first part is descriptive and examines the definition and dynamics of rurality. The second part provides an alternative view of rural America—a view that reconceptualizes, through a feminist analysis, some of the "truths" that are outlined in the first part of the chapter and that explores implications for social work practice.

The Parameters of Rurality

Before engaging in any discussion of the overall character of rural areas, one is confronted with the obvious task of establishing an operational definition of rural America—what it is and who its people are. Arriving at a standard or universal definition, however, is a continuing difficulty for all parties concerned about rurality, as one can readily determine by reviewing the literature.[1]

Rural America Defined. The U.S. Bureau of the Census provides the most common frame of reference for defining population aggregates in relation to land masses. According to the 1980 census definition, all nonmetropolitan areas with a population of less than 2,500 are classified as rural.[2] But because, for the purposes of social work practice, the concept of rurality includes a complex web of defining characteristics that extends beyond mere population density, the Census Bureau's definition of "rural" is limiting.

A definition proposed by Ginsberg is more suitable from a social work perspective because it allows for larger population aggregates with characteristics common to rural areas to be called rural as well. Ginsberg's definition of "rural" as an area with fewer than 50,000 people not contiguous to a metropolitan area— which is similar to the Census Bureau's definition of "nonmetropolitan"—is the concept of rurality used in this chapter.[3]

Current census data reveal that there are 62.8 million people living in nonmetropolitan counties, roughly one-third of the total U.S. population.[4] States in which the highest percentage of their population resides in areas of 7,500 or less are Vermont (66 percent), West Virginia (64 percent), South Dakota (54 percent), and Mississippi (53 percent). The least rural region of the country is the Pacific region, with only 10.6 percent classified as nonmetropolitan.[5]

Although rural populations, however they are defined, may share many common needs based on their rural existence, they are a heterogeneous group, including disadvantaged minorities **263** (such as American Indians, Hispanics, blacks, and Appalachians) who often face special hardships in rural areas where conservative value structures prevail and where minorities are much more visible than they are in metropolitan areas.

Not only does ethnic diversity cut across rural America, but dramatic regional diversity exists, with each region facing its own particularly prominent issues. Some regions, for example, face problems stemming from corporate or absentee ownership of land, and others face environmental issues, such as nuclear and toxic waste dumping, pesticide or herbicide spraying, or acid rainfall.

Although it is critical to highlight the diversity of rural America because this diversity needs to be considered in interventive efforts, it is equally important to elaborate some of the more prominent issues and salient values that are common to most of rural America, that is, the more homogeneous features of rural communities. Eight such features will be examined: (1) poverty, (2) lack of education, (3) unemployment, (4) living conditions, (5) the social welfare system, (6) health care, (7) mental health considerations, and (8) rural attitudes and values.

Poverty. Perhaps the reality of economic marginality is at the crux of many rural problems. About 39 percent of the nation's poor people live in nonmetropolitan America.[6] Rural poverty, in part, seems inextricably linked to the minority status of a large portion of rural people, although minority groups are not the only economically deprived groups in rural America. Current reports claim that agriculture is in a state of collapse.[7] Vinson and Jesberg note that the "farm poor have the highest incidence of poverty of any residential category"[8]; in 1981, this group represented 40 percent of the nation's poverty but only 2.4 percent of its population.[9]

Another cause of rural poverty is related to corporate and absentee land ownership and the economics that surround such ownership. This country's land is gradually passing into the hands of fewer and fewer people. Through vast holdings, 3 percent of the population own 95 percent of the 1.3 billion acres of privately owned land, and 568 large corporations control more than 300 million acres.[10]

Appalachia, for example, suffers the consequences of corporate and absentee land ownership. Mineral—namely coal—extraction is the backbone of parts of Appalachia, but the 1981 Appalachian Land Study found that corporations owned a total of 40 percent of the land and 70 percent of the mineral rights; furthermore, 84 percent of the corporately held land was owned

Feminist Visions

by absentee corporations. This situation has led to a failure of the property tax system in Appalachia. About 25 percent of the corporate owners pay less than 25 cents an acre in taxes; over 75 percent pay less than 25 cents in property taxes per mineral acre. According to the study, a concentration of absentee and corporate ownership is at least partially responsible for the chronic economic depression of the Appalachian region.[11]

Over the years, programs have been developed to alleviate rural poverty but have met with limited success. Communities applying for aid are often mystified and discouraged by the procedures. Sometimes program funds are drawn heavily to urban areas because the woes of urban poverty are more visible and city politicians have more political finesse in obtaining the funds.[12]

Poverty as a core issue in rural America does not stand alone, without cause or effect. Whether poverty itself is the cause *or* the effect, one can say with certainty that it finds itself in the company of unemployment and lack of education, the next two topics to be examined.

Lack of education. If, as Americans tend to believe, education is essential in the fight against poverty, there is little doubt about rural America's lot, as the following statistics show. In 1981, 59 percent of poverty-stricken nonmetropolitan family heads over age 25 had not completed high school, and 25 percent had not even completed the eighth grade.[13]

Dropping out of school is only one part of the education problem in rural areas. The *quality* of education is another dynamic to be considered. Rural schools often do not compare favorably with urban schools; therefore, rural students may receive an education that, in many ways, is inferior to that of their urban counterparts.[14]

In this day and age, the existence of illiteracy in rural America, regardless of the cause, is lamentable. The cuts in elementary education programs made by Congress can only exacerbate the problem and will undoubtedly contribute to future high unemployment rates.

Unemployment. Unemployment in rural America is a complex and chronic problem. Compared with urban areas, there is a disproportionate number of unemployed people in rural regions. According to U.S. Department of Agriculture Chief Economist Calvin Beale, the total number of jobs in rural areas declined 2 percent in 1982, while it remained stable in metropolitan areas; in addition, the ratio of unemployed to employed is 10 percent higher in rural than in metropolitan areas.[15]

265

Feminism and Rural America

In 1983, West Virginia, for example, led the nation in unemployment rates, which reached 21.5 percent in February of that year.[16] Many of the unemployed exhausted their benefits and had to be granted extensions. Many more probably needed extensions during subsequent years.

Several factors contribute to the rural unemployment problem. Basically, employment opportunities are more restricted in rural areas. "Rural communities tend to be one- or two-industry or company towns."[17] Although greater employment opportunities and more attractive jobs may be available in "neighboring" urban areas, rural areas lack reliable, efficient, and low-cost public transportation for the rural commuter. Of the rural poor or near-poor, 70 percent are without adequate transportation.[18]

Living conditions. Primarily because of the rampant poverty in rural areas, substandard housing is at a critical level. Rural America contains nearly 40 percent of the nation's substandard housing although it has only one-third of the nation's population.

Cochran estimated that there are 30,000 communities without a sanitary centralized water system—a figure that did not include families living in isolated areas.[19] His claim that federal funds for modern water and sewerage facilities were being misdirected was supported by a study published by the National Water Demonstration Project.[20]

The federal government has shown its lack of commitment to improving rural living conditions by making massive cuts in rural housing progams. For example, the Rural Housing Program of the Farmer's Home Administration, which provides housing loans at less than market rates to rural citizens, has been cut by 67 percent.[21]

The social welfare system. In the words of the Southern Regional Education Board, "Problems of rural areas tend to be more like problems of underdeveloped countries; that is, basic public services and necessities are lacking."[22] The paucity of agencies and professionals in rural communities is one of the most striking differences between the service sector of rural areas and that of larger cities. Geographically large but sparsely populated catchment areas add to the problems of service delivery in rural America. Overall, rural social welfare differs dramatically from social welfare in metropolitan areas.

One difference is in the types of programs offered. Only the most basic programs can be found in rural areas; more specialized programs usually cannot be found. For this reason,

266

Feminist Visions

the programs that do exist must often expand their services beyond the scope of what they might normally offer if the more specialized services existed.

Fiscal inadequacy created by a limited tax base makes it impossible for many rural areas to maintain specialized services and support a complex social welfare system. Tax concessions, which are used to attract new industries or encourage expansion of existing industries, often exempt billions of dollars' worth of property.[23]

The use of revenue-sharing money in rural areas is another factor that limits rural social service programs. Whereas urban areas often use revenue-sharing funds for social programs, rural areas often put these funds to use for "more basic, visible, and physical improvements and needs."[24]

In general, social welfare programs in rural areas are grossly underfunded. Moreover, the termination of federal funds for block-grant programs has meant the termination of some of the few services previously available in rural areas.

Rural America has always suffered inequities in the allocation of resources. Many groups that are active and knowledgeable about rural development, such as nonprofit organizations, often have difficulty qualifying for assistance from federal government programs because federal funds generally are allocated to help citizens via their municipality. The Task Panel on Rural Mental Health of the President's Commission on Mental Health also reported federal funding problems:

> Federal assistance guidelines for resource allocation,
> technical assistance, and program audit all flow through
> rigid access tunnels, which tend to deny the realities of
> rural social life. Allocation is based on presumed need
> for specific categories of service, a philosophy that
> penalizes practices that emphasize a holistic approach
> to community and individual needs.[25]

Because of the shortage of professionals and programs, the taxing job of operating on a shoestring, the task of being all things to all people, and the general lack of social supports, burn-out is an all-too-common problem of rural social workers. Consequently, a social service system that is already enduring many strains and tensions may become nearly immobilized when its few primary providers are on the verge of collapse.

Health care. Health care outside the confines of Standard Metropolitan Statistical Areas (SMSA) is a pathetic case of the **267** gross maldistribution of health care professionals and inadequate or nonexistent hospital facilities, juxtaposed with an overall population that is older and far less healthy than the urban population.

The vast majority of physicians practice in metropolitan areas; only 13.2 percent serve the entire nonmetropolitan population.[26] By and large, physicians are generally not attracted to rural areas, where modern facilities, professional stimulation, and ancillary services are lacking.

The provision of health care services in rural areas has serious limitations. Some rural counties lack hospitals, or existing hospitals may be old and inferior. Because rural hospitals are financially unable to keep pace with modern technology and to have the full range of specialists on staff, many rural patients travel to urban hospitals to obtain the care and services they need. Once they are introduced to technologically advanced and comprehensive health care, they may come to prefer the urban over the rural hospital. Hence, the rural hospital may experience a decline in the volume of patients. This loss of volume often leads to further discontinuation or limitation of services, which, in turn, compounds the inadequacies of health care in rural areas.

Isolation, poor roads, the lack of transportation, and limited emergency medical services restrict rural health care even further. For example, the ambulance service in most areas is either owned and managed as a service of a funeral home or is an all-volunteer unit relying on local funds for equipment and training. Some areas are totally without ambulance services.

What are the health care problems that intersect with this inadequate system of delivering rural health care services? Contrary to the romantic notion of many urbanites that rural America is the place to enjoy clean air, sunshine, and good health, good health may not be a part of the deal—or so the evidence suggests.

Statistics show that 50 percent of all maternal deaths occur in rural areas. Infant mortality rates in some areas run as high as 70 percent of the national average. Twice as many chronically disabled people reside in rural areas, as do 37 percent of the elderly, who need three times the health services of other groups.[27]

Decades of studies have shown that the three traditional occupations of rural America—mining, lumbering, and agriculture —are among the most dangerous occupations to workers.[28] A high incidence of work-related accidents is not the only form of

268

Feminist Visions

health hazard inherent in these occupations. In agriculture and lumbering, the ill effects of long-term exposure to herbicides and pesticides, although little documented, are not purely conjectural. In the Appalachian region, coal miners suffer from black lung— an insidious lung disease caused by exposure to coal dust. In the rural South, the textile mills produce a similar health hazard known as "brown lung," a chronic pulmonary disease caused by exposure to cotton dust.[29]

Not only are rural occupations more likely to be hazardous, but these industries generally provide fewer health benefits for their employees. Consequently, rural people, who already suffer economically, often find health care to be a basic economic issue.
Mental health considerations. Fear of being stigmatized and labeled "crazy" or mentally ill keeps many rural people from seeking help even when their need is severe. Rural persons suffering mental disorders seek no help 50 percent of the time,[30] primarily because of rural cultural barriers, such as mistrust of outsiders and "professionals," a belief in self-help and taking care of one another, and the fear of being stigmatized, coupled with the high degree of visibility in rural areas.

Furthermore, husbands and fathers, fearing that their authority may be undermined by the mental health professional, may obstruct the mental health needs of their families by forbidding them to visit a mental health facility.[31] Even when the family does engage in therapy, the father-husband often will not attend.
Rural attitudes and values. Rural America is more traditional and conservative—politically, morally, and institutionally—than is urban America, which often hampers social workers' efforts to provide formalized services. Rugged individualism, pride, and the self-help ethic keep people from seeking formalized help. Individuals believe that they must take care of themselves; communities believe they should take care of their own.

Generally rural people are intolerant of interference in what they consider to be their own affairs. Help and money from "outsiders," including professionals, may elicit suspicion and fear. Governmentally regulated programs are particularly disliked.[32]

The fishbowl existence of life in rural America also impedes the delivery of social services. Confidentiality may be a problem in small towns where individuals, families, and their problems are highly visible.

This section on values would not be complete without high- **269** lighting the impact of traditional rural values on rural women. The challenges of rural life have shaped women who are self-reliant, creative, and resourceful; however, the strength that rural women possess often does not seem to permeate their interpersonal lives in relation to their role and status in the home. Men generally make the major decisions in the family and are considered the heads of their households.[33]

Rural women, particularly those with limited incomes, are both confined and socially isolated. Young children, inadequate financial resources, lack of transportation, and a paucity of formal social supports reinforce conformity to the traditional female roles of wife and mother. The extended family, which gives rural women a sense of security, also strengthens the pressure on women to conform to traditional roles.[34]

Some rural women deviate from female roles by participating in the labor force; however, the role of these women in the family does not seem to alter appreciably. Women who work outside the home generally are concentrated in the low-paying female labor ghetto, that is, in "clerical and service jobs in industries and operative jobs in manufacturing."[35] Low financial returns tend to denigrate the women's financial contribution to the family's sustenance.

Farm women contribute significantly to the financial sustenance of family life as co-owners and co-managers of their operations. However, some elements of farming remain strictly "male activities," and women are permitted neither to intrude nor to interfere.

> Women are seldom seen as experts or decision makers in farming. Even with tremendous support, respect and encouragement from the men we live with, we still have to deal with the often gently disqualifying attitudes of the vet, the milktruck driver, the artificial breeder man, the feed company, the neighbors and even each other.[36]

In any case, rural women who share the breadwinning role with their mates do so at some risk. Complications escalate if the woman must enter the labor force out of economic necessity, which causes her husband to view himself as a failure in the role expected of him.

Thus far, this chapter has presented an analysis of rural America based on the literature and current demographic data. The view of rural America derived from these sources is stereotypic and unidimensional. Rural America as portrayed in

Feminist Visions

this way is a hopeless, helpless, powerless region of defeated, pitiable, and backward people. Although the "truths" delineated cannot be totally ignored, neither can they be used exclusively to define rural America.

Rural America: An Alternative View

Traditional definitions of rural America unidimensionally characterize rural people as being entrenched in sex-role expectations, steeped in ignorance of the outside world, contented with the status quo, and frightened of anything that might bring change. Although, at this level, rural America is ostensibly incompatible with feminist ideology, the feminist method of analyzing experience provides a mechanism for accommodating rural realities to present not only an alternative view of rural America but a more positive view.

> The role of [feminist] theory, then, is to articulate for us what we know from our practical activity, to bring out and make conscious the philosophy embedded in our lives.[37]

Feminist principles present a view of rural America in direct contrast to the traditional, fatalistic view. The feminist method of analysis depends on observation, conjecture, and insight to interpret and reconceptualize the "truths" presented earlier. According to Bunch, "Changing people's perceptions of the world through new descriptions of reality is usually a prerequisite for altering that reality."[38]

Validating Experience. Practitioners working with rural populations must be cognizant of the strengths of these people, rather than emphasize their liabilities. Rugged individualism, self-pride, a strong work ethic, a belief in self-help, and an ability to be resourceful are all potential untapped resources, on which the social worker can draw when planning interventive efforts.

The feminist principle of validating experience offers a sound approach to effective practice with rural Americans. It is undoubtedly a most powerful tool for puncturing the myths and eliminating the stereotypes associated with rural America.

The experience of the rural client is validated when the social worker understands and respects the culture, values, and **271** characteristics of rural people. Rural people are not shapeless lumps of clay to be remolded, repackaged, or relocated to suit the needs and schemes of others. The folk culture of rural America is important to the self-identity of its people. It follows, therefore, that validating experience can be a way to preserve the essence of rural America.

Making use of the strong sense of community that is characteristic of rural areas is another way to validate experience. Because rural residents share a life, a history, and a commitment to "taking care of their own," even those individuals who function at a marginal level are accepted and given a place in the community.[39] Commitment alone does not enable rural residents to take care of their own. The strength of the commitment, however, has spawned an intricate—although not highly visible—system of community supports and natural helping networks.

In keeping with the recommendations of the President's Commission on Mental Health, rural social workers can strengthen already existing community support systems and helping networks, such as lawyers, the clergy, physicians, and teachers, that traditionally carry out rural people's commitment to caring for one another.[40] Rural social workers cannot ignore the rural church as a resource for meeting individual, family, and community needs. In some rural areas, churches and other "civic" groups assume responsibility for many of the social welfare activities carried out by a variety of agencies in urban areas. These, then, are some of the support systems already in place that can be enhanced and strengthened by rural social workers.

In addition, practitioners must recognize the importance of natural helpers as resources to be used in the provision of social services. Natural helpers or caregivers can be defined broadly as persons "to whom others turn for instrumental (material) and/or expressive (emotional) support."[41] A natural helper may carry out his or her role as part of a formal occupation, such as the clergy, waitressing, or bartending, or natural helpers may be indigenous people who have no formal occupation but are recognized by friends and neighbors as having a special capacity for caregiving.

Natural helpers usually have neither formal training nor agency auspice; in addition, they may adopt helping approaches that differ in some respects from those of the professional social worker. Yet natural helpers are a vital extension of the provision of social services, increasing the outreach to individuals who might otherwise go unserved.

272

Feminist Visions

Aside from the natural helper being an additional resource in a land of scarcity, rural residents are more comfortable seeking help from "one of their own"; there is less stigma involved. Therefore, individuals who are reluctant to seek help from a local mental health agency, for example, may be far more inclined to consult an indigenous caregiver.

Some natural helpers may require some training if services are to be extended and enhanced. Training in basic communication skills may be advantageous for natural helpers, depending on their desire and need for such training. Teaching helpers to recognize serious mental disorders and how to refer when necessary could also be beneficial.

Whether to train natural helpers at all is an issue that has been debated throughout the literature on the use of indigenous caregivers. The concept of "trained" natural helpers seems a contradiction in terms. The "trained" natural helper may no longer be "natural," which tends automatically to alter his or her status in the community. The caveat is to exercise caution when entering rural natural helping systems. Existing processes should be disrupted as little as possible in order to preserve the integrity of the natural system.

The peer-oriented helping networks and associations that are burgeoning in contemporary society are extensions of the concept of indigenous caregivers. People who form these groups band together for the purpose of mutual aid.[42] Mutual assistance occurs through sharing information, insight, experiences, and coping strategies. Benefits may not only accrue to members, but may radiate to the public at large. Mutual assistance and self-help are viable alternative caregiving systems, the recognition of which validates the rural experience.

Natural helpers are not the only resources available to social workers. Individual community residents often can be mobilized to effect change or establish services when they are made aware of needs in their community. In many instances, rural women have been known to establish a much-needed service in the community by drawing on the organizational skills they possess in relation to their homemaker roles. For example, they have created "safe homes" for battered women and their children and have organized supportive networks for those in crisis or transition, such as widows, caregivers for terminally ill family members, or expectant mothers desiring alternative birthing methods.

273

Rural women are a valuable resource who should not be overlooked or underestimated. Historically, women have been the backbone of rural America, becoming the leaders and catalysts for change—to do what needed to be done. They supported strikes, fought for unions, and carried out many activities that enhanced the general well-being of a community.

Today, rural women continue to possess strengths, although these strengths often go unrecognized because rural women have assumed traditional roles—whether by choice or a lack of opportunity to assume other roles. Whatever the reason, rural women take pride in their homes and families, and in their role as homemakers. To do other than validate the experience of the rural homemaker would be a denigration of her sense of self.

Numerous women's groups are seeking opportunities to extend rural women's sense of self and to improve the women's economic situation by developing cooperatives and cottage industries, starting their own businesses, working out of their homes, and connecting with the outside world via computer. There is also a growing number of women farmers—women going into farming with other women, with a commitment to succeed.

> Economic developers in rural areas need to understand that for women development means training of the managerial, technical, and entrepreneurial skills that marshall rural resources and allow [them] to participate more fully in this vital sector of rural economies, *without compromising the traditional values of family which [they] genuinely espouse.*[43] [Italics added.]

Bauer asserted that training programs for new entrepreneurs are a necessity and that rural women should be included in the planning stages of these programs.[44] In sum, female entrepreneurial activity not only has many positive implications for economic development but is a response to rural needs that are harmonious with the culture at large.

Recognition of and respect for the people's tie to the land is another way to validate experience. Although the tie to the land is significant, rural people increasingly find that they are being squeezed out of opportunities to own land. Creative solutions to this problem have been slow in coming, yet the Community Land Trust (CLT) model offers some hope—and some possibilities—for social work. A CLT is a nonprofit corporation created to preserve land "for the benefit of a community and of individuals within the community."[45] Land is acquired by the

Feminist Visions

corporation through purchase or donation with the intention of retaining title to the land in perpetuity. Thus the land is removed from the speculative market and is available for leasing to interested individuals, cooperatives, or businesses in the community, which allows those who might otherwise be unable to buy land an opportunity to do so. In sum, the structure of the corporation and its board of trustees gives the community ultimate control over its land.[46] In this way, the tie to the land is preserved and strengthened, which is a huge step in validating the experience of rural people by providing an opportunity for them to retain what is precious to them.

Reconceptualizing Power. The use of alternative service delivery systems, such as informal helpers, indigenous caregivers, and mutual assistance networks, is not only an example of validating experience but also an illustration of reconceptualizing power—professional power in this instance. We social workers, as do other service professionals, firmly believe in our specialized knowledge and skill. We demand autonomy and the power of self-regulation. Indigenous caregivers and the like are generally relegated to positions of less importance in the helping system—often as *adjuncts* to the provision of services. *We* want to be able to determine where they fit and how they fit. We want to be the gatekeepers to our profession and its area of expertise.

Collaboration and cooperation with natural and indigenous helpers involve redistributing the power in our concept of "professionalism." Long before social workers and other helpers entered the rural ecological system, indigenous helpers were there, offering excellent and effective caregiving. Obviously, rural America can benefit from the efforts of both professionals and natural or indigenous helpers. There is room for both. There are roles and functions for both. The existence of one should neither preclude the existence nor denigrate the worth of the other.

Much of the helplessness and powerlessness experienced by rural populations is defined and perpetuated by the notion that power is a finite commodity: If someone else has it, you do not. The feminist principle that power can be both infinite and expansive is a principle that could serve rural areas well. It is a step toward regaining what rural inhabitants once knew and understood— a part of reclaiming their historical sense of self and pride.

Reconceptualizing power—helping to show rural people the power they can and do have—is often the most critical function **275** carried out by rural social workers. When a victim of black lung disease is helped to realize that he can articulate his plight to a congressional panel better than any outside expert could, even though his breath is short and raspy, he begins to see just how valid and powerful his everyday experiences can be. Similarly, when the isolation of rural people is overcome—via conferences, county fairs, or school meetings—and people begin to meet, they come to understand the common problems they face. Often this new understanding makes them quick to organize, to recognize their strength, and to use that strength to effect change.

The forces that shape rural people endow them with the power to change their communities—in essence, to change their plight. Who, better than they, can know rural needs? Who, more than they, has the vested interest to work toward meeting those needs? Rural people have been engaging in activities to improve their communities for years. A facilitator or enabler is often all that is needed to help them mobilize and focus their energies.

Social workers, as facilitators and catalysts of change, can empower residents to meet their needs via a citizens' advisory group, which can forge a common community goal. To be successful, planning must represent the genuine interests of the citizens. The social worker's main function is to empower the community to meet its needs; that is, the social worker *works with* people rather than *does for* them.

Reconceptualizing power also means recognizing that "different" should not indicate "lesser." This would pertain particularly to the minority and socially excluded groups in rural America, such as Hispanics, American Indians, migrant workers, blacks, and Appalachian whites, who are prejudged, discriminated against, and underserved.

These groups have a right to maintain their unique folk cultures without suffering denigration. Only in our more recent history have there been efforts to acknowledge the value of folk cultures and to preserve the structures and customs that were vital parts of those systems. The strength of American culture lies not in the homogenization of its people, but in the color and flair of their diversity.

Collaboration with natural and indigenous helpers, empowering rural people, and strengthening folk cultures are but three examples of reconceptualizing power in the feminist mode. Another example is validation of the form of power with which rural people are most comfortable. For rural people, the personal is powerful—personal relationships, personalizing common experiences, and, in general, operating at a personal level during all interactions. In rural areas, power is the result of face-to-face personal contacts. Resource networks depend on personal relationships. If only one farmer in the community owns a hay baler, those who want to use it develop a personal relationship with that farmer. Individuals in need are responded to on the basis of personal relationships that stem from the "sense of community" rural residents share.

In this same vein, consumer cooperative enterprises could increase economic opportunites in rural regions. Tools and equipment for harvesting, for building, or for dairying could be cooperatively owned, which would enable more individuals to engage in productive activities. The effect of cooperative enterprises on rural employment could be profound, and rural communities would have additional productive outlets, which would "facilitate a restoration of local pride, self-esteem and self-respect."[47] Cooperative enterprises, therefore, are an extension of the idea that personal-cooperative-collective networks can be power generating.

Eliminating False Dichotomies.   The ecology of rural systems, coupled with the paucity of human service resources, demands a service perspective that is different from approaches that are prevalent in metropolitan areas. Common artificial separations that serve as obstacles to the enhancement of rural life can be eliminated with the use of a holistic and ecological perspective stemming from a generalist approach. Thus, it is crucial for the rural social worker to relinquish a "specialist" approach to practice, for example, practicing exclusively as a clinician or as an organizer. Such a false dichotomy severely limits the effectiveness of the rural social worker, who must be able to intervene at any level—from the micro to the macro—depending both on the impact that social and physical environments have on a given system and how these environments can be actively used and changed to enhance social functioning. Generalist practice, therefore, is the most expedient method for planning change in rural America.

A holistic and ecological perspective keeps social workers cognizant of the interconnectedness between rural people and their social and physical environments. For example, the strength of rural people's tie to the land and what it symbolizes for them must be recognized and respected in all interventive efforts.   **277**

Renaming. If we as feminists are to form a coalition with our rural sisters, it is essential to rename some of our terms and models. At this point, our terms and models engender only negative responses and feelings in rural women. The word "feminism" itself is usually threatening. Rural women do not view themselves as anything similar to the way the media portray feminists. However, if one were to outline the underlying goals of feminism—choice and the freedom to be the best you can be—most rural women would give it overwhelming support.

The same holds true for the Equal Rights Amendment (ERA). The media, with Phyllis Schlafly's help and with their talk of unisex toilets and women on the front lines of combat, have done a good job of scaring rural women about the ERA. Informing rural women of the actual goals and ramifications of the ERA—and of the benefits to them—would dispel the negative, erroneous notions and give advocates of women's rights new allies. As it stands, rural women have not joined us in large numbers, and it is to our detriment.

Valuing Process and Product. A final feminist principle that is applicable to rural life is that of valuing both process and product. The understanding that is clear in the childhood of some rural people that "in the doin' you learn" is an adept way of restating this same feminist principle.

On the surface, the somewhat ritualistic pattern of the traditional lifestyle may seem purposeless, dull, and inert. But, in the old teachings, such tasks of everyday life built character, respect for nature, and a deep sense of one's self in relation to the world. This process of growth, of course, was always done "in due time" and therefore inhibited the progress of rural values to more cosmopolitan or metropolitan styles.

Yet, should this traditional lifestyle be viewed as necessarily negative? We think not. The process in which rural folks engage to achieve an end yields a sense of gratification that perhaps cannot be measured. As communities organize to meet a specific need, they gain much from joining together in a common effort; they fulfill their needs for affiliation and develop various skills, individually and collectively. These primary gains from collective efforts have a ripple effect: social support systems are broadened and individuals find their sense of self-confidence and self-worth increasing greatly.

278 Generally, the entire experience of forming coalitions for meeting needs is empowering. It gives the participants a new strength—a recognition that they are not helpless to alter their situation. Valuing process and product, then, ties into the principle of reconceptualizing power.

Summary and Conclusions

The first part of this chapter was primarily concerned with defining the term "rural America," giving a brief description of the diversity that exists within rural regions, examining the more common issues and concerns that cut across rural America and its people, and identifying the salient values held by rural inhabitants. The statistics presented generally supported the stereotypes associated with rural living.

The second part of this chapter outlined an alternative view of rural America through the application of feminist principles. In addition, feminist principles were used to suggest practice models for working in a rural setting. The view put forth in this section was a more positive and hopeful one that emphasized the strengths and potential of rural regions and populations.

Finally, we are led to the crucial question: Is the notion of a feminist approach to rural social work practice a hallucination or is it visionary? In some ways it is both, depending on the perspective of the person making the judgment. Most rural folks would surely and swiftly express a sentiment that feminism does not belong in rural America and could never have a place there. Feminism would be viewed as a nefarious force capable of vast destruction. Conversely, most feminists would view rural America as a target area that is in great need of enlightenment. The traditional and conservative lifestyles, in particular, would be aspects of rural life to be challenged.

Neither group is totally correct nor totally incorrect. Instead, the argument itself effects a counterproductive artificial separation that veils the more critical issue: how to enhance the lives of our rural neighbors in a manner that does no violence to the delicate ecology of cherished rural systems.

The use of feminist principles both to analyze rural dynamics and to suggest practice models offers great potential for meeting human needs in rural regions while preserving the integrity of rural life. In rural America, change as a positive entity can only be considered in context, and practice implications suggested by feminist principles show respect for the rural context. **279**

notes

1. For a detailed review of rural definitions found in the literature, see J. Bosak and B. Perlman, "A Review of the Definition of Rural," *Journal of Rural Community Psychology,* 3 (1982), pp. 3–34.

2. Additional Census Bureau definitions for "metropolitan," "Standard Metropolitan Statistical Areas" (SMSAs), and nonmetropolitan areas are germane to this discussion on differentiating population aggregates. A metropolitan area has a large population nucleus and a number of adjacent communities that have a high degree of economic and social integration with the nucleus. An SMSA is either a city with 50,000 or more inhabitants or an urbanized area (defined in terms of counties) of at least 50,000 inhabitants and a total SMSA population of 100,000 or more (75,000 in New England). All populations and land areas are not included in SMSAs are defined as nonmetropolitan.

3. L. Ginsberg, *The Practice of Social Work in Public Welfare* (New York: Free Press, 1983), p. 100.

4. C. Beale, "Rural and Small Town Population Change, 1970–80" (Washington, D.C.: U.S. Department of Agriculture, Economics and Statistical Service, February 1981), p. 1.

5. Ibid., p. 3.

6. E. A. Vinson and K. M. Jesberg, "The Rural Stake in Public Assistance: Summary of Findings and Recommendations," in E. Martinez-Brawley, *Seven Decades of Rural Social Work: From Country Life Commission to Rural Caucus* (New York: Praeger Publishers, 1981), Appendix 2, p. 153.

7. J. C. Clark, *How the Budget Cuts Undercut Rural Women* (Washington, D.C.: Rural American Women, 1982), p. 1.

8. Vinson and Jesberg, "The Rural Stake in Public Assistance," p. 154.

9. "Characteristics of the Population Below the Poverty Level," *Current Population Reports,* Series P-60, No. 138 (Washington, D.C.: U.S. Bureau of the Census, March 1982), p. 16.

10. These data are findings of a survey by the Economics, Statistics, and Cooperatives Service of the U.S. Department of Agriculture reported in J. Pekkanen, "The Land: Who Owns America?" *Town and Country,* 137 (May 1983), p. 176.

11. The study, conducted by the Highlander Center in New Market, Tennessee, and sponsored by the Appalachian Regional Commission, was reported in ibid., pp. 176 and 178.

12. B. Schorr, "Suicidal Rural Gap in Poverty War," *Wall Street Journal,* February 20, 1968, p. 16.

13. "Characteristics of the Population Below the Poverty Level," Table 20.

280

Feminist Visions

14. M. R. Reul, *Territorial Boundaries of Rural Poverty: Profiles of Exploitation* (East Lansing: Center for Rural Manpower and Public Affairs and the Cooperative Extension Service, Michigan State University, 1974), p. 32.

15. "Income, Jobs Still Lag in Rural Areas," *Appalachian Reporter* (Washington, D.C.: Appalachian Regional Commission, March 15, 1983), p. 3.

16. U.S. Department of Labor, Bureau of Labor Statistics *Supplement to Unemployment in States and Local Areas in 1983* (Washington, D.C.: U.S. Government Printing Office, September 1985).

17. L. Ginsberg, "An Overview of Social Work Education in Rural Areas," in Ginsberg, ed., *Social Work in Rural Communities: A Book of Readings* (New York: Council on Social Work Education, 1976), p. 4.

18. O. W. Farley et al., *Rural Social Work Practice* (New York: Free Press, 1982), p. 4.

19. C. L. Cochran, "Rural America—A Time for Decision," in R. K. Green and S. A. Webster, eds., *Social Work in Rural Areas: Preparation and Practice* (Knoxville: University of Tennessee, School of Social Work, 1977), p. 386.

20. The study, published by the National Water Demonstration Project of the Commission on Rural Water, was prepared by W. Moberg and reported in ibid., p. 386.

21. Clark, *How the Budget Cuts Undercut Rural Women,* p. 15.

22. Southern Regional Education Board, Manpower Education and Training Project, Rural Task Force, "Educational Assumptions for Rural Social Work," in Ginsberg, ed., *Social Work in Rural Communities,* p. 41.

23. B. J. Deaton, "The Impact of Altered Economic Conditions on Rural Community Development," in Green and Webster, eds., *Social Work in Rural Areas,* p. 33.

24. C. Jacobs, "Planning an Adolescent Drug Treatment Project in a Rural Area: The Patchwork Approach to Program Development," in Green and Webster, eds., *Social Work in Rural Areas,* p. 277.

25. U.S. President's Commission on Mental Health, *Report of the Task Panel on Rural Mental Health,* 4 vols. (Washington, D.C.: U.S. Government Printing Office, 1978), Vol. 3, p. 1169.

26. *Physician Characteristics and Distribution in the U.S., 1982 Edition* (Chicago: Division of Survey and Data Resources, American Medical Association, 1983), Table A-6, p. 23.

27. Clark, *How the Budget Cuts Undercut Rural Women,* p. 11.

28. L. E. Kerr, "The Road We Have Come: Rural Health Needs and Nonresponse," in Martinez-Brawley, *Seven Decades of Rural Social Work,* Appendix 5, p. 204.

29. J. Jankovic and D. Dotson, "Preparing Social Work Students in Occupational Health: Organizing around Brown Lung," in *Effective Models for Delivery of Services in Rural Areas: Implications for Practice and Social Work Education* (Morgantown: West Virginia University, School of Social Work, 1978), p. 98.

30. B. Berry and A. E. Davis, "Community Mental Health Ideology: A Problematic Model for Rural Areas," *American Journal of Orthopsychiatry*, 48 (October 1978), p. 675.

31. Ibid., p. 676.

32. L. C. Johnson, "Social Development in Nonmetropolitan Areas," in Green and Webster, eds., *Social Work in Rural Areas*, p. 225.

33. A. Angerman, "Overview of Mental Health Services for Women in Craig, Colorado" (Madison: University of Wisconsin–Extension, Continuing Education in Mental Health, 1976). (Mimeographed.)

34. E. L. Wilson, "Women Meet the Test of Rural Living," *Womanpower*, newsletter of the National Association of Social Workers, Committee on Women's Issues (September 1979), p. 2.

35. I. Bauer, "Homebased Industry," p. 1. Paper presented to the Rural Development and Capacity Building Council, Richmond, Virginia, July 14, 1983. (Mimeographed.)

36. S. S. Oberst, "Teachers and Learners: Reflections on Women and Farming," *Rural America* (January–February 1982), p. 32.

37. N. Hartsock, "Fundamental Feminism: Process and Perspective," *Quest: A Feminist Quarterly*, 2 (Fall 1975), pp. 75–76.

38. C. Bunch, "Not by Degrees: Feminist Theory and Education," in Bunch and S. Pollack, eds., *Learning Our Way: Essays in Feminist Education* (Trumansburg, N.Y.: Crossing Press, 1983), p. 251.

39. Farley et al., *Rural Social Work Practice*, p. 9.

40. U.S. President's Commission on Mental Health, *Report of the Task Panel on Community Support Systems*, Vol. 2, p. 154.

41. D. A. Bergstrom, "Collaborating with Natural Helpers for Delivery of Rural Mental Health Services," *Journal of Rural Community Psychology*, 3 (Fall 1982), p. 6.

42. U.S. President's Commission on Mental Health, *Report of the Task Panel on Community Support Systems*, Vol. 2, p. 171.

43. Bauer, "Homebased Industry," p. 3.

44. Ibid., p. 3.

45. M. Cirillo et al., *Community Land Trust Handbook* (Emmaus, Pa.: Rodale Press, 1982), p. 18. Available from the Institute for Community Economics, Greenfield, Massachusetts.

46. Ibid.

47. G. Mattera, "Commentaries," in H. S. Cochrane, ed., *Rural New York Conference Proceedings: The Plight of Rural Women in Upstate New York* (New York: Syracuse University, School of Social Work, 1977), p. 7.

Feminist Visions

integrating the lesbian/gay male experience in feminist practice and education

t his chapter explores and analyzes the need for integration of the lesbian and gay male experience within the context of feminist principles, ideologies, and politics, in particular as this experience relates to social work practice. The lack of integration must be understood within the context of the pervasive institutionalization of homophobia throughout U.S. society.

Weinberg defines homophobia as the "dread of homosexuality."[1] Homophobia is also defined as "the irrational fear of love and affection between members of the same sex. Homophobia and the discrimination it produces permeate our society."[2] Therefore, no analysis of the lesbian and gay male experience can be complete and valid unless a critique proceeds within the context of homophobia.

A feminist vision within social work cannot be realized without the validation and acceptance of the lesbian and gay male experience. To exclude that experience is contradictory to the meaning and definition of feminism. Thus, if social work is to demonstrate its commitment to a feminist vision that views **283** the human experience in a holistic and integrated way, committed to a high quality of life for all people, then the experience of lesbians and gay men must be validated. Otherwise, a feminist vision within social work will be fragmented.

For our purposes, it is important that homophobia be probed deeply. At its nucleus is the issue of power and empowerment. No one seems to challenge the traditional existing relationships of male power and authority as does the lesbian. She poses a literal and metaphorical threat to the ultimate power of the patriarchy. As an autonomous woman, she is free from the necessity of bonding with men, as well as from the social exchange between male and female that is based on the promise of protection, security, and supply of needs in exchange for denial of one's identity, autonomy, self-actualization, and self-determination.

Clearly a connection is made between lesbian and gay male experience and threats to the family, which is considered to be patriarchy's centerpiece. Religious fundamentalists and other conservative religious groups are fond of laying the responsibility for the "fall of the family" at the feet of the lesbian and gay male community. In fact, some opponents of the Equal Rights Amendment contend that its passage would lead to homosexual marriages! The granting of civil rights to lesbians and gay men has become a metaphor for the dissolution of patriarchal power.

There are a number of ways of defining patriarchy. Hartmann defines it as:

> a set of social relations which has a material base and in which there are hierarchical relations between men, and solidarity among them, which enable them to control women. Patriarchy is thus the system of male oppression of women.[3]

Hartmann also includes Muller's definition:

> a social system in which the status of women is defined primarily as wards of their husbands, fathers, brothers.[4]

It is essential that as we work toward incorporating feminist visions and values within social work practice, we must commit ourselves to integrating the experience of lesbians and gay men in order to achieve a holistic vision. Social work cannot advocate for social justice and deny protection of rights for lesbians and gay men.

284

Feminist Visions

Eliminating False Dichotomies

A commitment to the elimination of false dichotomies is basic to social work practice, as well as to education for social work, which should include curriculum principles and policies that are responsive to the needs of the lesbian or gay male client. There is an implicit and pervasive view held by many in the social work profession that issues of oppression of lesbians and gay men, the discrimination against lesbian and gay male clients, and the special needs of these clients are not serious concerns. For example, a long and acrimonious debate over the wording of the Council on Social Work Education (CSWE) Curriculum Policy Statement resulted in the declaration that content about minority persons and women "must" be included, whereas content on special populations, including those with a lesbian or gay sexual orientation, "should" be included.[5] There is a significant difference between "must" and "should." The effect is to encourage and maintain a dichotomy among oppressed persons and thus foster the establishment of a hierarchy of priorities, separating and dividing in the traditional manner of the patriarchy.

The feminist vision has been sensitive about the ways in which minority women are forced to identify their discrimination as primarily sexist or racist. However, feminists have not always been sensitive about the inclusion of lesbianism as a way by which women can be additionally oppressed. A holistic, integrated, and ecological perspective (also a feminist perspective) is successfully articulated only as it is sensitive to the inclusion of all oppressed groups.

The needs of lesbian and gay male clients cannot be addressed if their issues are relegated to "the closet." Gochros points out the following:

> Further contributing to the problems associated with homosexuality as well as the difficulties students and practitioners encounter in relation to homosexuality is its invisibility. No other large oppressed group is so invisible to the general public as those who are homosexually oriented.[6]

An urgent task, then, is to make the needs of lesbians and gay men visible. Being sensitive to the vulnerability of these groups is a way of ensuring that reality is viewed in a holistic and integrated way.

Another effect of the "must" versus "should" dichotomy is **285** that lesbian and gay male social workers can become enmeshed in homophobia by being invisible or remaining "in the closet." The implications of this dichotomy are far-reaching. Lesbian and gay male social workers are not available as role models, advocates, or teachers with special knowledge and information. They are not available as monitors of a homophobic system. The invidiousness of the dichotomy is inherent in a patriarchal system. Because closeted social workers are concerned with concealment of their own sexual preference, they tend to avoid openly addressing issues related to sexual preference. If the climate of social work fostered and encouraged their visibility, then they could openly advocate for lesbian and gay male clients.

Reconceptualizing Power

A second principle, reconceptualization of power, follows on the elimination of dichotomies. Empowerment for lesbian and gay male clients and social workers means making their concerns about homophobia visible, taking their issues "out of the closet." This is not possible if the social work profession continues to collude in a conspiracy of silence. The establishment of the National Committee on Lesbian and Gay Issues by the National Association of Social Workers (NASW) is an important step toward empowering sexual minorities by legitimizing the aspirations of this oppressed group. The committee also encourages and protects the visibility of its lesbian and gay male members. In addition, it provides an important formal arena for the explication of lesbian and gay issues and advocacy. Feminist visions require that social work not be blind to the oppression of lesbians and gay men who experience powerlessness because of their invisibility to society.

Renaming. Renaming by redefining one's personal experience is part of the process of empowerment. Being able to define one's experience by rejecting definitions of self imposed by others is, in part, regaining charge of one's own life. This is especially significant because the definition and names that "others" give to an individual are often denigrating, derogatory, and dichotomizing. For instance, homosexuality is seen as the opposite of heterosexuality, as though an individual is either one or the other. **286** Viewing human sexuality dichotomously negates the idea that

Feminist Visions

there is a continuum of sexual experience that includes richness and variety. Homosexuality is seen as an illness or as immoral; heterosexuality is seen as normal and healthy. Through the courageous efforts of lesbian and gay male professionals and their enlightened and supportive colleagues, the American Psychiatric Association in 1973 removed homosexuality per se from the *Diagnostic and Statistical Manual of Mental Disorders,* a significant step in the process of renaming.[7]

Nothing, however, illustrates the process of renaming quite as vividly as the renaming of the homosexual experience as the "gay" experience. The use of the concept "gay" counters the stereotype that such a sexual or affectional preference leads inevitably to despondency and despair, views reflected in such literary works as Radclyffe Hall's *The Well of Loneliness* and Lillian Hellman's *The Children's Hour.* The term "same-gender affectional preference orientation" is another example of renaming, as is, of course, the proud use of the term "lesbian" for women who are gay.[8]

Much of this renaming process is an effort to overcome the oppressive impact of the clinical term "homosexuality," which is sexist (in its usual application to gay men generically) and has the effect of objectifying persons. The renaming also helps counter the effects of obscene and stereotypical names given by others. In addition, renaming in this instance extends the meaning of loving one's own gender beyond a focus solely on sexuality by suggesting in a more integrative and holistic manner that "being gay" also represents a choice of lifestyle for lesbians and gay men.

The Personal Is Political

Renaming is also related to the principle that "the personal is political." For the lesbian or gay male, the most personal *and* political act is that of being visible, of "coming out." There is no doubt that coming out is perceived by others as a political act. We have all heard people make comments such as, "I don't care what they do in the bedroom. They don't have to rub my nose in who they are."

One objection to any civil rights legislation seems to be that it could lessen the threat inherent in coming out and in fact increase the probability that greater numbers will become visi- **287**

Figure 1
Interaction Between Institutional and Individual Change

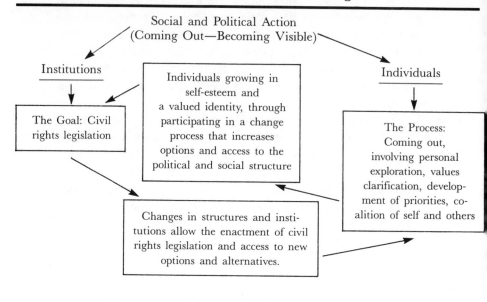

SOURCE: Adapted from a figure by N. B. Gluckstern, "Beyond Therapy: Personal and Institutional Change," in E. I. Rawlings and D. K. Carter, eds., *Psychotherapy for Women* (Springfield, Ill.: Charles C Thomas, Publisher, 1977), p. 429.

ble. Then, in turn, the more visible lesbians and gay men become, the greater the likelihood for passage of more civil rights legislation protecting them. Coming out is a political act in that it has the effect of increasing one's self-esteem through the feeling of empowerment; that feeling leads to further changes in social institutions and is, in turn, reinforced and confirmed by these changes. Figure 1 demonstrates the point that coming out, a personal-political act, has consequences for changing the individual as well as changing institutions and structures.

Coming out, becoming visible, is a complex and highly individualized process. It begins with a personal acknowledgment about one's own sexual preference. This is a complex development for some because it can proceed to a stage of denial or self-loathing, followed by grudging acceptance. In contrast, for others it may be an acceptance that is joyfully embraced and experienced as liberating. There are new stages in the process that involve sharing this acknowledgment with others; this experience is equally complex depending on how the acknowledgment is received by others and the circumstances of the sharing experience.[9]

288

Feminist Visions

Coming out can be and indeed is a social as well as personal process. It can also be a dangerous process. Not only may one suffer personal hurt, but the possibility of losing one's job is real, as is the possibility of losing one's home. However, taking the risks involved in coming out offers the greater possibility for a self-actualized life. Getting in touch with one's anger at the oppressive condition has the potential for directing energy toward changing that condition.

The lesbian or gay man's experience in coming out, becoming visible, is a process with complex meaning for the individual, and the process is as profound and important as the outcome. The process and the outcome are both political: They are self-validating, and they promote social change.

Coming out is a circular process that has impact not only on the individual but on social institutions as well. The process of coming out changes the individual, and it changes those around her or him. Social work as a profession must invest in this process. That is, it must allow lesbian and gay male clients and practitioners to come out of the closet. The social work profession must be more active in promoting civil and human rights for this group, and there must be an end to the dichotomies it has set up among divergent oppressed groups. An integrated holistic vision that includes the above feminist principles must validate the lesbian and gay male experience.

Implications for Indirect Practice and Advocacy

Assuming that at least 10 percent of the population, if not more, is homosexual, it is reasonable to assume that at least 10 percent of social work's clientele is made up of lesbians or gay men, as well as 10 percent of social work academics, practitioners, administrators, and policymakers.[10] Nevertheless, the social work profession has sorely neglected this significant minority and has often behaved as though it did not exist. This neglect is experienced in all sectors of social work. For example, schools of social work pay little attention to including content about this minority:

> Schools of social work generally offer courses devoted entirely to the elderly (who make up 11.3 percent of the population) and to racial and ethnic minorities, with an emphasis on blacks (who make up 11.7 percent of the population, while other groups constitute even

289

smaller percentages), yet only six schools include a course on homosexuality.[11]

Altman states: "Unlike other minorities, we lie within the oppressor himself, and our invisibility, the fact that we represent human potential that has been realized, makes the need to draw the line against us much sharper."[12] The issue of visibility is a key one in the analysis of the lesbian and gay male experience as well as critical to changing and reframing both indirect and direct social work interventions. It is also key to influencing the process of educating and training social workers in a manner congruent with the feminist vision. At the heart of these issues is the power of the patriarchal values that infuse our culture and the profession. Keeping the lesbian and gay male minority invisible is a patriarchal priority.

What would happen if lesbian and gay male social work practitioners, educators, administrators, and policymakers became visible? It is possible that the numbers would be astounding! Certainly, the presence of positive role models would have a healthy rippling effect on students and clients. The potential for confronting myths and stereotypes in order to eradicate them would be profound. Moreover, the empowerment of so many people could contribute significantly to the efforts of other minorities also trying to bring about changes in a system that currently deprives the oppressed of social justice as well as access to the structures of power and opportunity.

NASW's National Committee on Lesbian and Gay Issues and CSWE's Commission on Gay/Lesbian Issues in Social Work Education represent two major efforts at advocacy. Equally important, they provide a forum for visible lesbian and gay male professionals to define and name their experience and the changes that must occur to eliminate their oppression. The establishment of these committees is a beginning in the long process that must include purging the false dichotomies between oppressed groups within the profession.

An important step in this direction should be a concerted effort by the social work community to promote and ensure passage of civil rights legislation for lesbians and gay men. For example, advocating for legislation that leads to the protection of jobs and housing, regardless of a person's sexual orientation, makes the option of coming out more available. As more lesbians **290** and gay men become visible, the potential for eradication of

Feminist Visions

destructive stereotypes grows. The power of such political groups as the Moral Majority might diminish as more people become aware of the significant number of lesbians and gay men. Furthermore, as social agencies adopt policies that explicitly treat lesbian or gay male families as valid family units, as well as make adoption and foster parenting an option for lesbian or gay male couples, the process of eradicating false dichotomies is enhanced. Also, schools of social work should include in their statements of antidiscrimination a clause that would protect persons "regardless of sexual preference." Social work must also develop policies and programs that attend to the needs of lesbian or gay male youths.

The consequences of these actions will profoundly affect not just lesbians and gay men but the fabric of our social structure. The implications of these actions involve confronting patriarchal structures and values that form the foundations on which our beliefs about families and lifestyles are based. The process by which we begin to challenge these beliefs through changes that are shaped by feminist visions promotes alterations that move us toward a society that facilitates self-actualization for all persons.

Implications for Direct Practice

Principles of feminist practice are most useful in working with lesbians and gay men and their issues. For example, the feminist principle "the personal is political" is not only helpful but it is the most accurate framework for understanding, defining, and empowering a lesbian or gay man in personal distress. Many traditional, Freudian-based psychologies have been guilty of viewing and defining the lesbian and gay male experience as sick, pathological, or invalid, and thus of further stigmatizing and contributing to the low self-esteem, depression, and despair of lesbian and gay male clients. Any diagnostic evaluation or assessment of an individual's distress must include an analysis that explores the person's concerns from a feminist perspective. A client is encouraged to define and name her or his own experience, and the practitioner begins to work with that operational definition of the individual's experience. The premise that "the personal is political" is also included in a worker's analysis of a client's situation. The practitioner must understand the forced dichotomies that are **291** traditionally used in an analysis of an individual's distress, and not only avoid using them but also explore how those dichotomies themselves might contribute to the distress.

In my own practice, one lesbian client shared with her therapy group the confusion about her gender identity that she experienced when involved in intimate sexual experiences with women. For example, when she took the initiative and called for a date, she felt ambivalent about this action because it seemed to her to be "male" behavior, which made her very uncomfortable and anxious. Yet she "knew" that this anxiety did not quite make sense; *someone* would have to take the initiative. This and other experiences found her naming certain behaviors as "male" or "female." Her disclosure encouraged other women in the group to reveal similar experiences. When the discussion began, it was framed in the context of such questions as, "Why am I so confused? What is wrong with me? Why am I so upset?" The direction of the discussion shifted and was ultimately reframed by helping clients to rename their behaviors as androgynous, appropriate, and valid for their experiences. What the group had begun by identifying as personal aberrant behavior became reframed as being heterosexist concepts applied inappropriately to explain lesbian experience. The heterosexist framework falsely dichotomizes interpersonal behavioral transactions as "male" and "female." Androgyny, however, is a concept that is much more appropriate for same-sex relationships, because it validates the possession of both "male" and "female" attributes. The issue for the group then became framed as the problem of dealing with valid lesbian experiences in a heterosexist culture. With this redefinition of the problem, the group could then proceed with appropriate problem solving.

The traditional analysis of the client's experience, which generally begins with the client's internal or personal dynamics, is not a useful way to explore and analyze the lesbian and gay male experience because it does not adequately or accurately take into account the cultural variable of homophobia. Not only must the impact of this variable be understood but homophobia must be also included in framing the issue to be worked on.

The ecological model, consistent as it is with a feminist vision, is useful in dealing with the lesbian or gay male client.[13] It offers the opportunity for a more holistic view and one with the potential for encouraging the client to define and name her or his experience. It also makes possible a way of articulating "the personal is political" by valuing process as well as outcome.

292

Feminist Visions

A most important outcome of the feminist vision is collective sharing of experiences and problem solving. Group therapy must be valued as much as individual therapy. It is my professional experience that the group process is more valuable for oppressed clients than the individual work that we now emphasize. Lesbians and gay men suffer in varying degrees an internalized homophobia with serious consequences to self-esteem, identity, and validation of self. The group process, with its consciousness-raising potential, can bring about significant changes in self-perceptions. It provides a ready forum for empowering individuals by encouraging their exploration of ways to take charge of their personal lives by having direct impact on their environments. This is another specific way in which "the personal is political" is articulated. The shared experiences validate individual experiences and universalize them in an integrated and holistic manner.

Perhaps there is no more significant aspect of social work practice that has greater impact on the feminist vision, and is, in turn, more potentially influenced by the feminist vision, than work with the family. This is true not only in terms of direct practice, as in family therapy, but equally so for indirect practice, as in policy development. It is also politically the most explosive influence, as it is at the very heart of the patriarchal domain. There is little question that the renaming and redefining of the family must occur. The traditional definition of "the" family in terms of a nuclear unit must begin to give way to accommodate new alternative family forms. We can no longer tolerate the false dichotomies that have been set up between alternative families and the traditional view of family. There is an urgent need not only for the eradication of these dichotomies but also for providing the concept of family with a redefinition that accommodates new meanings.

For example, lesbian families that include a child or children by artificial insemination are a growing phenomenon. In recent times, George Annus, an attorney and faculty member of the Boston University School of Medicine, discussed on National Public Radio some of the new methods for inseminating and fertilizing women. He also talked about the legal and sociocultural implications of these new modes. The fact is that artificial insemination now makes it possible for a woman to bear a child without the involvement of a male. A large number of women are choosing this method and raising children as single parents or with another woman.

293

Moreover, many lesbian couples are raising children from their former marriages. Gay men are also raising children, either from former marriages or through adoption as single parents or as couples. The stereotype of the single lesbian or the single gay male contributes to the false dichotomy of family as a heterosexual experience and lack of family as the lesbian or gay male experience. Lesbians and gay men are also part of the families into which they were born and in which they were raised, as well as being part of the families they establish. This knowledge and experience of family life is denied to lesbians and gay men, who are stereotyped by large segments of the public as being antifamily. The consequences of these attitudes are far-reaching. For one thing, the richness and variety of these new family forms can provide important sources of data for social work practitioners, educators, and theoreticians. The social work profession could learn a great deal about these new family forms that would be useful for *all* people.

Also, many lesbian or gay male families are potential clients. Although these new family forms are exciting in their possibilities for expanding the human experience, they are also potentially problematic. Decker makes the point that although lesbian or gay male families struggle with issues similar to those experienced by heterosexuals, they do so in the context of a larger system that denies them their existence, a system in which the rules applicable to heterosexual families are not applicable to them.[14] Not only are there few rules but there are no sanctions and supports for such families. Often homophobic attitudes can exacerbate problems that might be experienced as minor in a heterosexual family; that is, problems can become generalized into questions about the soundness of the relationship, which could in turn confirm the homophobic view that such relationships cannot succeed. The consequence of such potentially self-fulfilling prophecies must be understood by practitioners. The social work practitioner working with lesbian or gay male families must begin by accepting the validity of the clients' definition of their experience of family. The lesbian or gay male's definition will differ from the traditional heterosexual definition of family, but will be just as valid.

An ecological systems perspective is the framework from which interventions should be shaped. This perspective helps both the social worker and the client understand the interactions and interplay of homophobia and familial distress. It helps to eradicate the dichotomies among the varied family forms and offers a client family the potential for feeling empowered to create structures and rules that would be useful for them. Perhaps most important is the attitude of the social worker and the need for the worker's commitment to feminist principles and visions enabling and facilitating the process of validation, protection, and commitment for lesbian or gay male families.

Implications for Social Work Education

Apparently no school of social work includes in its human behavior sequence a perspective, an explanation, a conceptualization about the development of a lesbian or gay male identity. For example, sequences continue to be taught as though *all* children and youths proceed through life stages toward a heterosexual identity. Anything else is an abnormal deviance. However, we know that at least 10 percent of children and youths do not follow this pattern. This information surely has implications for direct practice with children in residential treatment centers, foster homes, mental health clinics, child guidance centers, and family agencies. Explorations about the etiology of homosexuality need to be dealt with in curricula if for no other reason than to address the stereotypes that abound. Dr. Mary Calderone is often heard to comment, "If you can explain to me my heterosexuality, I'll try to explain homosexuality."[15]

It is a national disgrace that 10 percent of young clients of social service agencies are underserved, unserved, or inappropriately served because of homophobia within the profession of social work. The need for policies in this instance is critical. The Child Welfare League of America, for example, has not yet begun to deal with this issue in a forthright manner, nor has any other major social service agency.[16] The implication of this void is critical considering that direct service practitioners are supposed to be trained and educated to work with *all* youths. A grass-roots agency in New York, the Institute for the Protection of Gay/Lesbian Youth (incorporated in 1983), has attempted to provide services, to advocate, and to educate.

Curricula also need to include perspectives on the issues of adult sexuality, the middle years, and aging, and how these developmental stages are the same and different for lesbian and gay male clients as for heterosexual clients. Social workers must be trained, both in schools of social work and through in-service training programs, to work with *all* lesbian and gay male clients. **295**

Implications for Research

Finally, a word about research. Cummerton states:

> Feminist research is characterized by an emphasis on personal growth and reciprocity between researcher and participant. Because reciprocity characterizes every phase of the research process, the researcher and participant are seen as collaborators in the research. Feminist research is also seen as not only research on women but research for women. That is research that truly reflects women's experience and can be used to improve women's status in one way or another.[17]

The same may be said of the lesbian and gay male experience and research. Research can contribute significantly to improvement in the status of lesbians and gay men, but only when that research is *for* them, not *on* them. The degree to which patriarchy shapes the whole institution of research is the degree to which research becomes yet another method of oppressing lesbians and gay men.

Summary

This chapter has focused on several critical points with reference to the integration of feminist visions and the lesbian and gay male experience into social work practice and education. First, obstacles to the realization of this vision for lesbians and gay men have been explored, and suggestions have been made as to ways in which such visions might be achieved in both direct and indirect social work practice. Second, homophobia and the perpetuation of patriarchy have been identified as key obstacles to the attainment of feminist visions. It appears that the most virulent homophobes in our society have scapegoated the lesbian and gay male minority. They have focused their attack on this group as threatening patriarchal structures and values within our social institutions, particularly the family. Finally, it has been suggested that the fate of all minority groups is linked, and that the lesbian and gay male minority might in fact be the linchpin in effecting major changes that will promote social justice. It is essential that social work be openly and clearly active in behalf of all oppressed people and give up its ambivalent attitudes about lesbians and gay men for feminist visions to be realized.

notes

1. George Weinberg, *Society and the Healthy Homosexual* (Garden City, N.Y.: Anchor Press, Doubleday & Co., 1973), p. 2.

2. Alice E. Niessing, Robert Schoenberg, and Robert K. Stephens, "Confronting Homophobia in Health Care Settings: Guidelines for Social Work Practice," in Schoenberg and Richard S. Goldberg, with David A. Shore, eds., *Homosexuality and Social Work* (New York: Haworth Press, 1984), p. 65.

3. Heidi Hartmann, "Capitalism, Patriarchy, and Job Discrimination by Sex," in Martha Blaxall and Barbara Reagan, eds., *Woman and the Work Place* (Chicago: University of Chicago Press, 1976), p. 138.

4. Viana Muller, "The Formation of the State and the Oppression of Women: A Case Study in England and Wales" (New York: New School for Social Research, 1975), p. 144, n. 2. (Mimeographed.)

5. *Curriculum Policy for the Master's Degree and Baccalaureate Degree Programs in Social Work Education,* (New York Council on Social Work Education, 1982).

6. Harvey Gochros, "Teaching Social Workers to Meet the Needs of the Homosexually Oriented," in Schoenberg, Goldberg, with Shore, eds., *Homosexuality and Social Work,* p. 65.

7. *Diagnostic and Statistical Manual of Mental Disorders* (3rd ed.; Washington, D.C.: American Psychiatric Association, 1980).

8. Jack Louis Devine, "A Systemic Inspection of Affectional Preference Orientation and the Family of Origin," in Schoenberg, Goldberg, with Shore, eds., *Homosexuality and Social Work,* p. 9.

9. Scott Worth, "Principles for Psychotherapy with Families of Lesbians and Gay Men: Gay Youth Counseling Manual" (New York: National Network of Runaway and Youth Services, 1982).

10. Judd Marvin, *Homosexual Behavior: A Modern Appraisal* (New York: Basic Books, 1980).

11. Diana D. Dulaney and James Kelly, "Improving Services to Gay and Lesbian Clients," *Social Work,* 27 (March 1982), p. 178.

12. Dennis Altman, *Oppression and Liberation* (New York: Outerbridge & Dientsfrey, 1971), p. 2.

13. Carel B. Germain and Alex Gitterman, *The Life Model of Social Work Practice* (New York: Columbia University Press, 1980).

14. Beverly Decker, "Counseling Gay and Lesbian Couples," in Schoenberg, Goldberg, with Shore, eds., *Homosexuality and Social Work,* p. 40.

297

15. See John Money and Anne Ehrhardt, *Man and Woman, Boy and Girl* (Baltimore, Md.: Johns Hopkins University Press, 1972), p. 235.

16. Tracey L. Vergara, "Meeting the Needs of Sexual Minority Youth: One Program's Response," in Schoenberg, Goldberg, with Shore, eds., *Homosexuality and Social Work*, p. 19.

17. Joan M. Cummerton, "A Feminist Perspective on Research: What Does It Help Us See?" Paper presented at the Annual Meeting of the Council on Social Work Education, Fort Worth, Tex., March 15, 1983.

298

Feminist Visions

Katharine Hooper Briar
Michele J. Vinet

an expanded
mission for
occupational
social work

Over the decades, social workers have served diverse populations, but their professional attention to the world
of work and to workers as clients has waxed and waned.[1] The
current reinvolvement of social workers with the workplace has
been supported by some and criticized by others in the profession.[2] A feminist analysis of historical as well as current social
work practice in labor and industry offers a potentially useful
perspective on this reemerging field of practice and may help
to reduce the gulf between its advocates and its critics. Beginning
with an examination of the historical antecedents of occupational
social work practice, this chapter will draw on values, principles,
and world views that inform a feminist perspective. These include
the rejection of false dichotomies, promotion of more holistic
perspectives, validation of personal experience and intuition,
attention to process as well as product, and elimination of structures and relationships based on power differentials.[3]

Feminist thinking has generated alternative paradigms for
social work practice, thus potentially expanding perspectives,
choices, and options for practitioners. Feminist concepts are not

the sole domain of women; they are increasingly shared and advocated by men. This chapter tests their applicability, not just for the assessment of prior and current practice in labor and industry, but for the creation of expanded practice agendas and visions for both male and female practitioners.

Historical Interventions

In the late nineteenth and early twentieth centuries, when the profession was being established, social work practice centered on work and the workplace as a source of social problems and as an instrument of social welfare. Without work, one risked destitution and pauperism, yet work and work conditions were often exploitive, oppressive, and life threatening.

Contrasting views at the turn of the century about work conditions, worker needs, employer practices, and labor trends gave rise to divergent forms of social work intervention. One practice approach, exemplified by the work of Jane Addams, Florence Kelley, Josephine Shaw Lowell, and, in later years, Bertha Reynolds, saw workers as victims of uneven and sometimes capricious employer practices, without defense or recourse. These pioneer social workers developed resources and services as advocacy tools to strengthen worker autonomy and problem-solving capability. Their practice taught workers self-advocacy through the use of community resources and services. A contrasting approach, reflected in services and programs later entitled "welfare capitalism," saw workers as needing corporate-sponsored services to promote compliant, conforming behavior.[4] These opposing views of worker needs are relevant today as occupational social workers determine which strategies can best be advanced in labor and industry.

Jane Addams. Settlement houses served as one hub for service in behalf of the working poor and unemployed, who needed to get their bearings as they sought jobs or pressed for improved working conditions. Innovations at Hull House, established by Jane Addams in 1889, included the development of an employment bureau as well as a lunchroom and nursery for working women.[5] Addams's concern over workers went beyond the confines of the traditional workplace to address the problems of a special class of workers, prostitutes. Her efforts led her to write

Feminist Visions

A New Conscience and an Ancient Evil, an important book on the plight of this victimized group of working women.[6]

The settlement-house movement spawned an array of new community services and legislative reforms. Because it symbolized an abhorrence of social and economic stratification, it became a living testimony to the possibility of equality and fellowship among diverse populations. Settlement houses helped to advance a democratic ideal. They provided social workers with work structures more akin to women's preference for nonhierarchical, nonstratified settings. In Hull House, one's work was part of one's home life. For Addams, Hull House was a microcosm of the kind of community she sought to create. And in her work for women's suffrage, Addams viewed the vote as more than a right to be claimed by women: To her, it was a mechanism for infusing women's values into a world that was rife with war. The Nobel Peace Prize she received was as much a tribute to her efforts to develop community harmony through nonstratified community living as it was her mission to promote world peace. Her ability to see unity and connectedness in seemingly disparate events—a feminist principle—is vividly displayed in her work.

Florence Kelley.   Like Jane Addams, Florence Kelley devoted many years of practice to policy and service development in behalf of workers and their families. Beginning as a staff member at the Illinois State Bureau of Labor Statistics, she advocated improved factory working conditions, especially for women and children. Her practice helped to promote workers' compensation as well as to prevent industrial accidents.[7] One of her books, *Modern Industry in Relation to the Family, Health, Education and Morality,*[8] is a singular reminder of how central work and work problems were to social work in its founding years.

Josephine Shaw Lowell.   Such early reformers also determined that changing the workplace and its policies required the mobilization of consumers. Josephine Shaw Lowell, the founder of the National Consumers League, saw the social and economic power of consumers as an essential vehicle to press for reforms. Initially a founder of the charity organization movement, she later turned to social action strategies when issues such as the regulation of wages and working hours of women were at stake. The title of one of her books, *Industrial Arbitration and Conciliation* (1893), is indeed unlikely to reflect the interests of some of **301** her successors in social work, yet it reminds us of how much the profession has neglected such agendas.[9]

Exemplary vs. Anti-Union Practices. The often segmented, fragmented approach to client needs and service delivery that divides practice methods and arenas into specializations today and repudiates holistic feminist visions was not evident among these early practitioners. Jane Addams, for example, was as intensely committed to world peace as she was to child care provisions for working women. When she, Florence Kelley, and Josephine Shaw Lowell pressed for reforms in the neighborhood, workplace, or legislature, they demonstrated a "case to cause" mission, viewing individual problems, systemic causes, and societal responses as interlocking.

Not all social work practice in the world of work was as exemplary as that of Addams, Kelley, and Shaw. Social workers hired by management as "welfare secretaries" spied on labor union organizing activities to combat the development of company unions. Samuel Gompers of the American Federation of Labor (AFL) labeled these anti-union practices as "hell-fare work."[10] Such a legacy affects the profession today, as suspicion in the labor movement still influences some labor unions' view of corporate-financed social services. Labor leaders have also argued that excessive attention to the functioning or morality of individual workers would draw attention away from corporate causes and reform agendas. When unions define the corporation as the source of problems, then interventions to change the individual may be seen as harassing and scapegoating.

Bertha Capen Reynolds. Union-sponsored social work services have their own unique history. Such programs were pioneered by Bertha Capen Reynolds, who provided social services to seamen and their families through the National Maritime Union in the 1940s. The need to infuse services into the world of workers and their families is programmatically and philosophically described in one of her books, *Social Work and Social Living.*[11]

Mary Parker Follett. Often better known to the business and labor community than to social work is the path-breaking work of Mary Parker Follett. In the 1920s, she advocated for the "co-active" sharing of power among workers regardless of their rank and pay. Her understanding of the human side of the business

302

Feminist Visions

enterprise and her belief that all issues and decisions are embedded ultimately in human relations enabled her to infuse a social welfare perspective into work settings. She championed a human resource development approach to counter the rigid time-and-motion efficiency approach known as Taylorism. Her work has been viewed as visionary, given the more mechanistic approaches to human resource administration that have permeated the workplace.[12]

Follett's contributions were not limited to the workplace. Her commitment to integrating all points of view into an evolving, innovative process led her to organize gatherings with representatives from all socioeconomic strata. In her book *Creative Experience* she set forth prescriptions for valuing and building on the diverse views, ideas, and opinions of groups.[13] Her ideas are relevant to feminist approaches to planning and administration as well as to building democracy in the workplace. In her conceptualization of rationales for being "process- rather than product-oriented," she was able to provide employers and labor groups new ground rules for decision making. Applying the feminist value of "renaming," she helped the labor and business community progress by reconceptualizing and renaming what they were doing and whom they were serving.

Frances Perkins. Further testimony to the development of work interventions and innovations by our foremothers was the leadership of Frances Perkins, Roosevelt's Secretary of Labor during the 1930s. She is remembered for her extensive reform in behalf of jobless workers and labor unions. Many a social worker hearing her name or passing the building named for her in Washington, D.C., may have little awareness of her singular efforts and her professional status as a social worker.[14]

Other Interventions. Like the work of Follett and Perkins, other interventions by social workers in the world of work to promote employment and to mobilize workers have been overlooked by the profession. For example, annual community chest and United Way drives, evolving historically from the charity organization movement, ask workers to donate part of their paychecks to support human needs and community social services. In this effort, a distant but important connection between workers and the profession is forged. Sometimes, these workers who contribute to the United Way have found social services inaccessible and **303** possibly irrelevant for their own use. Why such workers cannot make use of the services they support requires a brief review of the more recent decades of social work involvement in the world of work.

Social Work Pulls Back from the World of Work

The demise of a focus on systemic change in the world of work and the loss of attention to the plight of workers have had immense consequences for the definition of social work practice. The passage of landmark legislation such as social security may have shifted the focus away from social action goals for the profession. In the corporate world, personnel officers helped to replace welfare secretaries. Moreover, concerns about professional status may have hastened a pulling back from social action as social workers became increasingly status-oriented.

In some cases, social workers themselves became the new class of workers with whom the profession was most concerned. By the 1930s, some social workers were involved in their own labor organizing as the profession became mainstreamed into public social welfare programs. Social workers also learned from past experience that "mission-oriented" practice brought them into conflict with the political system. Social work activists (including Jane Addams) who were investigated in the 1920s for anti-war and progressive sentiments found that their efforts had been fraught with professional peril. Thus, the reactionary climate of the 1920s may have diminished the reform-oriented practice agendas that had been intertwined with workplace interventions and issues.

One reason for the demise of an emphasis on reform in the workplace seems to have been the development of corporate capitalism and professionalism. Those phenomena appear to have affected social work, as witnessed by an increasing emphasis during the 1920s on the provision of clinically oriented services to employees. Such a focus served to redefine worker stress, viewed through a psychopathology model, as aberrant behavior.

The development of corporate capitalism and professionalism resulted in a clinical service methodology that redefined employment and economic stresses to fit a psychological frame of reference. This evolving psychological orientation of social **304** workers may have contributed to the decline in services to workers. The adoption of a Freudian approach to problems, with its emphasis on the intrapsychic life of the individual, may also have led to a diminished focus on the economic and employment needs of workers and their families. The mental illness focus created a stigma for those seeking help, which may have made it more difficult for men than for women to seek social work services. Moreover, practitioners, reflecting the widely held values of society, may not have seen work issues as relevant to their female clients.[15] Work outside the home had only recently re-emerged as a woman's right. Thus, the eclipse of workplace interventions left the profession more psychologically oriented and woman-centered; this approach overlooked for the most part conditions of work for both men and women.

Additional explanations for the exclusion of work issues from social work practice derive from what some perceive as the noxious association between income maintenance and compulsory work programs in the welfare system. Dislike for the degrading work required of welfare recipients and the nature of unjust work organizations with dead-end jobs may have blunted professional visions regarding the workplace as a practice arena.[16]

The denial of the importance of economic and employment problems as powerful shapers of human behavior, suffering, or growth may also reflect a perceived inability in the profession to solve work or income problems. Generally untrained in labor-market trends, vocational assessment, job development, or human resource development in the workplace, social work practitioners may have felt ill-prepared to aid the client with such concrete problems and resource issues.

A feminist critique of such trends argues that the severing of social work practice from the workplace and from workers as clients has deflected professional attention from the political economy. Yet by avoiding oppressive policies and organizational structures and the discriminatory and inequitable allocation of work opportunities, social work practice may unwittingly cushion and even mask the ills caused by the political economy. By removing workplace policies and practices from the social work agenda, the profession may help to reinforce a welfare state that takes a remedial approach to social needs. Moreover, of special concern to feminists is the false dichotomization segregating the work and home spheres of life; this dichotomization has historically relegated women to the family domain and men to the work domain.[17]

305

Current Practice in Occupational Social Work

The reentry of social work into the world of work in the last decade has taken the form of services to workers and family members afflicted by mental health, drug, alcohol, and family problems. Often called employee assistance programs (EAPs), these services provide assessment, referral, and case management for workers and family members whose problems affect their work behavior. In EAPs that are internal to the workplace, social workers are employed in departments of personnel, health, and employee relations. Other programs are operated through externally organized service arrangements, such as traditional social service agencies, the use of nonprofit or profit-oriented consultants, or employee assistance organizations.[18] For both internal and external service providers, practice rarely involves long-term counseling, but instead requires generalist skills spanning macro and micro interventions for change.

In addition to EAPs, social workers offer services for employers, unions, and consumers.[19] When the employer is the primary focus and recipient of services, the social worker may be engaged in such activities as organizational development or benefits coordination. In addition, social workers advocate for policy that extends health and welfare benefits or improves workers' job satisfaction, labor-management relations, and affirmative action practices.

Union-centered services entail a wide range of macro and micro skills and tasks. The union-based social worker may provide some of the same social services as in an EAP, such as drug, alcohol, mental health, and family counseling. In addition, the union auspices may provide a base to work on legislation to regulate plant closures and to promote benefits for strikers and the unemployed. Some argue that, unlike corporate-based services, union-centered services allow social workers to intensify their social reform agendas. Moreover, because a union's primary focus is on the welfare of its organization, union leaders may more readily see the value in social service programs that are beneficial to workers and thus help build membership.

Consumer-centered social work practice is being rediscovered as work organizations increasingly recognize the importance of addressing consumer needs. Some consumer-centered social work involves crisis counseling for such groups as airline passengers with a fear of flying or the survivors and families of those

306

killed in plane accidents. Other services to be offered may involve trust customers of financial or banking institutions. For example, a social worker may be employed by the bank or be on contract to deliver a range of social services to an individual trust customer, usually an elderly person.

Emergent Approaches

Given the developmental nature of these current services and trends, it is premature to draw conclusions about their long-term contributions. However, a feminist framework makes it possible to pose questions and to offer visions regarding future directions in occupational social work practice.

Multisource Capability. Each EAP or occupational social welfare program has the potential to deliver multiple services to the workplace it serves, just as multiservice agencies do in the community. Thus, the multiservice capability of EAPs is in keeping with the diversity of perspectives and choices promoted by feminist thought. Those EAPs that move beyond a single-issue focus (such as alcoholism) can offer more encompassing services to address the wide-ranging needs of workers and their families. However, broadening programs without addressing the needs of, for example, alcoholic workers may limit the programs' effectiveness and create a grave injustice for such clients.

It is not surprising that some of the same biases that women have encountered in community-based services are repeated in the workplace. The overriding focus on psychologically oriented services rather than on concrete resources, such as child care, caregiving benefits, and other family-oriented services as well as job security, suggests that EAPs may be limited in their relevance to the wide-ranging needs of women workers. Nevertheless, building on multidimensional perspectives, some EAPs are expanding beyond being counseling resources to addressing other needs and problems in the work lives of their clients. A number of EAPs, for example, now encourage health, wellness, and fitness services to deal with stress on the job. To be truly holistic or feminist in orientation, however, EAPs should move in the direction of advocating for the provision of indirect services—such as child care, parental benefits, and alternative work arrangements like "flextime," high-quality part-time jobs, and job sharing—that **307** can truly improve the quality of work life for many employees.

Evaluation.   Historical trends suggest that work and work conditions can be debilitating, or they can be enhancing for workers and their families. A feminist query might probe the extent to which current and future social work contributions address work and work conditions rather than symptoms. Certainly, employee assistance and related social work services offer critical help to workers and families suffering from social, psychological, health, and career-related stresses. However, the extent to which the work-related precipitants of such stresses are explicitly addressed remains an unanswered question.[20] Further study is needed. For example, could a supervisor who became more sensitive to a woman's dual jobs at home and in the workplace also become more supportive and less harassing? Would such changes at the workplace alleviate the depression and job dissatisfaction that may have engulfed the woman worker?

Most outcome studies to date focus on financial savings to the organization when an employee is treated for alcohol, drug, or mental health problems.[21] Indicators of most interest to employers include absenteeism, sickness and accident rates, and health insurance costs before and after the treatment. Thus, evaluations track individual data, which limits the conclusions that can be drawn about a program's total impact.

A feminist critique of such evaluative approaches suggests that to describe benefits solely in terms of cost savings to the employer rather than a changed organizational environment implies a constricted service mission. Little empirical documentation has been generated about the impact of such programs on changes in the work organization, supervisory practices, relationships among co-workers, or other quality-of-worklife effects. Inattention to the impact of a program on multiple parts of the work environment reduces the value of evaluations and tells an incomplete story. By stressing the costs savings to employers, evaluators minimize the positive as well as the negative effects of the programs on workers and on work conditions.

Reform.   It may seem difficult to envision current occupational social work roles, which are client-centered, moving into the policy-development realm. Likewise, it may seem premature to conjecture that social workers in macro roles, such as planning and employee relations, would be able to parley their jobs single-handedly into reform-oriented instruments. Yet if reform-oriented practice in such work sites is not feasible, should social work practice occur there in the first place? Unclear social work norms have heightened the difficulties occupational social workers encounter as they enter corporations that produce nuclear weaponry, those that are multinational, and those with long histories of exploitive labor relations policies.

In examining the service-based movement that dominates current developments in occupational social work practice, one must ask whether services by themselves historically reflect the contributions of the profession, its legacy, or feminist visions and values. Clearly, service initiatives may be significant job-saving and life-saving supports to some stressed workers and their families. Are service-oriented programs unable to address systematically the causes of problems: the inequitable allocation of jobs, opportunities, income, and benefits? Can services promote social welfare values and thus become a moral force to counter or balance the market values of the workplace?

It is too early to tell whether services are conduits to workplace reforms, but such issues must be posed as questions to guide the review of progress in this emerging practice arena. For instance, it is unclear whether a change-oriented social work mission can best be supported by auspices that are union, consumer-based, or industry-based. Such roles as employee relations manager, affirmative action officer, or employee assistance director need to be evaluated for their long-range potential for change. Clearly, the auspice for one's work greatly determines the boundaries for practice. However, such social work issues as individuals' service needs, reforms of work conditions, and inequitable work opportunities cut across more than one auspice. Eventually, occupational social welfare may compel the mainstreaming of such issues into all social work practice.

Employment and Unemployment. A broadened perspective on occupational social work from a feminist point of view also needs to address the problems of the unemployed. Historically, high unemployment rates have been tolerated in the belief that unemployment controls the upward trends in salaries and worker benefits. A deliberate, but unnecessary, instrument of the political economy, involuntary unemployment persists unabated. The jobless and the underemployed, many of whom are women, ethnic minorities, the aged, the young, and the disabled, are under- **309** served, high-risk populations requiring social work intervention. Traditional psychological approaches to these workers must be balanced with strategies based on knowledge of employment, job development, labor market, and career trends. These workers are often indoctrinated to believe that their joblessness or under-employment is a psychological, health, or interpersonal problem or are forced to redefine their problem in one of these ways in order to use traditional services. A feminist vision for the future of social work practice would regard the unemployed and under-employed as a central client group, whose needs and rights must be systematically addressed. Practice in behalf of this group might entail the development of a continuum of service and policy initiatives that reduce or prevent the hardships of joblessness and underemployment, while promoting full employment as an entitlement.[22]

Currently, despite the emergence of innovative programs for workers and their families, few social workers in labor and industry address the service needs of workers who face temporary or permanent layoffs. The hiatus in a community care system for this group—those who lose income and job security through industry-wide recessions—compels the emergence of a new focus of practice. Filling this gap and addressing this victimized group with work-sharing policies and other worker advocacy goals will add a new dimension of service to the profession.

A much overlooked arena of practice for social workers has been the array of employment services in the state employment service departments and federal departments of labor and commerce. Public job creation programs, training, career counseling, and vocational rehabilitation programs offer social workers important arenas that reclaim our heritage as a profession. The few social workers who are employed in these settings have not been identified as occupational social workers even though they are concerned with the allocation of jobs and training to disadvantaged and disabled workers. The exclusion of these social workers from the purview of occupational social work reflects an unnecessarily constricted view of this arena of practice.

A feminist perspective would seek to broaden the base for practice by including social workers practicing in any employment setting as occupational social workers. Furthermore, a feminist vision would promote the infusion of knowledge gleaned from this "forgotten sector" of practice into mental health and family counseling services in the community. In a feminist vision,

310

Feminist Visions

job development, the assessment of labor market trends, and career planning should be part of the well-equipped social worker's repertoire, as clients undoubtedly bring employment problems to their counseling sessions.

Infusing Feminist Principles in the Workplace

Feminist principles of empowerment and the elimination of oppressive and discriminatory structures should figure squarely within occupational social work. A feminist analysis is a powerful vehicle for infusing into the workplace knowledge about differences due to gender, age, ethnicity, disability, and sexual and lifestyle preference. Feminist visions offer alternative paradigms to the hierarchical distribution of power and responsibility. "Win-win" relationships and shared power arrangements can be infused within private, for-profit organizations.[23] Elements of such rearranged power relationships are beginning to be reflected in "quality circles," worker teams, and other collaborative problem-solving efforts that seek to counter traditional hierarchical structures. Just as feminist principles might help to inform structural change efforts, they are essential in promoting an appreciation for gender, ethnic, age, and class differences, which, in turn, may alter biased workplace policies and practices. Thus, a feminist analysis may help to interpret why a woman union member shies away from being promoted to a supervisory role. Even though she is invested in the workplace, the normal hierarchy may be antithetical to her values.

Women taking supervisory positions experience more harassment and testing of their competence than men. Expected to be better than their male counterparts, many women may choose not to subject themselves to the added pressure to perform. Because there are so few women at the top of hierarchies, those who are may fall into narrow roles and be expected to emulate their male counterparts.[24]

Sex-segregated labor markets, where men and women are in separate occupations and where women earn less than 60 cents for every man's dollar even in the same occupation,[25] mean that only a few women have been admitted to positions of power in hierarchies. Thus, few women have opportunities for traditional high-status and high-paying jobs, given the fact that women are disproportionately represented in low-wage, dead-end jobs. In 1980, fewer than 1 percent of working women made over $25,000 **311** per year. The median annual income that year for women employed full time was $11,590, as opposed to $18,428 for men employed full time. Less than half the earnings gap between men and women can be explained by differences in job commitment or work qualifications.[26]

A feminist analysis fosters a reexamination of the formal and informal rules of the workplace that have often deliberately created inequities in work opportunities, wages, and occupational and socioeconomic status. Differential and discriminatory treatment of persons based on ethnicity, age, gender, sexual preference, disability, and class or job status will persist until opportunity structures are changed. To effect such a change, a feminist agenda could promote full employment, worker ownership, and cooperatives. It could increase work sharing to diminish layoffs, improve access to permanent part-time jobs, promote employment of women in jobs not traditional for them, and alter wage and career ladders to eradicate low pay and underemployment. The latter is especially important as it particularly affects women, ethnic and sexual minorities, and the disabled, as well as both the young and aged, despite the comparable worth of work they perform.

The Family as a Workplace.   From a feminist perspective, the family as a workplace is as important to occupational social work as is one's place of paid employment. Currently, the segregation of family work functions and responsibilities from other occupational roles reflects inappropriate dichotomization. Variants of the work roles assumed by family members, usually women, are also performed by nurses, counselors, housekeepers, child-care providers, police officers, gardeners, and chauffeurs, to name a few. It seems unjustly ironic that one set of workers is remunerated for such responsibilities while another goes virtually without pay or validation for family-centered careers. This discounting of family work roles may account for the low self-esteem expressed by women who describe themselves as "just a housewife." Caregivers, such as welfare mothers, are subjected to compulsory workfare schemes that erode the value of the work they already perform. Feminist visions for the future might recast such issues as discriminatory responses meted out by society for the work of caregiving.

Feminist visions may involve the reconceptualization of family work roles as "real" jobs. Otherwise such work roles are

Feminist Visions

reinforced by the welfare state, maintaining women as unpaid laborers who are often, because of their multiple responsibilities, either prevented from working outside the home or overwhelmed by the dual roles of their jobs in and out of the home. Moreover, such family workers represent a most unprotected and vulnerable class of workers, especially those whose jobs may involve care for impaired family members and extend around the clock, seven days a week.

Without respite, through publicly provided caregiving services, vacations, and other resources to alleviate work stress, caregivers can become financially, emotionally, and physically crippled by their at-home jobs. In fact, emerging data suggest that some caregivers become more impaired than those for whom they are caring. Other data indicate that for some women, paid employment outside the home is preferable to that in the home because it is their only respite from their caregiving tasks.[27] Paid employment outside the home should be organized to support family work roles without afflicting market values on the family.

Family work roles should be as accessible to men as to women, so that equalization of work roles in the home occurs when both men and women are working outside the home. Feminist visions might include employer-sponsored family sick leave, funds to purchase caregiving services, time off for caregiving chores, and support for men to assume more of the housekeeping and caregiving roles. Not only should there be improved societal supports and certainly partial remuneration for women and men who labor at family work roles, but such work must be validated by employers and educational institutions.[28] The movement toward alternative work patterns like job sharing and part-time careers could affect the way men and women share their home and work responsibilities.

Moving Toward Occupational Social Welfare

Feminist advocacy for more multidimensional thinking about human needs suggests that the entire profession, rather than a small cadre of occupational social workers, needs to be promoting workers' welfare. Feminist analysis acknowledges that work and work conditions are central to individual, family, and community functioning, and, as such, social work interventions must be expanded to reduce work problems in order to promote well- **313** being. Moreover, to attach such a mission only to social work specialists in labor and industry is to abdicate responsibility for problem solving that should be borne by the rest of the profession. Without a full commitment from the profession, those currently employed in occupational social work cannot advance a more multifaceted approach.

One does not need to be practicing occupational social work to promote occupational social welfare, which may be done by practitioners in all fields using new forms of practice and service arrangements. For example, residential treatment centers may hire job developers to aid in the transition of emancipated youths to the world of work. Mental health interventions might include an assessment of employability and job acquisition as a treatment goal. Occupational social workers might develop regulations regarding plant closures or seek remunerations for women working outside the home while also juggling roles as primary family caregivers. The prevalence of occupational issues in clients' lives makes them pervasive components of all social work practice.

Because the array of social, psychological, economic, health, and family problems with which social workers deal are directly or indirectly linked to work issues, these problems must be tackled head on rather than masked by psychologically oriented interventions that exclude work-related problem solving. Even if occupational social work had not emerged as a practice field, social work reinvolvement with workplace issues would have occurred to ensure more comprehensive interventions with clients. Just as our predecessors advocated a "case to cause" model as they pioneered new services and reforms in the public and private sector, so, too, can their paradigm guide our current and future practice.[29] This vision for broadened interventions will help to answer the charges that social workers using a narrow intervention repertoire blame the victim.

Occupational social welfare could be conceived of as a foundation for all social welfare. Thus, a feminist scenario for the social work profession of the future involves the linking of occupational social welfare issues with all other dimensions of human welfare. Social welfare of the future would address all forms of work and would promote equitable, nonoppressive, and nondiscriminatory structures, as well as work opportunities, conditions, and benefits that enhance well-being. A feminist mission for the profession may help to ensure that such issues are central rather than peripheral to future practice.

314

Feminist Visions

Transcending Market Values

Once the profession infuses occupational social welfare into its mission, it is possible to envision an end to the false dichotomies that segregate market considerations from social welfare principles. Moreover, it is important to imagine a time when social welfare decisions transcend market concerns for all sectors of society. How might this happen? For those who envision a world evolving from feminist principles, such a futuristic model may seem plausible. This is because feminism in essence compels the preeminence of female values; historically, this is what the social work profession and social welfare issues originally represented. While women in recent centuries have been prepared for the family as a workplace where nonmarket values prevail, men have been groomed for roles outside the home in which market principles predominate.[30] As women gave birth to the profession of social work, they saw the world as a family requiring the same nonmarket values based on care that they offered within their own homes.

As women and the profession of social work reclaim this historic feminist vision in which female values or nonmarket family caregiving values have their place in the world, they will not only increasingly help to counter or balance market considerations but will transcend them. It is possible, then, to envision a time when decision criteria are not limited to those that solely promote the economy or the market, nor even to those that merge economic and social welfare considerations. Instead, criteria will reflect the preeminence of social welfare values. Ultimately our feminist agenda requires that we disconnect the grip that market forces have on all of us that works to deaden the humanist in us and subject human needs to market-related criteria. This will require personal struggle. If there is no struggle, there is no change. Our feminist challenge centers around mainstreaming the core issues of caring that have dominated women's lives. Thus, the profession of social work, if it carries out its mission, will intensify its advocacy for values, making occupational social welfare the center stage on which value differences and value challenges are played out. When such ultimate visions of a caring society are realized, feminism and occupational social welfare will have brought to those people we serve some of the promises of social work's heritage and the potential we have only begun to discover.

315

notes

1. Irl Carter, "Social Work in Industry: A History and a Viewpoint," *Social Thought*, 3 (Winter 1977), pp. 7–17, notes that the very term "social work" evolved from German derivations in which practice comprised social care and stabilization of the work force.

2. See Rosalie Bakalinsky, "People vs. Profits: Social Work in Industry," *Social Work*, 25 (November 1980), pp. 471–475.

3. See the Introduction to this book.

4. See Stuart D. Brandes, *American Welfare Capitalism, 1880–1940* (Chicago: University of Chicago Press, 1976).

5. Jane Addams, *The Second Twenty Years at Hull House* (New York: Macmillan Co., 1930), pp. 129, 169, 221.

6. Jane Addams, *A New Conscience and an Ancient Evil* (New York: Macmillan Co., 1912).

7. See "Florence Kelley," *Encyclopedia of Social Work* (15th issue; New York: National Association of Social Workers, 1965), pp. 440–441. When Florence Kelley was head of the Illinois Factory Inspection Department in 1893, she was responsible for upholding the newly enacted eight-hour working day and for prohibiting employers from hiring children less than 14 years old. Later, as head of the National Consumers League based in New York City, she worked toward a national policy of workers' compensation for accidents occuring on the job.

8. See Florence Kelley, *Modern Industry in Relation to the Family, Health, Education and Morality* (New York: Longmans, Green, & Co., 1914).

9. Josephine Shaw Lowell, *Industrial Arbitration and Conciliation* (New York: G. P. Putnam's, 1893).

10. See Sheila Akabas, "Labor: Social Policy and Human Services," *Encyclopedia of Social Work*, Vol. 1 (17th issue; Washington, D.C.: National Association of Social Workers, 1977), pp. 737–744.

11. See Bertha Capen Reynolds, *Social Work and Social Living: Explorations in Philosophy and Practice* (New York: Citadel Press, 1951) (reprinted; Washington, D.C.: National Association of Social Workers, 1975).

12. John Naisbitt, *Megatrends* (New York: Warner Books, 1982), pp. 85, 93.

13. Mary Parker Follett, *Creative Experience* (New York: Longmans, Green & Co., 1924).

14. For more about her work, see *The Anvil and the Plow: A History of the United States Department of Labor.* (Washington, D.C.: U.S. Government Printing Office, undated).

15. This idea was suggested by Naomi Gottlieb, School of Social Work, University of Washington, Seattle.

Feminist Visions

16. Katharine H. Briar, "The Meaning of Work and Its Implications for Social Work Education." Paper presented at the Annual Program Meeting, Council on Social Work Education, New Orleans, La., February 26–March 1, 1978.

17. See Carl N. Degler, *At Odds: Women and the Family in America: From the Revolution to the Present* (New York: Oxford University Press, 1980).

18. See Katharine H. Briar et al., eds., *Initiating Industrial Social Work Services* (Silver Spring, Md.: National Association of Social Workers, 1984). See also Michele Vinet and Constance Jones, *Social Services and Work: Initiation of Social Workers into Labor and Industry Settings* (Silver Spring, Md.: National Association of Social Workers, 1981).

19. See Briar et al., eds., *Initiating Industrial Social Work Services*, Chap. 1.

20. Katharine H. Briar et al., "Occupational Social Welfare in Hard Economic Times." Paper presented at the Seventh Professional Symposium, National Association of Social Workers, Philadelphia, Pa., 1981.

21. See Robert L. Leavitt, *Employee Assistance and Counseling Programs: Findings from the Recent Research on Employer-Sponsored Human Services* (New York: Community Council of Greater New York, 1983).

22. Katharine H. Briar, "Lay-Offs and Social Work Intervention," *Urban and Social Change Review,* 16 (Summer 1983), pp. 9–14.

23. Cheryl Ellsworth et al., "Toward a Feminist Model for Planning for and with Women," in Ann Weick and Susan T. Vandiver, eds., *Women, Power, and Change* (Washington, D.C.: National Association of Social Workers, 1981), pp. 146–157.

24. See N. J. Sokoloff, "Motherwork and Working Mothers," in Allison M. Jaggar and Paula S. Rothenberg, eds., *Feminist Frameworks* (New York: McGraw-Hill Book Co., 1984).

25. Claire S. Thomas, *Sex Discrimination in a Nutshell* (St. Paul, Minn.: West Publishing Co., 1982), p. 191.

26. See D. J. Treiman and H. I. Harman, *Women, Work, and Wages: Equal Pay for Jobs of Equal Value* (Washington, D.C.: National Academy Press, 1981).

27. Katharine H. Briar and Rosemary Ryan, "The Anti-Institution Movement and Women Caregivers," *Affilia Journal of Women and Social Work,* 1 (Spring 1986), pp. 20–31.

28. The valuation of the competencies acquired in such unpaid jobs might result in accelerated entry into schools and employment outside the home. For example, one experimental program fostering the return to school by older students, primarily women, gave up to two years of college credit for prior learning, in part from such family competencies as counseling, interviewing, community resource mobilization, and health systems work acquired in tradi- **317**

tional women's caregiving roles. Recognition of such competencies should also help to accelerate job acquisition, which for the most part is currently based only on experience derived from paid employment. For more information, contact the AURA Program, Pacific Lutheran University, Tacoma, Washington.

29. Let us take, for example, the case of a worker who suffers from terminal cancer but wants to continue working. A medical social worker whom the patient is consulting advocates that the patient be allowed to reenter his firm, but on the job, he is met with hostility and some overindulgent reactions that intensify his worry about losing his job. Should such problems be accepted as a given, or does the medical social worker have the repertoire, resources, and support to intervene, directly or indirectly, to alter the patient's stress in the workplace? For a description of the "case to cause" paradigm, see Porter R. Lee, *Social Work as Cause and Function* (New York: Columbia University Press, 1937).

30. Degler, *At Odds*.

Feminist Visions

contributors

Nan Van Den Bergh, Ph.D., is Associate Professor, Department of Social Work, California State University–Fresno. She coordinates the research sequence, is a member of the Women's Studies Executive Council, and organized a university-wide interest group, the Women's Caucus, for women faculty and staff. She has also worked as an organizer for rape crisis centers; battered women's shelters; and the antipornography, reproductive freedom, and nuclear disarmament movements.

Lynn B. Cooper, doctorate in criminology, is Professor of Social Work and Coordinator of the Women's Studies Program, California State University–Sacramento. She specializes in child abuse and family violence and has recently completed a videotape on mothers in prison. She is active in the reproductive rights and anti-apartheid movements.

Mimi Abramovitz, DSW, is Associate Professor, School of Social Work, Hunter College of The City University of New York, where she chairs the Social Policy Sequence and the Committee on Women's Issues in the Curriculum. She has published extensively in journals and is currently working on a book about women and the U.S. welfare state.

Ruth A. Brandwein, Ph.D., is Dean, School of Social Welfare, State University of New York at Stony Brook. She has been involved in women's issues since the late 1960s and from 1980–83 chaired the Women's Commission of the Council on Social Work Education.

John Brekke, Ph.D., is Assistant Professor, School of Social Work, University of Southern California, Los Angeles. He has worked extensively with men who batter.

Katharine Hooper Briar, Ph.D., is Assistant Professor, School of Social Work, University of Washington, Seattle, where she teaches courses on social policy, women and social change, and social work and employment. She has served on various national and state NASW committees involving the world of work and currently is writing a book on unemployment to be published by NASW.

319

Susan Meyers Chandler, DSW, is Associate Professor, School of Social Work, University of Hawaii, Honolulu. She chairs the Social Development Concentration and teaches in the areas of social policy, community organization, and child abuse and neglect. Currently, she is serving on the Women's Commission of the Council on Social Work Education.

Roslyn H. Chernesky, DSW, is Professor, Fordham University Graduate School of Social Service, New York City, where she teaches administration, program planning, and organizational theory and chairs in the macro-practice area and the health field of practice. She has published extensively on women and management.

Joan M. Cummerton, DSW, is Professor, Department of Social Work Education, San Francisco State University, California. She teaches in both the micro- and macro-practice concentrations and has taught research courses and supervised student research for many years. Recent writing has focused on the application of feminist theory to classroom teaching and learning, and the influence of homophobia on social work practice with lesbians.

Rosemary Cunningham, MA, is a doctoral candidate, School of Social Work, University of Washington, Seattle.

Miriam Dinerman, DSW, is Professor, School of Social Work, Rutgers–The State University of New Jersey, New Brunswick, where she teaches social policy and social work in health care. She also directs the Center for International Comparative Social Welfare at Rutgers. Her interests have centered on social work education in this country and abroad and on the condition of women, especially those heading families with children. She is currently Chapter President of NASW in New Jersey.

Gloria Donadello, Ph.D., is Professor, Fordham University Graduate School of Social Service, New York City, and is in private practice, New York City. She was formerly a member of the NASW National Committee on Lesbian and Gay Issues.

Becky Fowler, MSW, has served as Membership Director and a board member of Rural American Women, a national organization based in Kempton, Pennsylvania. Her interests include developing rural women's networks, innovative economic development models, and the relationship between land and power.

Patty Gibbs, Ed.D., is Associate Professor, School of Social Work, West Virginia University, Morgantown. She has published articles on women and economic development, female sexuality, and field learning in women's studies programs.

Hilda R. Heady, MSW, is Director, Preston Birth Center, Kingwood, West Virginia. She has many years of professional experience in rural community development and organization, teaching, program development, women's health, and direct practice with women and their families.

Nancy R. Hooyman, Ph.D., is Associate Dean and Associate Professor, School of Social Work, University of Washington, Seattle. She is co-editor of *Not for Women Only: Social Work Practice for a Feminist Future,* published by NASW. In addition to her work in feminist practice, she has published extensively in the area of gerontology, particularly with regard to older women and women as caregivers for the elderly, and has recently completed two gerontology textbooks.

Linda E. Jones, Ph.D., is Assistant Professor, School of Social Work, and an associate member, Women's Studies faculty, University of Minnesota, Minneapolis. Her work has focused on the relationships among poverty, welfare, and employment. She has published articles on long-term AFDC recipients, career patterns of social work students, and androgyny and mental health; she is co-authoring a book (with Diane Kravetz) about feminist organizations providing social services for women.

Diane Kravetz, Ph.D., is Director and Professor, School of Social Work, University of Wisconsin–Madison, and a member of the Women's Studies Program. She teaches courses on practice, sexism and social work, and women and mental health and has published articles on women's consciousness-raising groups, androgyny as a standard of mental health, and several areas related to women in social work education and administration. Currently, she is working on a book (with Linda E. Jones) about feminist organizations providing social services for women.

Donald D. Mowry, MSW, is Lecturer and a doctoral candidate, School of Social Work, University of Wisconsin–Madison. His clinical experience with family violence includes work with child **321** abuse, child neglect and incest. He has worked through The Program to Prevent Woman Abuse, Madison, with men who batter.

Barbara Smith, MA, is a co-founder of Kitchen Table: Women of Color Press, New York City, and a board member of the National Coalition of Black Lesbians and Gays. She recently taught a course on racism through the School of Social Work, New York University, New York City. Her books include *All the Women Are White, All the Blacks Are Men, But Some of Us Are Brave: Black Women's Studies; Home Girls: A Black Feminist Anthology;* and *Yours in Struggle: Three Feminist Perspectives on Anti-Semitism and Racism* (with Elly Bulkin and Minnie Bruce Pratt).

Richard M. Tolman, Ph.D., is a postdoctoral fellow at the School of Social Service Administration, University of Chicago, Illinois. He has worked in several states with men who batter, and his current research focuses on evaluating the effectiveness of intervention with men who batter. He is Associate Editor of *The Journal of Interpersonal Violence.*

Michele J. Vinet, MSW, is a doctoral candidate, School of Social Work, University of Washington, Seattle. Her dissertation focuses on the multiple roles of working mothers, particularly single mothers. She has conducted research in occupational social work on the roles of social work professionals and ethical dilemmas they face.

Marie Weil, DSW, is Associate Professor, School of Social Work, University of Southern California, Los Angeles, where she teaches organizational and group behavior, and administration and community organization. She has helped develop women's programs and services through the Southern California Rape Prevention and Study Center and has held a variety of administrative and planning positions in Office of Economic Opportunity, public housing, and settlement programs. She recently co-authored *Case Management in Human Service Practice.*

Diane Goldstein Wicker, MSW, is a Jewish feminist who has taught social work and women's studies courses in Sacramento and Long Beach, California. Based in San Francisco, she has a full-time private practice and conducts antiracism workshops **322** in the community.

Feminist Visions

index

323

324

Feminist Visions

personal, 9–10, 257
  direct services and, 23–24
  for lesbians and gay men,
    287–89
  radical, 50
  transformational, feminism as,
    1–2
Pornography, 72
Positivism, intuitive knowing invalidated by, 14
Poverty
  feminization of, 150, 155,
    231–37, 241–43, 253
    social policy and, 211–28
  historical perspectives on,
    229–31
  official line to determine, 230
  precipitants of, 231–33
  Reagan Administration's budget
    cuts as cause of increase
    in, 234–35
  reasons for persistence of,
    235–37
  in rural America, 264–65
  social policy and, 253–54
  work incentives and, 241–43
Power
  reconceptualization of, 5–6,
    15–18, 168–69
    by lesbians and gay men,
      286–87
    in rural America, 275–77
  redefining of, 152–53
Process
  male attendance to, 72–73
  product valued equally with,
    6–7, 19
  in rural America, 278–79
  value in women's organiza-
    tions of, 178–80
  valuing of, 170–71
Prostitutes, 300–301
Psychological development, female
  subordination and, 102–7
Psychotherapy, sex bias in, 111
Public assistance, 213–19
  (*See also* AFDC)

Quality circles in supervision, 144
Quotas, hiring, Reagan Administration's opposition to, 243

Racism
  combating of, 29–44
  definition of, 33
  female mental health and, 109
  male opposition to, 68–70
  myth of black matriarch and,
    105
  personal work to combat, 35–37

Radloff, Lenore, 109
Rankin, Jeanette, 192
Rape, 49–50
Rape crisis centers, 2
Rappaport, Bruce, 76
RAVEN (Rape and Violence
  End Now), 72
Rawlings, Edna I., 114–15, 119–20
Reagan Administration, 59
  AFDC policies under, 218
  affirmative action, 156
  budget cuts by, increase in
    poverty as a result of,
    234–35
  hiring quotas opposed by, 243
Reagon, Bernice Johnson, 48,
  54, 59
Reid, William J., 82
Renaming, validity of, 7–9, 21–23
Research
  as agent of change, 95–96
  challenging false dichotomies
    in, 14
  client empowerment facilitated
    through, 17
  comparison of perspectives in,
    89–92
  ethical issues in, 94–95
  feminist perspective on, 80–100
  generating concepts vs. hypo-
    thesis testing in, 96
  issues related to feminist per-
    spective in, 88–95
  lack of, on women, 84
  nonsexist perspective in, 83–85
  patriarchal paradigm in, 81–83
  societal sanction for, 96–97
Reynolds, Bertha Capen, 11, 25,
  302
Roberts, Robert W., 189
Roosevelt, Eleanor, 259
Rothman, Jack, 188–89
Rothschild-Whitt, J., 165–66
Rural America
  alternative view of, 271–79
  definition of, 263–64
  feminism and, 262–82

Salsa Soul Sisters (New York), 58
Sapphire Sapphos (Washington,
  D. C.), 58
Scherz, Frances H., 129–30, 134,
  137
Schlafly, Phyllis, 278
Science, female "inferiority" ex-
  plained by, 103
Second Sex, The (Simone de
  Beauvoir), 192
Settlement houses, 149
  women's involvement in, 191

Feminist Visions

United Way, 303
Upward mobility as measure of
    liberation, 165

Valentich, M., 254
Van Kleeck, Mary, 11
Vinson, E. A., 264
Violence
    family, 110
    male, 71
        intervention and, 76
        police, 45–46

Wald, Lillian, 149, 189, 191, 260
Walker, Alice, 34
Wasserman, Harry, 131
Watkins, Mary, 58–59
Wax, John, 133
Weinberg, George, 283
Welfare recipients, stigmatization
    of, 236
Welfare rights movement,
    women involved in, 191
Well of Loneliness, The (Radclyffe
    Hall), 287
Westkott, Marcia, 86
Whites
    racisms's damage to, 31–32
    as racists, 30–31
Williams, Robin, Jr., 154
Wise, Sue, 87
Women
    as administrators, 164
    American Indian. *See* Native
        American women
    Asian American. *See* Asian
        American women
    battered, shelters for, 57
    black. *See* Blacks
    child care and employment of,
        240–41
    community and organizing
        and, 187–210
    community organizing by,
        192–94
    disabled, social security pay-
        ments to, 220
    divorced, social security and,
        222–23
    elderly, poverty rate among,
        219–20
    family ethic and, 211–28
    Hispanic. *See* Latina women
    historical understanding of ex-
        periences of, 66
    Latina. *See* Latina women
    male support for efforts of, 68
    mental health and, 101–27

Native American. *See* Native
    American women
    percentage in labor force of,
        2, 237–38
    poor, systems to aid, 233–35
    psychological development and
        subordination of, 102–7
    rape committed against, 49–50
    research on nonfamilial roles
        of, 83–84
    rural, 270
    scrutiny of men by, 67–68
    sexual activity by, public
        assistance and, 217–18
    social work's origin with, 61
    suburbanization's impact on,
        255
    value of perspectives and ex-
        periences of, in adminis-
        tration, 167–68
    violence against, male oppo-
        sition to, 65
    as wage earners, 155–56
    in work force, 237–39
    working, Social Security Act
        penalization of, 219–23
Women Strike for Peace, 192
Women's health movement,
    women involved in, 191
Women's International League for
    Peace and Freedom, 192
Women's issues
    feminism not limited to, 2
    people of color and myths
        concerning, 50
Women's movement
    racism in, 47
    theorists of, 192
Women's organizations
    funding for, 177
    study of, 171–81
Women's Pentagon Action, 192
Wood, Katherine, 82
Work, poverty and incentives
    for, 241–43
Work force, women in, 237–39
Workers
    median weekly earnings of,
        239
    poor, taxation of, 234
Workplace, feminist principles
    in, 311–13

Young, Alma T., 142
YWCA, feminist values and,
    166

Zurcher, L. A., 182

330

Feminist Visions